The Last Witness

The Child Survivor of the Holocaust

The Last Witness

The Child Survivor of the Holocaust

Judith S. Kestenberg, M.D.,
and
Ira Brenner, M.D.

American
Psychiatric
Press, Inc.

Washington, DC
London, England

Copyright © 1996 American Psychiatric Press, Inc.
ALL RIGHTS RESERVED
Manufactured in the United States of America on acid-free paper
98 97 96 95   4 3 2 1
First Edition

American Psychiatric Press, Inc.
1400 K Street, N.W., Washington, DC   20005

Library of Congress Cataloging-in-Publication Data
Kestenberg, Judith S.
      The last witness : the child survivor of the Holocaust / by
   Judith S. Kestenberg and Ira Brenner.
            p.   cm.
      Includes bibliographical references and index.
      ISBN 0-88048-662-7 (alk. paper)
      I. Brenner, Ira, 1950-   .   II. Title.
      [DNLM: 1. Stress disorders, Post-Traumatic.   2. Holocaust--
   psychology.   3. Concentration Camps.   4. Survivors--
psychology. 5. Cohort Studies.   WM 170_20K42L 1996]
   RC451.4.H62K47   1996
   616.85'21--dc20
   DNLM/DLC
   for Library of Congress   95-26268
                                                              CIP

British Library Cataloguing in Publication Data
A CIP record is available from the British Library.

This book is dedicated to
Milton Kestenberg
and
Leo Brenner

Contents

Contributors

Judith S. Kestenberg, M.D.
Clinical Professor of Psychiatry, Division of Psychoanalytic Education, New York University, and Training and Supervising Analyst in Adult and Child Analysis, the Psychoanalytic Institute, New York University Medical Center, New York, New York; Founder, Child Development Research, Sands Point, New York; Codirector and Cofounder, International Study of Organized Persecution of Children, and Cofounder, Group for the Psychoanalytic Study of the Effect of the Holocaust on the Second Generation, Sands Point, New York

Ira Brenner, M.D.
Training and Supervising Analyst, Philadelphia Psychoanalytic Institute; Clinical Associate Professor of Psychiatry, Jefferson Medical College; Attending Psychiatrist, Institute of Pennsylvania Hospital; and private practice, Philadelphia, Pennsylvania

Janet Kestenberg Amighi, Ph.D.
Professor of Anthropology, West Chester University, West Chester, Pennsylvania; Faculty, Laban/Bartenieff Institute of Movement Studies, New York

Milton Kestenberg, Esq. (deceased, 1991)
Member, New York Bar; Cofounder, International Study of Organized Persecution of Children, and Cofounder, Group for the Psychoanalytic Study of the Effect of the Holocaust on the Second Generation, Sands Point, New York

Preface

I recently visited the Holocaust Memorial in Miami and witnessed a powerful exchange between two men of vastly different cultures. Most of the visitors had left for the day, and a silent emptiness was descending upon the grounds. There, in the waning moments of daylight, the huge sculpture of a tattooed arm, reaching for the heavens, cast an eerie reflection in the surrounding pool. One of the last tourists, a Hispanic man, was hurrying through, explaining the significance of the photographs and maps to his son. They paused in front of a photograph of a barracks in a concentration camp, which showed the emaciated prisoners with shaven heads in their striped uniforms, locked in their cagelike bunk beds. A man with a European accent was standing by the photographs also, pointing to the same scene, and sadly, but matter-of-factly, he stated to his own family, "I was there." The Hispanic man immediately spun around, his mouth dropping open as he confronted the silver-haired man, and asked incredulously, "You were there? You really were there? Did you know Elie Wiesel?"

The European man, seemingly unfazed by the stranger's curiosity and forthrightness, simply replied that yes indeed, he was there, but no, he never met Elie Wiesel. Still astonished and apparently not convinced, the man searched for words in English and asked many questions. Still unconvinced, he finally asked, "You have the numbers?" The survivor nodded, silently raising his forearm to show the man and his son.

The Hispanic man gasped and started to cross himself, exclaiming, "Dios mio! Dios mio!" He yelled for the rest of his family, urging them to come see this man—it was very, very important. He stood in awe, and whispered, "Worse than the holy wars!" He then asked more questions, which the survivor patiently answered. He became visibly shaken, and in the end all he could mutter was "Then it really happened."

This dramatic encounter illustrates the challenge of meaningfully describing the Holocaust and putting it in any kind of perspective. The questioner was obviously knowledgeable, caring, and interested in the history of the Holocaust, but it did not become real to him until he had living proof. His proof came in the form of a man with "numbers"—an eyewitness. But he still could not comprehend it and compared it to the holy wars. His historical perspective seemed to remove it from the modern twentieth century and cloak it with a religious aura. He became overwhelmed and had a profound experience when his extended conversation with the survivor finally broke through his denial. It became so important for both men to communicate about the reality of horror that they struggled to overcome the language barrier between them.

This tendency toward denial in the face of an overwhelming reality can be exploited by perpetrators who count on general incredulity at reports of their misdeeds—whether incest or the Holocaust. In addition, the feelings of shame and guilt that are mobilized during victimization may keep those who have experienced trauma from speaking up. Survivors of the Holocaust, however, whose numbers are ever dwindling, have clearly recognized the crucial importance of sharing and documenting their experiences. We hope that this volume becomes a suitable forum for their voices, while at the same time broadening our understanding of the psychological aspects of survival.

■

As the reader will note, we offer no photographs, tables, graphs, maps, blueprints of the gas chambers, copies of incriminating Nazi documents, or extensive statistics. Such information is available, and with access to the archives in the former Soviet Union, more data will certainly emerge to add to the already enormous amount of historical evidence. What we offer is an in-depth study of the traumatic effects of genocidal persecution on the child's psychic structure and on development throughout the life cycle. Although this book is essentially about the victims in one particular instance of genocide—though one that has become almost paradigmatic—we suspect that some of our findings will be replicated in other situations.

The upsurge of nationalistic strivings and ancient ethnic hatreds associated with the collapse of the Soviet Union, the "ethnic cleansing" in Bosnia, and the deadly tribal war between Tutsis and Hutus in Rwanda are just a few of the many instances of mass violence today in which genocidal aggression shows itself. The advent of psychodynamic sophistication in the realm of international conflict resolution has brought hope, however, that through understanding the psychology of neighbors and having an appreciation of national unresolved mourning, groups can work out their differences (see the work of Vamik Volkan, especially Volkan 1988). The signing of an agreement between Israel and the Palestine Liberation Organization finally to recognize each other can be seen as a very positive step in that direction.

It has been more than fifty years now since the liberation of the concentration camps and the hiding places, so we have been able to see some of the long-term effects of trauma on child survivors and their offspring. For those whose suffering persists, help is available through support groups in the various survivor organizations and through professional channels. We hope that our contribution will help mental health professionals be more aware of some of the issues confronting these patients, whose lives have been touched by the flames of the Holocaust. We may be able to alleviate some of the pain of the survivors, but the memory of those who perished endures. It endures as a somber reminder that the future of humankind hangs in the balance between the forces of creation and the forces of destruction.

As a participant in this project, I have learned a great deal and am deeply appreciative of Dr. Kestenberg's wisdom and support. However, I have lost count of the number of times, over the last ten years, that I have considered ending my involvement in this overwhelming project. After all, I was quite busy with the demands of my practice, my psychoanalytic training, my teaching, and of course my personal life. I further rationalized that I did not think of myself as a researcher and had not originally envisioned my career as taking this direction. So I preferred not to think of it as "giving up" each time Judy Kestenberg, whose tireless energy, inspiration, and absolute commitment to intellectual integrity, spurred me on: "We were invited to present a paper at. . . . " or "Can you write a paper for . . . ?" or "Can you speak on a panel at . . . ?" So I kept going, pushing myself a little more, to get another interview, to present one more time, to "survive" in the project just a little longer. I quickly realized how hard it was to set ordinary limits on my time when it came to this extraordinary group of people, many of whom had pushed themselves beyond imagination in order actually to survive from one day to the next. The emotions stirred up in me each time I listened to their stories were profound and utterly exhausting. It is little wonder that for several decades after the war the world did not want to hear about the suffering of the survivors. And now "the children," many of whom are in their fifties and sixties, have long since come of age and have needed to be heard from also. They have much to teach us, and I was compelled to listen.

When Dr. Kestenberg felt that we needed to reach more psychiatrists with our findings, I responded. With the encouragement of my friend the prolific writer Salman Akhtar, I contacted the publishing arm of the American Psychiatric Association with the idea. Much to my pleasure, it was eagerly accepted. The result is this book, a tribute to all of the last witnesses of this all too human tragedy. It could not have been put together without the expert secretarial efforts of Lorraine Amato-Margasak and Ellen Young, as well as the loving support of Roberta Brenner, whose own endurance was put to the test on more than one occasion.

■

This volume consists of previously published articles and new material. Although the book is a collaboration, Judith Kestenberg is primarily responsible for Chapters 1, 2, 5, and 9, and I take authorial responsibility for Chapters 4, 6, and 8. Janet Kestenberg Amighi assisted in writing Chapter 1, Chapter 3 is a joint effort by Judith Kestenberg and me, and Chapter 7 was written by Judith and Milton Kestenberg.

Chapter 2 combines two presentations. The first is a contribution to a panel, "The Psychological Impact of Being Hidden as a Child," held at the Meetings of the Hidden Child, May 26, 1991, New York, NY, chair Dr. Sarah Moskovitz. The second was read at the Nürnberg-Erlangen Meeting on Persecuted Children and Children of the Persecuted, October 18, 1991, and was published in German in 1994 by Vandenhoeck and Ruprecht.

Chapter 3 is reprinted in revised form from an article in the *International Journal of Psycho-Analysis,* published in 1986.

Chapter 4 is reprinted in revised form from an article in the *Psychoanalytic Review,* published in 1988.

Chapter 9 is translated in revised form from an article published in German, "Kinder unter dem Joch des Nationalsozialismus," in *Jahrbuch der Psychoanalyse,* in 1992. It also appeared in shortened English versions in the *British Journal of Psychotherapy* in 1992 and in *Mind and Human Interaction* in 1990.[1]

Ira Brenner, M.D.

---

[1] Complete publication information for these chapters can be found in footnotes in the individual chapters and in listings in the Bibliography.

Introduction

T he last witness to the near destruction of European Jewry by the Nazi Third Reich will survive well into the twenty-first century, as he or she will be fifty-some years old in the year 2000. The fate of this last witness is as yet unwritten; but, like other aged survivors of major historical events, this person, yet unknown, will probably live to be more than a hundred and will be remembered in obituaries as the last living survivor of the Holocaust.

By then, this person's memory of that part of life—ravaged by time and doubtful in the first place (the child was "too young to remember")—will have faded into the barbaric ancient history section of the twentieth century. By then, revisionist historians will have done their best to "prove" that the Final Solution of the Jewish problem never existed, or that if it did, the death toll was "only" in the thousands, not the millions. By then, the world will have seen numerous genocidal attempts by the stronger against the less powerful; and the word *Holocaust,* which already is thought by some to have become overused and even commercialized, may have taken on totally new connotations.

Consequently, it is not difficult to envision the problems of psychohistorical research in that far-off time, which will include the accuracy and reliability of eyewitness reports and the limited degree to which they can be corroborated. The effects of time on one's recollections add merely another level of doubt in sorting out the validity of memories of long ago, especially if children are involved. My first contact with child survivors came via my husband Milton, an attorney who spent many hours helping children remember what had happened to them so that they might qualify for compensation. When we joined the Group for the Psychoanalytic Study of the Second Generation, he stood by me and participated, and when I began to interview child survivors, he did too, with an open ear and heart.

My attention was then drawn again to survivors who were children during the war, by several parents who attended the Center for Parents and Children, where we did research and practiced primary prevention. We could observe the effects of child survivors' hiding on the development of their own young children, and we were amazed to see how very early these parents transmitted to the children their own fears of being abandoned and never returned to their parents. One survivor had to escape from his homeland when only four years old. He had to learn a new language and for a long time could not communicate with other children. This led to an attitude that was later reproduced in his own son, a four-year-old who, because encouraged to speak his parents' European language, could not learn enough English to talk to other children. It was the son's assigned task, it seemed, to resurrect the dead, which he did symbolically by holding back his feces and not dropping them into the toilet, where they might drown.

Some twenty-five years ago, faced with my first patient who was a child of survivors, I became concerned with the generationally transmitted effects of persecution, but I still knew very little regarding the adult fate of children who were themselves persecuted. I read several stories of how children rescued themselves, but I still knew very little about these young children except for my knowledge about the Theresienstadt children brought to Anna Freud's Hampstead nursery and clinic after liberation. But nothing I read had the same effect on me as the analysis of a man who was born during the Holocaust and spent his first two and a half years in ghettos and two more in a concentration camp. The effect on his cognitive and moral development was overwhelming. I knew then that I must learn much more about the adult fate of young children who suffered under the Nazis, both those who survived with their parents and those who were left to make it on their own.

So I began to read the literature from abroad. It was in the midst of reading about newborn babies' being killed, about very young children in concentration camps and in hiding, about a mother on the way to the ovens holding her daughter, deploring that not even her little child would be allowed to survive, about starving ghetto children begging in front of a bakery frequented by rich Jews—it was in the midst of all this that I knew. I knew then that with the tactics of the Nazis, some people's attitude toward children could be made to change. Adam Gawalewicz, a Pole who survived several camps, has observed that those of us who were not there cannot entirely understand that the principles of ordinary morality did not hold under conditions of horror: this was a time when the Nazis systematically used their victims in innumerable ways to carry out their criminal acts.

The task of resolving conflicts such as having children or having an abortion is intensely aggravated in people who once lived with death as an everyday occurrence. They had to harden themselves as they saw corpses lying around while people stood in line for soup. In the ghetto, children played while in their midst one of them may have lain lifeless, dead of starvation. In the ghetto courtyards, children played the deadly game of Jews caught by Nazis, of being shot or beaten. In the garden of the assistant superintendent of the Auschwitz camp, his wife and his two children frolicked among the flowers while two inmates, exhausted, starved, infected, and swollen from hunger, laid out lovely walks with gravel made of human bone.

Despite the prolific Polish literature on the Holocaust, very little had been written about the psyches of survivors and their children. Just how widespread, we wanted to know, are the repercussions of the massive regression of Nazi persecution? And could we have begun to understand the survivor's guilt so clearly described by Niederland (1968) had we not studied the working of the superego under these extreme conditions?

So we studied history, not as historians, but as psychoanalysts who wanted to know what happened to the human psyche during the Holocaust and in its aftermath. One of the things we found is that children under the persecution were more outspoken to the Nazis than were grown-ups. They joined the resistance and fed their families. They had to become old before their time, while often their elders regressed. We also found that the strength of these children and the strength of those who resisted regression brought them a new zest for life, which was then transmitted to the second generation.

Under the auspices of the International Study of Organized Persecution of Children, a group of interviewers followed a semistructured, psychoanalytically informed protocol, audiotaping these heroic and remarkable people for hours at a time. Although we were interested in the internal consistency of their testimony and gently confronted them when chronological or historical contradictions were obvious, the more important aspect of the interviews, for our purposes, was their experience and understanding of what they had undergone. Approximately ten years and fifteen hundred interviews later, the data are being deposited in the Wiener Library of Tel Aviv University for long-term study.

It is gratifying to have the opportunity to bring together some of our early findings in this volume. Though it is a modest contribution about a subject that ultimately must defy comprehension, we hope that readers will come away with a better understanding of how the developing child can be affected by the trauma associated with persecution. We did not see this work as merely a study of the pathology of a traumatized group. Nonetheless, although our metapsychology cannot do justice to their suffering (and indeed the use of too much psychoanalytic jargon can have a trivializing effect on their experience), we have felt it necessary to communicate some of our findings in our professional language. We hope it will be received in the spirit in which it is intended.

The chapters show considerable overlap (as might be expected, given that the stories they tell are of people who managed to survive the same genocidal onslaught). Although the chapters might have followed a different order, we have decided on the following progression. Chapters 1 and 2, each of which presents a number of vignettes and histories, show the similarities and differences in the experiences of children of various ages facing the two main situations that could befall them in those dire years of the Holocaust: that of being in hiding (sometimes even from oneself) and that of being in the concentration camps. Chapters 3 and 4 then focus on recurrent themes relevant to both situations: the effects of this experience on superego development and the role often played by transitional phenomena in mastering the attendant trauma and object loss, even much later in life.

With Chapter 5 we move from issues of early childhood and latency to consider the effect of the Holocaust experience on adolescent development, as seen here in a young girl's diary. Continuing this progression through the life cycle, Chapter 6 looks at these child survivors from the perspective of adulthood, examining typical patterns of parenting and grandparenting—at times disturbed, at others adaptive and even salutary, but always bearing the indelible stamp of a harrowing childhood experience. The aging process is next considered from an unusual double perspective: Chapter 7 first considers the premature aging of children in the Holocaust—both the physical wizening of children exposed to extreme trauma and deprivation and the psychological phenomenon of the "little adult," so often a stage-skipping adaptation that later becomes maladaptive. The chapter then goes on to consider child survivors in their chronological old age. Chapter 8 presents an instance (not unique in our experience) of how some of these unresolved issues were dealt with, however belatedly, as a result of survivors' participation in our research interviews. Finally, Chapter 9 presents an overview of what has preceded and advances a partial hypothesis, admittedly speculative, regarding the cause of this most demonic episode in human history.

We have tried to present some of the complexities of understanding the interplay of genocidal persecution and the development of the child, keeping in mind the uniqueness of the experience of each of these "last witnesses." We hope that readers will be able to tolerate the anxiety, horror, and sadness that this subject invariably evokes. It is a necessary experience if we are to prepare ourselves better to understand and assist the survivors of massive trauma.

Judith S. Kestenberg, M.D.

Children in Concentration Camps

Judith S. Kestenberg, M.D.
Janet Kestenberg Amighi, Ph.D.

A wide variety of experiences is revealed in our interviews with child survivors, reflecting not only the differences of living in concentration camps, being hidden in stifling spaces, or being concealed by foster families and others, but also differences in individual circumstances. This chapter will attempt to show some of the effects the age of the concentration camp child survivor may have had on his or her outcome in later life. The special circumstances and outcomes of children in hiding at different developmental stages will be considered in the next chapter.

We have been impressed with certain patterns in the outcome of infant, latency, and adolescent survivors, patterns presented here in four case histories. These cases have been chosen as representative based on a reading of a large number of interviews, published and unpublished, with child survivors in each of these age groups. The degree to which they fairly represent the approximately fifteen hundred interviews with child survivors in our data base will be further determined when the interviews have been coded and analyzed, and a more quantitatively based assessment can be made.

A preliminary hypothesis here is that the younger the survivors (and the greater their suffering), the more psychosomatic symptoms they experienced in later life. However, the effects of age differences on later outcome of child survivors is a subject of some controversy. Keilson (1979), discussing a large sample of primarily hidden children, found that those who were very young during the Holocaust have later suffered from character neurosis, whereas those who were preadolescent at the time have later experienced anxiety neurosis. Robinson (1979), studying a clinical population of survivors, found that severity of symptoms is inversely correlated with the age of the child survivor at the time of the trauma. However, in a later investigation (Robinson et al. 1994) of a nonclinical population, was unable to find any clear correlation of symptoms with age. Some of the differences in findings may reflect differences in methodology and sampling.

From a psychoanalytic perspective, one would predict that the specific long-term effects of trauma would be related to the age or developmental phase during which the trauma was experienced. Infants and very young children do not have a coordinated kind of cognitive memory. However, they can remember on a bodily level. This would lead us to expect that the trauma experienced during infancy would be somatized (McDougall 1989). Let us take the case of Dorothy.

Dorothy: An Infant Survivor

Dorothy's family was deported from Czernowitz in Bohemia to a concentration camp in Balta, Latvia. This happened at the end of 1941 or the beginning of 1942. Late in 1943 they planned an escape to Odessa, hearing that partisans were there. Although Dorothy's father left the camp, her mother stayed on, because she discovered suddenly that she was pregnant. Not having menstruated for some time because of malnutrition, she had not suspected a pregnancy, and it was already too advanced for her to make an arduous trip. Luckily, her mother was in the same camp and so was able to help her out with extra food. However, she was frightened, having heard that pregnant women were killed or simply disappeared. She had heard also that the Germans had once found a baby in the fields, and, when no one claimed it, they had torn the baby apart in front of everyone. (Relating this to the interviewer, Dorothy began to cry.) However, Dorothy's grandmother was a strong, determined woman who gave her daughter the strength to go on. She would tell her daughter, "This is the only way we can win that war—if there will be another generation. This [birth] is going to be our victory."

Dorothy was born one night in January 1944 with all the women of the camp looking on. "When my mother gave birth, it was as if everybody gave birth." The event was experienced as a victory for all of them. Dorothy's mother managed the experience by denying what was happening to her and allowing the grandmother to handle the situation. The old lady wound a rag around the baby's mouth and hid it inside a hole in the wall. In the evening the guards would give them soup and bread or a potato. Dorothy described how her grandmother used to "save it up for me and chew it and feed it to me" because her mother had no breast milk. When the family was liberated, Dorothy had survived to the age of five months.

She does not remember much from her early childhood:

> If I remember anything, it is just the covering of my mouth. Sometimes I wake up at night . . . with my hand over my mouth. I have this double feeling about myself, about being a very weak person and having that incredible strength. Today I am not very strong. Sometimes I feel I can't stand up for myself . . . that I don't have any rights . . . but when it comes to somebody else, I can become Hercules.

She proceeded to tell the interviewer that she had a "very heavy package." She explained, "I have tried all my life to get rid of that victim within me. I am still trying."

As a baby in the camp, she learned to stop crying. Asked when she started crying again, she said that it was not until she was four years old and she and her mother and grandmother were in Rumania. They had remained in the area in the hope of finding her father. One day her mother had been singing in a theater, and the director gave the child a song to sing about a father. She started crying and could not stop. Later, she said, she found herself unable to breathe:

> My grandmother slapped me to bring me back to life. I started crying and now I cry quite a lot. That's why acting is my life, because I am given permission to express all the pain that is just there. I carry all those dead people with me. *[She then showed pictures of her deceased father and grandmother.]*

When she was still a small child, a friend had given her a doll. As the family was leaving Rumania to cross into Poland, the customs officer tore open the doll. "It was like straw inside. I learned at a very early age not to scream. My mother said I had an 'alten Kopf' [old head] like a grown person, not like a child." Asked what had happened to the doll, she replied that her mother had lost it.

Her earliest memories include sleeping between her mother and her grandmother, which gave her a feeling of closeness. When asked to imagine being fed with a spoon, she connected it with what her mother had related to her. She was constantly hungry as a child. "They used to feed me with two spoons, that's how desperate they were." But it was primarily her grandmother who raised her. Her mother was too involved with running away from the past, although Dorothy remembers her mother braiding Dorothy's hair—that was a pleasant memory. Her grandmother, though a good caretaker, was not affectionate. "Being held is being protected," Dorothy explained. She had had none of that. She carries her father's picture, however, and this gives her a sense of his presence and perhaps a feeling of being held. She said, "His picture makes me pretend he is here."

They settled in Israel and her mother remarried. She became uncomfortable speaking about her stepfather:

> He was an intruder and not a nice man. He was a vulgar man, and he had no understanding of children. He and mother fought all the time, physically. I ran away a few times, but Mother always brought me back.

She had many nightmares:

> I was running and somebody was running after me and trying to kill me. I would get a brilliant idea. I would play dead. And that's what I did. I was terribly afraid of the danger. Those dreams started at an early age and lasted for a long time. There was a knowledge that they are going to kill me, but there was no one there.

Dorothy married in Israel and had three children. She found it very hard to hear a baby cry; if her child cried, she had to run and pick it up right away. She described herself as an ignorant mother, one who ran away from her babies and left them to the maid. (Perhaps she did it to escape their cries.) Describing this, Dorothy became agitated and lost her breath as she was talking. She explained that when things got difficult, so too did breathing.

> I was just thinking—if someone tied me up so I could not cry and I got a lot of tears under my nose, then I would not breathe with my mouth closed and my nose full. But that does not ring a bell. I am on the wrong track.

A medical emergency, a ruptured ovarian cyst causing severe hemorrhaging, led her to medical care and later to therapy. When the doctor told her she might not make it, she could not breathe. "I was tired of life and fighting and struggling and having so many problems. I wanted to retire and take it a bit easier." Her recovery felt to her like survival, but after the surgery, I again could not breathe, and then I started to go to therapy. I had already three children, so I had a lot to live for. Then I discovered that my breathing had to do with facing death. I went back to [acting] in the theater. That and my therapy helped me a lot.

In 1978 she came with her husband to the United States and entered therapy there. "I could go to therapy all my life," she said. "I get hopeless. It's forever dark and I want to cover up and hide. Sometimes I feel I run on a thin line. I just run to therapy."

Finally she told the interviewer about her relationship with her mother and father. "I am definitely like my father," she insisted. She could remember her mother and grandmother whispering about him at night, and she would hide because it was too painful. As for her mother, she doesn't have a very good relationship with her. "She tells my children I was an angel, and I wasn't. That's why I can't have a relationship with her." She feels it is her un-angelic anger that has allowed her to survive—an anger she wants to hold onto.

In her last meeting with the interviewer, she related that she had stopped therapy and that she and her husband had separated (though he wanted them to go back to a marriage counselor, which they eventually did). As with other relationships, she finds this one hard to maintain without intermittent times of distancing.

Discussion

Dorothy's experience of being gagged and hidden seems to be a recurring metaphor for her life: her problems in breathing brought on by fear; her angelic behavior, from which she wants to escape to free herself from being bound by anger; and her dreams that she can escape danger by playing dead. Her difficulty in maintaining intimate relationships, common in child survivors, seems more closely connected to her not very affectionate grandmother, her distant and depressed mother, the loss of her father, and a difficult stepfather—hardly a school for learning intimacy.

In sum, Dorothy can be assertive in identification with her grandmother, but more often she seems to feel suffocated and fearful of death in identification with herself as an infant. It is hard for her to connect her symptoms to her early experiences, because the experiences were so remote and seem so unlikely; the symptoms are therefore that much harder to overcome.

Sarah: An Older Infant Survivor

Sarah was born in 1942 in Vienna. Her parents, taken away when she was three months old, eventually died in the concentration camp at Auschwitz. She was raised by her grandmother and Catholic grandfather, so she was protected until he died. She was also hidden by nuns for a while and was baptized. However, in 1943, she and her grandmother were taken to the concentration camp at Theresienstadt.

Sarah does not remember anything about the Holocaust, but she has vivid memories of the following era. Her grandmother befriended a man who molested the little girl. "He was the kind of man who would change religion if it suited him,"she said contemptuously. "He obviously did not go all the way, but he grabbed me a certain way. I shudder to think that this man was around me for a long time."

Sarah also remembers receiving confusing messages from her grandmother about other things. Her grandmother took her to the synagogue every Friday night, but then would say, "There could not be a God if he let your parents die." Sarah's uncle was no more comforting. He said, "Your mother did not have to die, because her father was not Jewish. But she loved her husband and went with him." This uncle is a bitter man who did not tell her anything of the past. (Neither the grandmother nor the uncle seemed to focus their anger on the perpetrators.)

One can sense the grandmother's bitterness. She was unable to give her granddaughter any affection the entire time she was growing up. "I hugged my grandmother once," Sarah remembered, "and she said, 'That hurts, stop.' I never hugged her again." But all Sarah ever had, she said, was her grandmother:

> She was a strong individual to give up her country for me, put up with all the suffering. She never let on what she went through. But I was very unhappy growing up with her, and I don't know why. I have a son who is the same way. Since he was fifteen he has been talking about moving out.

Sarah also resented the way her grandmother used her as a showpiece of Jewish victory: "She wanted me to join a choir and wander around with them even though I couldn't sing. I was always on display. I had to play several instruments and do acrobatics, which I hated." She still feels unconnected to her grandmother and turns instead to the image of her mother:

> I am told that I am just like my mother. My family hurt me a great deal, and I think it is all connected. In high school I took a test for careers, and it showed that I had too many mother images in my life. At that time I went to see a psychologist, and I totally changed. I never had had moods before. After that I had moods and explosions and more of a temper. The interview with a psychiatrist a few years ago totally unglued me.

It seemed that searching for her past and for her connections was alarmingly disturbing for her. She had too many mother images, but not enough mothering.

Raising children was a challenging experience. She related that she nursed all her children and wanted to do the best for them and for her marriage, but clearly it had not been easy.

> My youngest used to vomit all the time, I thought he was going to die on me. I was afraid he would choke to death, and then I had him sleep with me. I didn't sleep for like

three years because I was awake fearing he might choke to death. It turned out he was allergic to his own bacteria.

Sarah was recuperating from hepatitis, which had recurred off and on for years. She had a spastic colon and ulcers, both typical survivor problems. "I am recovering from an ear infection, I have nausea, and I feel like vomiting. Now I have been getting rashes and scratches. I break out in hives, but I will not go to an allergist." When the interviewer suggested that she dreads certain ways of being touched, she agreed, relating that dread to the sexual abuse she suffered as a child.

"I used to love motherhood," she said. "Now you can have it. My kids don't care about me. My son mouths off at me and yells at me—but there is something special between us." Regarding her parents, she said that when she was growing up she didn't miss them, because you can't miss something you don't know anything about. Sarah had no recollections about the concentration camp or her parents. "I don't ask questions. I don't want to hurt them [her family]. I think I am protecting myself." Later, however, she offered a different perspective:

In my mind, I am my father's pet. I also have a couple of dolls that were my mother's. My mother knitted a little dress for me. I have it; I save everything. Everything is important to me. My house is a mess because I can't part with anything.

She noted that her illnesses probably stem from the concentration camp and the absence of milk in her diet there. To another interviewer she said, "I just can't cope with hunger and I can't stand being cold. My husband does not understand all this."

Her interviewer suggested that much of her memory is bound to her somatic symptoms in a perpetual reliving of her camp experiences. He noted that she seemed lost and sometimes bewildered. Later, when he saw her in the company of older child survivors from Theresienstadt, she appeared more "complete" as a follower of older children.

Discussion

Sarah, like Dorothy, appeared to somatize her trauma. She also seemed to want to be taken care of in a way that she missed as a young child. It was not only the concentration camp that affected these young children and ruined their childhood, but also the depression of their caretakers afterward.

Sarah's relationships with her parents were ambivalent. On the one hand, she said she could not miss what she never had, but on the other, she identified with and cherished both of them. She kept everything because she could not bear to part with "anything."

Loss of a parent or parents intensifies the search for the past. Robinson (1979) suggested that infants in the Holocaust were too young to remember relatives who were lost. However, in both the cases just discussed, infant survivors held onto the memories created out of the partial narratives of others. In particular, Dorothy and Sarah held onto material objects, a mother's knit dress or the photo of a father, that offered a kinesthetic connection to the past, their primary mode of connecting.

There are many similarities in these two women—similarities seen in others who were infant survivors. Mazor et al. (1990) spoke of the efforts made by child survivors to remember their past in order to render their personal histories coherent. This characterizes infant survivors as well. But it seems that the limited memory of very young children persecutes them with incomplete images and uncertain feelings. As Sarah says, she has too many mother images. Lacking cognitive memories, children carry their memories primarily in their bodies. Thus somatized, these memories, rather than bringing release from the past, resurrect the suffering.

Harriet: A Latency Survivor

Latency children tend to be cooperative, work well with adults, and are relatively reasonable and emotionally stable, qualities that usually served them well in the camps. Further, those who were in latency during their concentration camp experience can later remember much more and can therefore cope better with the aftereffects.

Harriet was born in Rumania in 1933. The first ten years of her life were very happy. She had spent summers in Maramoresz with her maternal grandparents, and she had wonderful memories of Jewish holidays, relatives, and playing with other children. She could close her eyes and remember her nana, a Russian woman engaged to nurse her. The nana was then suckling her own son, too. Harriet claimed to remember the nana holding both of them, one at each breast: "I almost have no doubt in my mind that that's the way it was." Later memories included the following: "I remember bringing the poorest children home and feeding them with marmalades, and then Mother came—I saw her shoes first. 'Will she be angry or not?' Then she started laughing." She also recollected being terribly afraid of ghosts and her father's telling her, "You are much stronger than any ghost you will ever meet." Later she walked toward an object she feared was a ghost, and it turned out to be a sheet the maid had forgotten to take in. "I had such a wonderful childhood," she said. "That's why I think I survived."

She has other memories too, less pleasant—of being sick, of being locked in a closet by her aunt as a punishment, and of being deprived of things by her parents. Sometimes she would be teased by Christian children; they would call her Zyda (grandfather) or make up rhymes about dirty Jews. They would say, "You are Jewish, I am not. I am clean, you are not." The peasant girl employed by her family told her that Jews killed Christ, and that Jews took the blood of Christian children to make bread for the holidays. The children told her that too, but that was only children's talk. When there was more serious talk in school, she would go home and cry and would tell her parents about it. Her mother would say, "We have to understand this. There are those who hate and those who love, and the best thing is not to look for trouble." Both her parents and her grandparents inculcated in her a pride in her Jewish identity. They would tell her, "We are the people of the Bible and the prophets, and we are taught how to behave, to love other people. This comes from our great sages and from Moses. The Gentiles do not have such an up-bringing."

She recalls at the age of five seeing bedraggled people coming in hordes:

> I asked who they were, and the teacher told me they were Christian Poles, escaping from Hitler. I offered them my lunch and said, "Here is lunch." And they said, "We want nothing from Jews." Why were they so angry? I had tears in my eyes, and I asked, "What's wrong with the Jews?" I had difficulty falling asleep that night. Many years later my own child in Montreal asked me, "Mommy, what's wrong with being Jewish?" My main concern was not to instill prejudice in my children.

Signs of impending trouble increased gradually. One day her best friend told her that she did not like Jews. She said, "I like you, but you are an exception." She explained that Jews are not really nice people, "but we have to be nice to them, especially to the rich ones." Harriet believed it was March 19, 1941, when Hitler came and it was announced that Jews must wear yellow stars.

> I said, "I want mine very big." Later, I heard we were going on a trip to Hertobagy. I was happy because we were going to ride Hungarian horses. But they came for my father and took him away along with other intelligentsia. He said he was going to do some work and we would all meet in a few days. I was told we are going to a ghetto. It was still dark and my mother said, "It's very cold, you must put on several things." The maids were crying, and I told them not to cry: "After the war we will be back."
> The Germans were so rough. There were carts and carriages full of Jewish people. And then I saw a terrible sight: I saw some man, a poet, who was about a hundred years old, and I saw this man being hauled up in a sheet. He was crying

and begging in Yiddish, "Please let me stay. I want to die here." Then I began to understand what pain and suffering were. I became very angry. *Don't they have a heart? How can they do it?* They threw him at other people. People were crying and hugging, and when these uniformed men saw that, they would strike out with whips. It gave me a terrific rage in my stomach. The Hungarians were not sad; some were smiling.

Now I shall talk about the trip to Auschwitz: the stench, the lack of food, and so many of us—I could not understand how I could stand without my feet being grounded. And then somebody died. They threw him out on the way. People had to urinate over themselves. It's beyond words. This was four days and three nights. My mother was always hovering around. Then when we got out, there was a long convoy and a line here and a line there. I was pushed and shoved, and a man in stripes came and asked me how old I was, speaking in German. Then very quickly in Yiddish he said, "Say you are eighteen and this is not your mother." And he pushed me in the line where the adult people stood and my mother too. This man saved my life. Otherwise I would have gone straight to the crematorium.

All of a sudden I saw myself in the line with the big people, and I felt big and tall. I understood that I had to toe the line. We had to undress and were shaved. I was upset seeing my mother naked—it was so humiliating. I was trying to be close to my mother, but [was] not speaking to her. We got into this huge barracks, and there were one thousand people in there. No sooner [had] we got into the barracks [than] there was someone yelling, "Zahlappell" [roll call]. Then I remember getting a number with striped clothes. We got black coffee and black bread and sometimes a piece of margarine. I used the coffee to wash my face. There was a common latrine, and each time we sat down, Irma Greese would come through with a whip. She was a lovely-looking creature—and she held a whip. Several times I got hit with it. Some women had scars all over their breasts and everything.

At night, mother and I slept together and held each other closely. There was a danger that they would separate us.

They would come in the middle of the night, drunk, and whoever they put the rifle on had to get out, and these women never came back. They were abused. When two women held each other, they would say "Scheisse" [shit] and separate them. It was just holy terror. They were laughing and hitting them apart.

One morning they put something mushy in my hand—a dead baby—and said, "Bury it." I was obedient and did what I was told. I went to the back of the barracks and tried to scoop earth with my hands. I was trying to make this hole and I succeeded. I see a pair of boots standing in front of me, and it was Hanna, the kapo [prisoner who was supervisor of work details], and when I looked at her, she turned away.

For Harriet this was an important moment. She felt she had prevailed. A similar incident of momentary confrontation occurred later, when Harriet was taken to Salzwedel, a labor camp in Germany.

One day when I returned from my work at the ammunition factory, I saw the kapo führer beating down on something in a hole. Then I saw a woman's head bobbing up and down, and he beat her into this mass with his boot. The background to this horror scene was the setting sun. He was screaming in German, with foam on his mouth, in a rage. I retreated, but he came toward me, advancing, still the saliva dripping from his mouth and his eyes really bulging, and my heart was pounding. So I kept walking. He said, "verfluchter Jude" [damned Jew] and held his gaze on me. Trying not to let my voice tremble, I said "the setting sun" in German. And inside I was thinking in Hungarian, *You scum, I hate you and you don't even know it.* And I consider that a triumph. Even though my heart was beating, I was not consciously aware that I was afraid. I did not need nightmares, because this is what I did with my aggression. I thought, *I am a child and you are thirty or forty years old and I am so much younger than you and so weak and helpless. But you don't know what's on my mind.* I never told anyone what I saw, not even my mother. Telling it to Dr. S.M. on TV, I felt a tremendous relief.

Harriet's assertiveness and clinging to her dignity also expressed itself in her attitude and behavior toward other camp workers. She told this story:

> When the Americans bombed Salzwedel, we, the women, had to clean up, and there were three SS women with us. There was an old lady there shoveling. So I said to her in Yiddish, "Pretend you are shoveling, and I will do it for you." I did, and I got a whack with a shovel on my back. I stood there and saw an airplane and said, "Look," and they screamed that we should lie face down. But [their] attention was attracted to the plane and this worked beautifully. I went on my back and was able to see the most unbelievable fireworks of my life, and flashes of lightning between planes. What was even more fascinating, this SS woman was urinating, excreting, all at the same time over her boots. She was shivering and shaking in a panic. When it was over, I got up and pretended I did not see, and it worked. I was more afraid of being whacked again than of the bombs.

Harriet's disobedience here was another triumph that allowed her to keep her dignity and sanity. It was important also that despite being made to feel like animals, the prisoners were able to keep to a higher moral standard than their "superior" tormentors, Harriet said.

She recalled liberation and her post-camp experiences:

> On April 14, 1945, the Americans came, and I saw a soldier crying. He looked at me and said, "Frei [free]. Leave frei." I jumped on the tank and fell. I was skin and bones— I weighed maybe sixty pounds. They took everyone into the infirmary, but many people died from overeating. My cousin and my aunt died the same day.
>
> One day a civilian German took me aside and asked me, "Who are you?" I told him, "Jews." He asked me, "What did you do?" I told him, "Nothing. We are Jews." He had not known. He was bewildered.
>
> From Salzwedel, we went to Hamburg, because we did not

want to stay with the Russians. I was afraid of the Russkies.
People from Israel came to take children to Israel, but my
mother did not let me go.

Her mother wanted to go back to Hungary to find her jewels,
but Harriet refused and eventually prevailed. The two remained
in Hamburg, waiting for her father to reappear. He never did.
(They heard two stories, equally painful, of how he died.)

Harriet's adultlike independence led her to leave Europe.
When a man started courting her mother, she decided to leave
and joined a transport of children going to Canada. Still only
fifteen, she passed for twenty-two and was taken on as a chap-
eron. That was in 1948. She began working in Canada, married,
had children, and was later divorced. Always fiercely independent, she created a career for herself and became a relationship therapist, helping people who do not get along with each
other. She has not suffered psychosomatic symptoms, although
when she visited Hungary once, she felt sick and left immediately. It was a place where she had not been wanted, and she could
not remain. She felt she could deal with the past and could discuss it. She told her children, "I have been in Auschwitz. If you
want to know about it, ask me." (For many years, they did not.)

Asked how she has been affected by her experiences, she said
that they gave her a greater depth of feeling. She had a strong
anger against the Nazis and vividly described what she would do
to one if she caught him.

Recollecting it all, she said, "This is how I grew up. The instinct to survive jolted me into growing up. And I never lost my
faith. The most amazing thing is that I prayed to God every night
in Auschwitz too." And she retained her dignity, her anger, and
a sense of pride in herself. She says, "Until today, whenever I am
asked if I am Hungarian, I say I am Jewish."

Discussion

Harriet was a girl who went through hell, aged quickly, and yet
retained her bravery, dignity, and strength. She used her stability

to remember the past and her anger to cope with it. She has suffered no psychosomatic symptoms, fears, or nightmares, although she has been depressed at times. Her pride in being Jewish, developed in the prewar period, included a fear of not being wanted, a reminder of those many times when she was rejected.

Harriet spent all of her latency and part of her early adolescence suffering persecution. She appeared to have managed well in the post-Holocaust era by focusing on the qualities particular to latency children. She spoke always of integrity and dignity, and in a way was a latency superwoman. Although she aged rapidly, in the sense that she had to act the part of an adult, developmentally she persisted in the latency–early adolescence pattern, which earlier had served her so well.

David: An Adolescent Survivor

Adolescents understand reality better than latency children do. Often they are physically strong, proud of their work, and able to undertake it. Survival and successful adaptation are common among this group.

David was born in Zydowska Kalwarja in December 1925. His parents had a bakery. There were two girls in the family in addition to David. He attended a Polish school with only five Jewish children, in a very anti-Semitic town. He recalls,

> I went to school five days a week, and we had to beg the Polish children to give us the homework that was given on Saturdays. I gave them white bread in exchange for homework. My father was not fanatic, but he was religious. I studied in the cheder.
>
> When the teacher asked the children what they will be when they grow up, they said fireman or carpenter, and the Jewish kids said doctor. The Polish kids made fun of us and called us doctors.

When the war broke out, David and his father fled toward Russia, but when they reached Cracow, the Germans had already arrived, and they were forced to return home. His mother and sisters also fled and returned. In the early period, they had permission to keep the bakery open, and they gave out bread "on cards." After six months, though, Jews were ordered not to walk outside except on side streets. David relates,

> They had their little hunts. The Judenrat[1] did the dirty work for the Germans, and the Jewish police helped them also. The Polish women waited for the Germans with flowers in their hands. They pointed out Jews to them. However, there were instances where the Poles helped us, especially in the countryside.
>
> In the winter of 1939 they took away our skis, our furs; and they would always collect something from Jews. Then they began taking people to work building roads for the Germans. I was very young; they took my father more often. They did not beat us, but were harassing us something terrible. They took over a church or a synagogue and made a stable out of it for horses. Then they would take Jews to work with the horses.

One day they took David to a labor camp. However, they gave him a chance to say good-bye to his family. His mother cried, he said, but "my father was always quiet, did not show his feelings. It was something not unordinary that during the war children kept quiet and hardly ever cried. So my sisters never cried. I never saw my family again."

At the camp, David said,

> We had terrible masters. One day I was told to clean the offices and bring water. When I was finished, I was afraid to sit down, so I came to the boss and told him I had finished. So he liked that and he gave me easy work. I always tried to be reasonable and dependable. I did not speak nothing but Polish, but the German civilians seemed to trust me. In the

---

[1] Council of Jewish representatives set up in communities and ghettos under the Nazis to carry out their instructions, ensuring passivity and compliance.

summer of 1942 they closed the camp because of incidents
of typhoid. We had gone to the hospital, and I was feverish
and unconscious for seven days. Then I fell out of bed. The
medic saw I was not dead and gave me an injection. I was
like a stick. I had to come back to my room on my hands and
knees. The feldsher [medic] kept me with himself and gave
me extra bread and soup.

David was often resourceful, never fully giving way to a feeling of hopelessness. After work he searched around for dead
people and took their bread. Other times he was simply lucky.
Selected for a work crew, he was warned by the Jewish police to
give money and jewelry, but he had none. He was then selected
for Erhohlung (recuperation), which generally meant death. But
instead, his group was sent to Schindler.[2]

Then we were taken to the kitchen for some food. Schindler
came and said if people felt weak they could go to the hospital, but people did not believe him because sick people
used to get killed. I was about fifteen or sixteen. Some Poles
called me Jidiszek [little Jew] . . . , or Moishek [nickname
for Moshe or Moses], but names no longer bothered me.
That's how they used to call us before the war.
At times we worked twenty-four hours. When the Russians
neared, we worked disassembling the factory, loading the
stuff onto railroad cars to go further into Germany. In the
new factory, a man came with a whip and beat some of us.

From one place to the next, they were moved, always
working long, hard hours. David, however, had recurring
incidents of good luck. One master was a fair man and
asked him if he was in touch with his family. He replied that
they had all been killed. The master said, "Impossible." Then

---

[2] Oskar Schindler, German Catholic profiteer industrialist, Direktor of
a prison camp, who saved more than a thousand Jews from the gas chambers
by having them work at his factory-camp—at greater personal cost than any
other single person during World War II.

he tried to console David by saying that after the war David would
go to Palestine.

> Near the end of the war they took us by foot to Czechoslo-
> vakia. We were dragging our feet, seeing the Germans flee
> from the Russians. One day they took us to Theresienstadt,
> and there we were awaiting the end of the war. We would get
> a portion of bread every day. I was so surprised to see Rus-
> sian prisoners of war about my age who were anti-Semitic.
> They divided everything among themselves, but they said
> that Jews were parasites, sitting in offices, while they are
> workers. First they would eat, and then when nothing was
> left, they called us in. We were so hungry—reduced to an
> animal state. We would dream of a loaf of bread. We would
> eat flowers, yellow ones, and sometimes coal.
>   When the armed Russians came in, we opened the gates.
> After liberation, we thought to take revenge, but it did not
> work out that way. I met an officer with boots on. I called
> him over and asked for the boots, and he gave them to me
> and was barefoot. His boots were excruciatingly uncomfort-
> able, and I came back to Poland that way.

David hoped to find someone from his family still alive in his
hometown, but he did not. He ran away from there very quickly.
Not to find anybody was quite painful. On his return to Cracow,
he found a youth group being organized for aliya (immigration
to Israel). He met his future wife and left for Palestine in 1945.
He was in Atlit, a receiving camp in Israel, when the British
caught him, but when he was freed he went on to Palestine
proper, met up with his wife, and helped found a kibbutz called
Fighters from the Ghetto. He said,

> I could no longer be religious. I joined the Kibbutz Shomer
> Hatzair [a group of kibbutzim of socialist orientation]. I had
> some fears. I was afraid of Poles, even my own age. I still was
> afraid to walk the streets at night in Poland. I used to be
> afraid of dogs, but not anymore.

The kibbutz provided an environment of emotional and physical security. There he also found a former friend from the labor camp and other Jews who had gone through the Holocaust.

He says, "It would have been too painful to name my children after their grandparents or my sisters. So my older is Nurit and another Edna, who is in the army now." But in a group of survivors, one does not forget the past.

Asked what was the worst experience for him during the Holocaust, he responded,

> It was such a long period of suffering that there was no incident that was worse than another. For instance, before I was taken to the camp, at home the worst time we had was when my father used to go to town to buy some food and not return on time, and we all would sit at the window and worry.
>
> Today's discussion disturbed me. There were a few spots where—but I have to learn to control myself. I cry when I am alone. I have just thought about it recently [crying]. The train would arrive in an area where the people practically knew that it would mean death to them—none cried, as if they were made of cement. I think when one is chronically hungry, one does not permit oneself to think of anything else but food. I remember that I always kept a small piece of bread from the day before for a bad moment. It was easier to be hungry with that piece of bread in my pocket. Then one night someone stole it from me. It was worse than if someone stole from me today a sum of money. I used to steal too, but I never used force because I was too weak. When we got out of the barracks in Germany and a woman passed with a child, we would not stop her for food because she was with the child.

Discussion

Being an adolescent meant that David was strong compared with younger children. He could work harder and deal with his hunger better and more creatively. In many cases, adolescents were stronger than adults as well. They understood the reality of survival and adapted to it. Proud of their work, they did a good job for the Germans and often found a German who liked them and would help them out, as David did on several occasions. In contrast, most middle-aged adults became emotionally and physically debilitated in such conditions. They were not physically prepared for the hardships, whereas children—especially the stronger, older ones—could fix their minds on survival and continue on. David did so without giving up his integrity. He stole bread only from the corpses, refusing to take food away from a mother and child. He was not forced to give up all the values with which he had been raised, and this kept him from complete humiliation.

In contrast to smaller children, David, even more than Harriet, was quite accustomed to anti-Semitism. No one could offend him by calling him a dirty Jew. He knew the aggressor was wrong, and his self-esteem did not suffer as much as did that of younger children. Also, in contrast to smaller children, both Harriet and David were old enough before the war began to have developed a sense of identity and pride in being Jewish. They had already established protective mechanisms to deal with anti-Semitism. Understanding what was happening allowed them to seize the moment, become adultlike, and cope. Further, older children had memories of their family and a part of their earlier childhood. In many cases they were able as adults to re-create families—through marriage and parenthood, and, in David's case, by joining a kibbutz.

Small children and infants grew up to find that they had had no childhood and no parenting. A lost mother or father who could not be remembered was gone completely, as if childhood had never existed, as if a loving, protective family never was. Such persons often become persecuted by their search for this past, and their memory of it becomes expressed in somatized forms. Although they too marry and have children, they must work much harder to create a family from such elusive memories. Rather than suffering less because of their limited memories, they seem in fact to suffer more.

Mixed Experiences

In some cases, children suffered the experiences of ghetto life, concentration camps, and being hidden or taken in by foster parents. Separation from one's mother is often the most traumatic aspect of these experiences. There is also a fear of being hurt in other ways, but with children who were taken in by foster families, there is often a confusion concerning identity and concerning modes of forming and breaking off relationships with others.

Guta's Experiences

For example, Guta was born in 1940 and spent her infancy in a ghetto and in a labor camp. However, her parents were able to send her into hiding with a Polish couple. Her adopted Polish father was good to her and adored her. Her adopted mother, however, made her afraid of Jews, telling her that they would kill her if they found her. When her uncle came for her after the war, she refused, saying she did not want to go with a Jew. However, she did not stay with her foster family either.

What has happened to her? What does she repeat from her infancy? She cannot imagine back to her childhood and recapture visual images, but she retains bodily memories of childhood. For example, she showed her abdomen, from which as an adult she hears noises that she thinks were related to feelings from her childhood. Specifically, she recalls feeling the birth of her little sister in her own abdomen, a sister she lost when she was fostered out. Today when she is scared she feels it in her abdomen too, and she has developed psychosomatic disease.

In her creative work she recapitulates aspects of her experiences in infancy and childhood. She is highly educated and is a great painter and poet who paints and writes about the Holocaust. She was married for many years and had two children, but she said that the marriage had no passion in it and ended in divorce. With another man, she had a passionate affair that lasted for two years. It is possible to see in this leaving of her husband and then her lover a repetition of her separation from her mother (by whom she may have felt abandoned) and from her foster father, who had loved her so much.

Benjamin's Experiences

Similarly, Benjamin was born in 1940 in the ghetto and was then taken to a labor camp for a while. Eventually he was hidden with a very good foster mother, who raised him as a Catholic and—again we hear this—frightened him with warnings about being shot by Jews so that they could make matzoh from his blood. When reunited with his mother and sister after two and a half years, he did not recognize them. There followed several successive separations from his mother and sister in various countries.

What has happened to him? In adolescence, he was obsessive-compulsive, and traces of compulsive touching have remained with him. He was treated for this disorder and substantially recovered. Afterward he began to wander from one place to another, always becoming depressed when he left one place and found himself alone or separated. Once he was so depressed he married a Jewish woman with whom he was not in love. After having two children with her, he left, perhaps as his mother had often left him. He was remarried—this time to a Gentile, with whom he had two more children. Like others discussed here, he appears to recapitulate aspects of his past. He even re-creates his original nuclear family of husband, wife, and two children. His greatest problem is his identity; he does not know where he belongs. When he finally found a substitute for his lost Polish mother, he was faced with her insistence on bringing up their children as Christians.

Discussion: Guta and Benjamin

In both Guta and Benjamin, we have examples of *acting out*, a term that probably overlaps with Keilson's (1979) *character neurosis*. As an adult, Guta began searching for her roots when she was twenty years old. Part of her search involved the re-creation of "just the right family" and leaving those that cannot satisfy her requirements. Similarly, Benjamin wandered around profoundly dissatisfied with himself before winding up with his "Polish mother." Problems of identity affect making relationships and dealing with separations.

Their instability may also be attributed to the age at which they underwent these experiences. Unlike latency children, these infants did not have a firm base onto which to integrate their disorienting experiences.

General Discussion

Certain patterns tend to recur in persons who experience similar trauma at similar ages. The stage of development of a child suffering a trauma affects not only the immediate pattern of coping with the trauma, but also posttraumatic symptoms. Those who experienced concentration camps as infants, having little cognitive memory upon which to draw, often recapitulate their early experiences through psychosomatic symptoms in adulthood. Latency children not only draw on a developmentally based stability to cope in the camps, but use their clear memory, sense of integrity, and dignity to work through their sufferings in later life. Adolescents' commitment to work, their energy, and their focus on survival often serve them well in finding sources of aid in camps and in making their labor valuable. Unlike many adults in the camps, they did not become physically or emotionally debilitated, but could adapt to harsh conditions. In adulthood, they were able to draw on their good childhood experiences (in the prewar era), on an established sense of identity, and on a sense of capability to cope with posttraumatic stresses.

A recent study by Robinson et al. (1994) suggests that there are no clear correlations between age at the time of the trauma and later outcomes. The cases presented here suggest otherwise. It is difficult to compare the two studies, however: Robinson's material is based on a large number of questionnaires, whereas the material here is drawn from a smaller number of long, intensive interviews. The upcoming analysis of our fifteen hundred interviews will, we hope, shed additional light on this question.

We and other researchers agree, however, that the suffering of all children in concentration camps was tremendous. Many hidden children were also hungry and in fear and suffered frightening separations. Analysis of age-group patterns should not detract from the uniqueness of each experience and the importance of each story. What we hope to accomplish here by focusing on age is to validate the experiences of infants and small children, who are often told by their parents or other relatives that they were too young to remember. Relatives may find comfort in denying that the experiences had traumatic impact on the children, but this distances the grown-up child even further from his or her past and from the means of coping with the residues. Robinson, Keilson, Mazor, many other authors, and we ourselves all agree on the important point that a very young age did not insulate child survivors from the horrors of the experience and posttraumatic repercussions.

From recent work with survivors, we are learning how crucial it is to attend to people after severe trauma is experienced, no matter what their age. It is disturbing that after the Holocaust, when these children first came to the United States and to Palestine, no one listened to them. Often, having no one to whom they could unburden themselves, they lapsed into silence. We have learned a lot for today's children, and we hope that these lessons will be universally applied in the unfortunately numerous circumstances in which children continue to suffer trauma.

Hidden Children: Early Childhood and Latency

Judith S. Kestenberg, M.D.

Perhaps the first experience of hiding is the peekaboo game of the infant, who is indefatigable in pulling off the diaper from his mother's face and his own. He controls both his own disappearance and how long his mother can abandon him. This helps him overcome the frustration he experiences when his mother disappears from sight and does not come back for a while.

By the end of the first year, a baby develops stranger anxiety. In her mother's arms, she hides from the stranger, feeling safer being held than being alone and closing her eyes so as not to

---

Translated and revised by the author from "Versteckte Kinder. Latenzalter im Holocaust," in *Ein Ast bei Nacht kein Ast*. Edited by Wiesse J, Olbrich E. Göttingen, Vandenhoeck & Ruprecht, 1994, pp. 61–82. Used with permission.

see. She trusts that her caretaker will protect her from harm. When the protector leaves her for too long with a stranger in a strange environment, she becomes afraid and sad and loses her zest for life. It takes her some time to accept a trusted substitute to whom she becomes attached (Bowlby 1960, 1973; Spitz 1965).

As children grow older, they are taught not to go away with strangers and to make sure parents know where they are. Still, the hide-and-seek games continue until adolescence. They become longer and longer, and the aim shifts. The child does not want to be found quickly, but as a seeker, he wants to find the hidden person as quickly as he can. The frequency with which children play this game illustrates the fact that the child still tries to overcome his fear of being abandoned or lost, in addition to his wish to abandon his mother and make her disappear (A. Freud 1967). He still needs to feel that he can control the disappearance and the reunion.

In adolescence, the drive for independence becomes exaggerated. Many teenagers play the hide-and-seek game by going off, disappearing, and "abandoning" their parents without telling them when they will return. We know it is a hiding game because they come back in their own time and then want to see their parents immediately. An important aspect of development, therefore, is to become free of shackles without losing one's love of parents and friends.

During the Nazi persecution, the progressive developmental process, which usually ends in the adult's ability to separate without conflict, was interrupted and distorted. Hiding took on an ominous feeling. For children, it meant not only separation from the familiar and a feeling of abandonment, but also an exclusion from the mainstream of their contemporaries. It interfered with the development of trust and hope. Instead of voluntarily hiding, as before, now the children were forcibly hidden and confined. These hidden children became especially sensitive to even short separations, which they interpreted as disappearance and abandonment. The children became vulnerable to any sign of exclusion or rejection.

Varieties of Hiding

Children were hidden in convents, with Christian families, and in orphanages. Most of them had to hide their Jewish identity and change names. Some had to dye their hair or conceal it with a kerchief. Some moved freely in the hostile world, passing as Gentiles—Dwork (1991) refers to them as "visible"—whereas others never went outside for fear of being recognized as Jews. There were geographical differences also. Greek families hid in the mountains, some in monasteries. Yugoslavian children hid with the partisans and were protected in Italian camps. Many families were sheltered in Italian mountain villages. In Germany, children were hidden with Gentile families, often moving from place to place to avoid detection. In the final stages of the war they mingled with German refugees fleeing the advancing Soviet army and received lodgings and hot food from German relief organizations. Quite a few Jewish children in Poland passed as Gentiles and hired themselves out as farmhands. Some three-year-olds, taken by their rescuers to peasants, had to tend cows. Many of them understood the danger.

Many children roamed the countryside, begging and sleeping in fields and barns. When they were caught and the Nazis did not believe their stories of being Polish children whose homes had been bombed, they had to recite prayers to prove they were Catholic. So-called good Aryan looks and fluency in Polish were greater protection than false documents. Children were hidden in holes in the ground, in coal boxes, and in false wardrobes. In ghettos they were hidden in specially built bunkers. In Transnistria (Rumania) and in Polish labor camps, children were not officially allowed to stay and had to be hidden when SS controls came. In Buchenwald, Jerzy Zweig (1987), a boy under three, was hidden under garbage until the SS left. Once he heard the word SS, he never uttered a word or coughed. Several children in Auschwitz were hidden among corpses. One child hid herself among the corpses, reasoning that her captors would not kill the dead. In a few cases, children were hidden by maids or by friends of the family they had known for a long time. Some children lost their parents and never saw them again; others received visits, but each meeting raised the child's hopes, and good-byes were always painful. In convents in France, Belgium, Italy, and Poland, many children found a refuge and attached themselves to nuns. They were taught that Jesus loved them and that his mother, who was Jewish, looked out for all children (Kurek-Lesik 1991).

Many child survivors, especially in Eastern European countries, in effect are still in hiding. Afraid to disclose their identity, they have not told their children that they are Jewish. Some who vowed they would become nuns or priests, if only Jesus would help them to survive, have kept their vows. But none of those we interviewed have given up their Jewish identity, only their religion. They still hide in convents and in churches, which give them protection. Even today, many have a tendency to hide their stories; there is still a fear of exposure and a need for reassurance that they will no longer be penalized because they are Jews.

Quite a few children, thinking they were the only Jews left, did not come out of hiding after the liberation. Others did not want to leave their rescuers. For years they did not give up hope that the lost ones would come back. Seeing someone on the street who resembled a father or mother raised new hopes and occasioned renewed sadness when it was only a mistake (Keilson 1991).

Franciszka Oliwa (1986) wrote about Karolek, who arrived in Oliwa's home for children dressed like a girl. He responded only to a girl's name, Marysia, and never made a mistake about hiding his gender. It took a long time before he could accept himself as a boy and no longer needed to hide his genitals.

Many children constantly relived their traumatic experiences. At night, they screamed and called for their mothers. One girl had a nightmare during which she exclaimed, "No, no, don't kill my daddy, let go of my mommy." The nightmares usually persisted into adulthood. After about six months, the children calmed down and stopped talking about their wartime hiding. Soon, however, they experienced new rejections. The Polish schools in Otwock refused to accept them because the school staff feared the anti-Semitism of the other children. When they finally did attend schools, the Christian children, envious of the Jewish children's good food and clothing sent from America, called them names, threw stones at them, and took their books away. In most schools, Jewish children excelled in their studies. Obedient and industrious, they enjoyed learning, which they had missed. Another tragedy befell children who were sad, skinny, and underdeveloped and perhaps lacked blond hair and blue eyes. They were shunned by adoptive parents. Once more their "bad looks" caused their rejection.

A Note on Christian Children in Hiding

Polish Christian children reporting their wartime experiences recall how bad they felt when they saw Jews mistreated. Some gave food to Jewish children, and others assisted their parents in rescuing Jews. Sometimes they were envious of the attention their parents gave to the strange children, but only rarely did they give away the secret to the Nazis. In contrast to the Jews, quite a few Polish Christian children had to hide precisely because of their "good Aryan" looks. The Nazis kidnapped such children in order to Germanize them and forbade them to speak Polish. Those who could not be Germanized were sent to special camps. To avoid either danger, Polish families often hid their children. Today there are a great many Polish adults who were persecuted as children and who suffer the effects of childhood trauma. However, relatively few experienced the wholesale assault on their identity that was the lot of Jewish children.

The Hidden Child's Problems in Adulthood

The primary conflict besetting the hidden child's life was the conscious or unconscious uncertainty whether one wanted to be a Jew or a Gentile. Those in convents and in religious rescuer families, who found solace in Catholicism, still look back lovingly at their feeling of being protected and peaceful in church. The Nazi propaganda that Jews are inferior, the anti-Semitic indoctrination that they had killed Christ and that they drank the blood of Gentile children, made it difficult for some children to accept their Jewishness. As adults, they still feel at times that they are inferior to others. After the war and their immigration to other lands, this feeling was often reinforced when Western European or American children teased them because of their accents and lack of skill in their new language. In Eastern European countries, many child survivors married Gentiles and reared their children as Catholics. In the United States it is rare, but not unheard of, for children of Jewish survivors to do what their parents dared not do—marry out of their faith.

Unfortunately, many parents, adoptive parents, and rescuers tried to protect the children from knowing too much and from remembering the atrocities they had experienced. This attitude was continued after the liberation, and the prohibition against remembering was reinforced by communities, social workers, teachers, and even psychiatrists. As a result, quite a few still hide their innermost feelings for fear of being rejected and made to feel ashamed.

Those who lost their parents tend to idealize them and feel disloyal, as if they were desecrating their memories, when they are about to recall how angry they have been at them in the past. Those whose parents survived feel freer to profess anger at them, say, for having given them away to strangers instead of keeping them. Many still find it difficult to trust people and get close to them; some are loners who feel most secure when they can hide in their sheltered apartment and need fear rejection by no one. Instead of being excluded, which they fear, they exclude themselves. Some are angry at the whole world for not protecting them, and almost all are afraid of helplessness or any loss of control over their destiny. To combat this painful feeling, some vie for control and exclude others. In their great need to provide their children with a happiness they had lost, many have become overprotective of their children and are unable to share their sad stories with them. This silence may interfere with successful mourning, as does a persistence of guilt feelings related to survival. The fear of being alone flares up especially when children leave home. The reexperience of feelings related to hiding, such as anxiety, depression, and anger, is common when a husband or a child fails to return home on time or leaves on an extended trip. The more the child survivor tends to repeat what happened to her, the more difficult it is for her to enjoy to the fullest the ordinary pleasures of life.

A Young Child's Trauma and Its Sequelae

The following is an example of how symptoms in adulthood are connected with early childhood experiences in hiding. Only one such experience that affected the development of several symptoms is highlighted, but in fact this individual suffered a multitude of such traumas.

Janine never enjoyed life like other people. She tried to laugh off her depression, but she did not always succeed. When interviewed, she was phobic, uncomfortable in elevators, afraid of falling and of driving alone, and especially concerned about her children. Asked to relate her earliest memory, she told how at the age of eighteen months she suddenly awoke in a "grave." She found out later that she had been drugged and taken to a Christian family to be hidden. She remembered vividly that the walls of the "grave," the floor, and its ceiling were made of mud. She lay on a wide bed. She was afraid because she had never lain on a bed by herself before. There were strangers there whose language she did not understand, as she had just begun to speak and Yiddish was her native tongue. Although she had many traumatic experiences before and after the awakening in the "grave," this episode became an organizer of her life. She had not told this story to anyone before because no one had asked her.

The fright and the feeling of loss had never really left her. However, her fears of being enclosed in an elevator, of falling, and of becoming lost while driving alone were all belated attempts to master that terrifying and depressing episode of her early childhood in hiding. Reexperiencing her fears as an adult, she had a chance to resolve what she could not overcome as a toddler. She became especially depressed when her child left home for a while. She took to a couch, and—reenacting the scene in which she lay on the bed as in the grave—lay there terrified and sad, unable to do her housework.

The anxiety and depression seen here are normal enough responses to severe and chronic stress. Despite these burdens, many young hidden children learned a great deal from having been hardened and used to overcoming obstacles. Having been helped themselves, many hidden children have become altruistic people who respond well to groups of peers, as they did before and after liberation (M. Kestenberg and J. S. Kestenberg 1988). Their expectation of finding lost parents has waned through the years, as have their nightmares. The self-healing abilities of many are remarkable. They need help only when they encounter obstacles on the way to self-healing or mourning. The more they are able to talk about their experiences and share them with their children, the easier it is for them to mourn what they have lost with the family and the larger community.

Hidden Children of Latency Age

Children of latency age tended to be more obedient and more adaptive to the strange new requirements imposed by hiding than were preschoolers and reckless adolescents. Children from nurturing families had more trust, and thus a greater hope that they would survive, than those who came from dysfunctional or motherless families and could not identify with loving parents. The older they were, the more they could participate in their own rescue, and the less encumbered they were by having to hide their identity. The more steeped they were in Judaism or a belief in a good Jewish God, the less threatened they were by the new identity they had to assume for a time.

Franciszka Oliwa, a Jewish woman who headed the orphanage in Otwock, Poland, after World War II, describes vividly (1986) how children behaved after the war in the orphanage. The older children, once their initial distrust was overcome, actively guarded her. Once, when an ambulance came to take her to a hospital, several boys sent it away. Instead they brought a surgeon to examine her infected leg and thus saved her from an amputation. An eight-year-old boy, Jozio Rochman, periodically fell into states of wooden paralysis. Unable to move his legs during an attack, he did not lose consciousness, despite a high fever, but talked incessantly about his beautiful mother who loved him. When he had almost lost hope that he would ever see her again, she found him. Jozio was overjoyed, and from that time on his attacks disappeared. Such children in Polish Jewish homes had a great need to tell their stories, and representatives of the Jewish Historical Commission interviewed many of them.

After the Warsaw uprising in 1944, the families of resisters, whom the Nazis called bandits, could save themselves from deportation or slave labor in Germany only by going into hiding (Mazurczyk and Zawanowska 1983). Among them were Jewish children who passed as Gentiles in Warsaw. (Eventually, these older children or adolescents preferred to be sent to Germany rather than be deported to Auschwitz; once in Germany, they had to hide their identities.) Sometimes in Poland the children spoke Yiddish in their sleep, but the Poles did not give them away to the authorities. At the end of the war, many Polish rescuers and their children, for fear of persecution by their anti-Semitic neighbors, had to hide the fact that they had harbored Jewish children (Fogelman 1994).

The older the child in hiding, the more he was capable of understanding what happened and of remembering the Jewish customs and holidays from the pre-Shoah (pre-Holocaust) time. The older and the more active the child in hiding, the more she was taken into confidence by adults, and the more capable she became of acting courageously and enduring and hardship.

What happened to the hidden children after liberation depended not only on their pre-Holocaust experiences and their

ordeals during the Holocaust, but also on the social circumstances in which they found themselves after liberation (Danieli
1981). Some discovered that they had no relatives left in the
world; others were reunited with their parents or found relatives
to take care of them. Many had to stay in orphanages; others
were adopted by people who cared for them. A majority had to
keep their sorrow to themselves, and even more were forced to
live from day to day, adjusting to new circumstances over and
over again. Unlike adults, these children tried to assimilate to
whichever country they found themselves in at the time.

What follows is a discussion of latency-age children who were
forced into hiding in Poland. Their reaction to the initial separation from their mothers, their struggles to save their lives by
faking a new identity, and their subsequent lives growing up in
Poland after the war are all touched on. Most of the data are from
the reminiscences of Katarzyna Meloch (1987, 1989, 1990),[1] referred to here as Kasia, and from an interview conducted with
a child survivor we call Maniek. We acknowledge gratefully here
the work of our interviewers in Poland, primarily R. Raduszewski
and J. Witkowski.

Kasia

Kasia, born in 1931, lost both her parents in Bialystok, Poland.
In an essay (Meloch 1989), she compared her fate to that of other
hidden children who were about her age or younger. She read
about "herself" in the biographical accounts of Hanna Krall
(1985) and Henry Grunberg (Meloch 1990), both of whom she
envied. Hanna, who hid in the homes of several of her mothers'
clients, was not alone in an alien world. Her mother kept in touch
with her. Henry fought for his life alongside his mother.

Because Kasia's mother was a Communist, she accepted her
own death as inevitable, but she enjoined her nine-year-old

---

[1] Translations of Meloch's work by J. S. Kestenberg.

daughter to survive; she "fated her to life." Kasia, who came from an atheist family, heard the word *Jew* for the first time when policemen came to take her mother away. One of them said, "A Communist," but when he looked at her Russian passport, he added, "of course, a Jewess." Kasia's mother departed with the Germans, and Kasia never saw her again. Since her father had disappeared much earlier, she was left all alone except for relatives in the faraway Warsaw ghetto.

Mothers and Children

Many mothers fought for their children's lives and prepared them for life without them. While Kasia's mother drummed into her the address of her relatives, Maria Perlberger, Kasia's friend, called out to Kasia when they parted, "Go already, go already." In Birenbaum's fictional story of Martha, cited by Meloch (1989, p. 97), the mother did not allow farewells to be too long, saying "Do you want that we should both perish?" Like the others, Martha's mother wanted to safeguard her child; in the house, Martha heard family members speak about the need to give her into "safekeeping." The little girl pondered, *Is it like giving the furs into safekeeping?*

All these children felt abandoned by their mothers. Kasia must have had a long-standing resentment, because her mother worked for and devoted a lot of time to the Communist cause. Janka Herscheles (1946) wanted to die with her mother, but her mother enjoined her to live, no matter how much she would suffer, and refused to give Janka the poison that she herself took. Only after Janka became a mother herself could she forgive her own mother for not letting her die with her. However, not all parents had a say about the fate of their children. Quite a few were deported without being allowed even a word of good-bye (Vegh 1979). Reminiscing about her childhood in a French convent, Jessica could remember sitting in a meadow and looking at the back of her departing mother. Her mother visited Jessica more than once, but Jessica could not remember her coming, only her going. Parting after a visit was very painful. In many instances, children were already in hiding or were temporarily absent from home when their parents were deported.

Maniek

Maniek, born in 1931, escaped death because he was not home when his mother was taken away. At the age of nine or ten he became caretaker of the family; periodically he would take the train to the large city his family had lived in, where his aunt, who was married to a Gentile, remained. He would then return, with food for his family, to the small town where they were hiding. He did not share the resentment of children who felt abandoned by their mothers. Perhaps he too would have been resentful had he not been able to look back on his mother as a cheerful person, always smiling and nurturing. He may have enjoyed the experience of becoming the breadwinner of the family; it allowed him to play the role of his deceased father. It may well be that the less resentment generated in children by parents before the occupation, the less the children felt abandoned when forced to part.

Reactions to Separation

One of the greatest fears of children during the Holocaust was the fear of dying alone. Even sensitive mothers had difficulties in handling separations. Some did not want to prolong the agony of farewells; others were afraid that their children's refusal to leave right away would bring on a disaster. Many admonished their children to obey their caretakers for fear that they would be sent back if they rebelled or cried. Quite a few made the children feel that they had been chosen to survive and that it was their duty to do so (J. S. Kestenberg 1987a). Fathers were particularly likely to enjoin their children to live to tell what happened to Jews. Many fathers had joined the army and left their children when the war started. In Poland, many fathers tried to run away to Russia. However, even when both parents were instrumental in "sending" the children away, resentment was directed primarily against the mother. Most children treated their parents' parting words as a last will and testament. They began to take care of themselves in identification with the lost parents. Children who hid with their parents felt more secure, but the children lived in fear that their parents, who would have to leave periodically to go in search of food, would not return. In addition, parents' fear and depression contributed greatly to their children's lack of trust. Some children prayed not to be spared, but to die before their parents so as to not witness their murder.

Double Identity

When parents were able to plan separations, the children were often given Christian papers; it was drilled into them never to reveal their real names and to say only that their parents had died in a bombing raid and that they had no other relatives. Other children were given little preparation for their new lives. They would wake up suddenly in strange surroundings, terrified and bewildered. In some cases, children would enter a convent in the false expectation that they would find there a familiar home, only to experience the shock of being in a strange place where they knew no one.

Regardless of the circumstances of transition into the Christian world, all the children understood sooner or later that it was important to blend in and not be recognized as Jews, and some did not want to be Jewish. Krall (1985), born in 1935, was envious of Polish Gentile children, who could go to school and belonged, while she was just a "subtenant." She suffered most from the fact that she was different. As a child, she depicted herself in fantasy as the child of Polish aristocracy, a rescuer's child who hid a Jewish child. She did not want to be herself; she wanted to be the "other," the hider, not the hidden.

During the Warsaw uprising, Hanna Krall (1985) gleefully ran out of the house despite the bombing on the streets. She did not mind the danger as long as she was not singled out for attack as a Jewess. Similarly, the fictional Martha did not want to be different; she tried to emulate the Polish children with whom she played in the courtyard. "She learned quickly to behave like a born Christian" (Meloch 1989, p. 98). The influence of the street children was so strong that Martha even laughed with them "on the other side of the wall" while the ghetto burned.

Kasia too wanted to be like the "real Poles" (Meloch 1989, p. 98). In Turkowice she mingled with Germans, as did Gentile children, until her sister Irena reminded her that she should not attract the attention of the Germans. Maria Perlberger (Meloch 1989) believed what the Germans and some Poles said about Jews, whom she learned to despise, even though she missed her own family. In the house of Kasia's rescue, there hung at that time a poster with the caption "Jews—lice—spotted typhus." The Jew depicted on the poster was despicable-looking, but this figure did not arouse pain in her. It did not "touch" her; she felt separate and safe. For her, as for Maria, "mine" were those close to her—parents, aunts, uncles, grandparents—not Jews. They had never talked about themselves as Jews. Now the children's self-identification as Polish became a safeguard for survival.

Parents' lack of allegiance to Judaism allowed their children to separate themselves from their own people with ease. They learned to lie in order to live (Begley 1991). It was not easy to convince themselves that they were Christians, but the pretense became reality for quite a few. They prayed in churches in which the words of the Evangelist, full of accusations of Jews as Christ killers, were read. Kasia never doubted that this was true. The church and the chapel were the children's oases of safety. Kasia said the church gave them a spiritual nurturance they needed but did not receive in their atheistic homes. She did not feel stigmatized; she did not think that the blood of Jesus fell upon her own shoulders, because she did not belong to the daughters of the "guilty" tribe.

Kasia's false birth certificate bore the name of Irena Dabrowska, daughter of Anna, baptized in the church of Targowek. At first the certificate was something to study and to memorize. Over time, however, it became more than that; it became her identity. By contrast, children who came from religious or Zionist families or who were enjoined never to forget their origins only pretended to be Christians, though they kept their secret well. In some instances, continuous persecution and the fear of being caught did not allow children to forget they were Jews.

Maniek never had a baptismal certificate. When he lost his father to tuberculosis because proper care was unavailable, Maniek moved with his mother and his brother to a small town where they hoped to go unnoticed. One day, however, while he was in the city procuring food, his mother and brother were discovered and rounded up. When the Germans searched his aunt's apartment at about the same time, he was hidden in the pantry and not discovered. After that, he was sent off to a farm, where he was put to work. However, when Maniek's aunt was seized by the Nazis, the farmer made the child leave. For a while, Maniek found refuge with a friend of his aunt, but she too made him leave for fear of discovery. These fears were justified; a concentration camp or death was the penalty for harboring Jews.

Maniek literally had no time to think about his mother, his brother, or his aunt. His mother did not abandon him or send him away. She only sent him on necessary errands to secure food. Even though he does not say so, it seems evident that he felt honored he could perform the duties of an adult. Up to this point, however, he clearly had been a child. He and his friends looked on the German occupation as an adventure, and not until lightning struck did he perceive the peril of their situation. Left all alone, he acted in an adult fashion and took care of himself. Like Kasia, he came from an assimilated family, but he did not need to pretend to himself that he was Christian, even though the fact that he had a Gentile uncle might have encouraged it. Nonetheless, he could readily pass as a Pole because of his "good looks"—blue eyes, blond hair, a fair complexion.

Before the war, Maniek had experienced anti-Semitism—pogroms in his native town and cries of "dirty Jews"—but he himself had not felt any discrimination at the Polish school he attended. Thus, he was not directly touched by the scourge of being Jewish. During the war, however—especially after he was left alone—

things changed dramatically. For him there was no rescue in the
church and there were no nuns to succor him. He was hidden
only for a short time, and he then had to fend for himself like
a hunted animal. For a time he slept under a bench in the railway
station, where he was periodically picked up by the railroad police and beaten up. Perhaps at some level he considered the railroad a last link to his mother.

At no point during this ordeal did Maniek feel any resentment against his parents for not having protected him; he was
too busy protecting himself. However, he could not really protect
himself in an adult way. He was not prepared for capture, as he
had not made up a cover story and did not have a false birth
certificate. However, he did take care of his needs. He developed
a trade in cigarettes and became "rich." From time to time, he
would wash his hair and bathe his louse-infested body in a mu-
nicipal bath. Unlike the child cigarette vendors of Warsaw
(Ziemian 1963), he was alone except for a few weeks during
which he befriended another Jewish boy who was living in the
station. One day, however, the friend jumped off the trolley car
directly into the hands of the Gestapo, and Maniek never saw
him again. But there was no time for mourning or anger. He had
to go on. For a few months he was lucky; he found a "grandmother" whom he supported in exchange for a clean bed and
shelter. Then he was caught and brought to the Polish police for
interrogation. He knew that as a Gentile, he would be taken to
a children's camp; as a Jew, he would have to perish. To lead the
gendarmes on, he extemporized, giving them a random Polish
name and, to protect the "grandma," a false address. When
a routine check revealed that he was lying, the Polish gendarme
asked him point blank whether he was a Jew. Dumbfounded and
completely unprepared for the question, he confessed. He knew
then that he would have to die and thought constantly about how
they would "finish" him. He decided that a shot in the neck while
escaping would be his choice.

For the other children described here, an alienation from
their Jewishness helped them but also made them overconfident.
Maniek was perhaps not alienated enough, but his forthrightness

had an unusual effect on the gendarme, who delivered him to a children's home without disclosing that he was a Jew. Maniek, foreseeing that he would be sent to a notorious camp for Polish youth in Lodz (Witkowski 1975), spent only a night at the children's home and escaped once more. Afraid to be caught again, he traveled to Warsaw, expecting to find refuge with a friend of his aunt. Instead, he found Warsaw completely devastated by the Polish uprising. As he had done before, Maniek proceeded to the railroad station, where he took the first train out. It took him to a small town that was holding a market. His luck held, and he was promptly hired by a farmer. No one guessed he was Jewish. The farmer wanted him to marry his fourteen-year-old daughter, but Maniek, thirteen or fourteen himself, was not interested in girls, nor did he look forward to inheriting the farm. All he wanted was to survive. After liberation, having been interned briefly by the Soviets, he escaped once more and took a train to his hometown, where he found his aunt, who had survived. It must be added that taking a train at that time was no small feat. Thousands of people were migrating, and they would even ride on top of the train or cling to its sides. After this last dangerous journey, Maniek settled down to study.

The central theme in the lives of these hidden children was a need to pass as Gentile and be saved. Meloch (1989) has described what she calls the "Holocaust culture":

> Life in a situation where lying and tricking was necessary in order to be saved, and lying does not evoke moral opposition, that is one of the elements of the "Holocaust culture." Another element of this culture is the growing up in the role of a Catholic hating Jews and pretending to be Christian, knowing well that one is a Jew. (p. 99)

To live with a double identity, the children had to undergo a split in the ego, coupled with habituation to their situation. A similar split was operative when the children were confronted by death (DeWind 1968; Gampel 1988). Meloch (1989) describes a scene in her life and then comments:

I saw corpses on the street of the Warsaw ghetto. They were the steady element of the street landscape; they lay everywhere. I did not wonder about them. The disappearance of those close to us was such a natural thing that it did not evoke opposition.

In many cases, children did not face death as a natural end of life. For them death was equivalent to murder. But Jewish death was something which comes from people and is not proscribed by the order of nature. My people perished in the ghettos, in the camps and fighting, but never from illness or old age. . . . [Many, of course, died in the camps and ghettos from typhus, dysentery, or tuberculosis, but Kasia was not witness to it.] To this day, I cannot believe that death is calculated in the human fate. It seems to me that Germans invented it. (p. 6)

Two German authors, a filmmaker and a historian, would seem to agree: their book, a work of nonfiction, is entitled *Death Is a Master from Germany* (Rosh and Jäckel 1990).

Sudden Maturity

How did these hidden and hunted children deal with the extreme stress under which they lived for years? How did they handle their feelings while trying so hard to blend in with the Christian Polish environment? It is often remarked that they became adults at an early age. No doubt children who suffered physically, from starvation and disease, did indeed age (see Chapter 7). But did the hidden children who did not suffer from extreme hunger become adults prematurely?

Although hidden children had a measure of protection, they had responsibilities not normally expected of children. They could not cry when they felt anxious, lonesome, or abandoned. They could not confide anything about themselves to others. If they overplayed their Polishness, they endangered their lives, as Kasia did. Maniek hardly pretended; he was conscious of living in constant danger without protection. He said,

It is not possible to describe or understand it; it transcends human imagination. For so many years I lived on the edge between life and death; rather, death every day, every hour, threatened me.[2]

In contrast to more sheltered children, Maniek could not use isolation or splitting to dissociate himself from impending death. Dealing with Germans, he had to endanger himself to make a living:

All the time, I thought I lived illegally on credit. I looked the Hitlerites in their eyes, in which, at the end, also lurked an eerie fear, but if they recognized me, they would not hesitate nor blink an eye and would murder me—not even just a Hitlerite, any German would do that.

In this passage, Maniek concurs with Kasia. For him, too, death came from the Germans. Confronting them daily as he did, he faced death every day and could not ignore it. Can we even properly describe him as hidden child? Might it not be more appropriate to call him a hunted child—or a hunted, prematurely aged boy? An alert, intelligent child, he became the family breadwinner shortly after his father's death. Because his parents had treated him kindly and lovingly, and because he had a solid background of family safety before the occupation, he was able to become self-reliant and take charge of himself. We heard from him that he had a beautiful, elegant, and always cheerful mother and a father who made an art out of his craft. He admired them both and identified with them.

Initially, Maniek was saved by chance, simply because he happened to be away when his immediate family, and later his aunt, were caught. Thereafter, like a clever adult, he learned to escape

---

[2] Quotations by Maniek in this chapter are from R. Raduszewski and J. Witkowski, unpublished interviews, translated by J. S. Kestenberg and located in the archives of the International Study of Organized Persecution of Children (J. S. Kestenberg, Codirector).

in time and to take as good care of himself as he knew how. Yet throughout his tribulations we recognize the child in the hunted boy. He made no attempt to secure Polish papers, which would have enabled him to rent a room. The question arises whether it was Maniek's immaturity and lack of experience that prevented him from providing himself a new identity, or whether it was his social isolation that kept him from making his life safer. It seems that both factors played a role in shaping his fate.

Unprepared for being recognized as a Jew and apparently confident in his own ability to outsmart the gendarmes, he was caught with his guard down. All his resourcefulness gone, he admitted that he was a Jew. An adult interrogator outsmarted the child, whose reliance on his Gentile "good looks" was suddenly shattered. However, his superior adaptation came to the fore again when he was confronted with impending death. His almost immediate response was to cope with it as if it were an external adversary. In an attempt to control his own destiny, he began to choose the manner of his death. It is not difficult to imagine how this appealing and resourceful youngster impressed adults (Moskovitz 1985). A Polish gendarme let him go; a Polish farmer chose him for his future son-in-law and his heir. Still, not unlike the other children, Maniek too remained a child while at the same time acting in an adult way. Although seemingly quite brave, he was vulnerable as well.

Examining Maniek's case more closely, we see a latency-age child transforming himself into an adult and beginning to skip his early adolescence. The latency-age virtues of taking care of oneself, as parents used to, persisted and overtook the child's need to play. At first, the eight-year-old saw the invasion as a fascinating adventure—a view he shared with his friends. However, left on his own, he instituted a moratorium on his childhood and adolescence in the service of survival (see the opposite effect on an adolescent in Cahn 1988b). He became his own educator and his own protector. When after the Allied victory the danger was over, he could suddenly join a group of youngsters playing war with live grenades and shooting guns. As soon as he could, he retrieved his childhood.

Liberation and After

At the end of February 1945, Maniek returned to his native city, where he and his aunt were "free but hungry and without anything." Looking back at that time as an adult, he made the following assessment:

> From then on, life was normal, without the occupation and Hitlerites; but the occupation, the ill treatment, the humiliation, and the continuous fear left an indelible trace not only on me, but on everyone who conquered hell and survived.

After liberation, he began to think about his lost family. At the age of sixteen, he went to the small town where his mother and brother had been seized by the Germans. He wanted to know exactly what had happened to them, but could find not a trace of his mother from the time after she was deported. "I don't even know where her dust is settled," he reflected bitterly, "and that hurts me very much. How can one deprive a human being of a space for her eternal rest?"

Although burdened by being left alone in this world, Maniek pursued his studies, supported by his relatives. He thought that perhaps he had been a bit lazy but that still he was successful and lucky. As soon as he finished his studies, he was given a good job; unlike many of his compatriots, he never suffered from lack of funds. He was "rich" again; he married a Polish Gentile woman and had a child. He never concealed the fact that he was a Jew, though he did not advertise it either. He told his son about his origins.

And what did Kasia have to say about her life after liberation?

> Evil lasted in us after the war. Was it possible to leave one's hiding place with a protective hand, leave the daily lies, the childhood on false papers; was it possible to leave it without internal damages—I think not. We started out life in peace with the false wartime papers, without discernment [of] who we are and who we want to be. It took long years in Poland

before we were ready to own up to our own life story, to use
our own name from before the war. (Meloch 1989, p. 99)

Kasia thought that things were different in Israel. Living
among Jews, most children gradually gave up their wartime identity. In a letter to the editor of the periodical *Wiez* in 1990,
Meloch wrote that in 1987, when she read in that journal the
confessions of a child hidden in Turkowice, the town in which
she was hidden, she did not yet know how to get in touch with
her Jewish past. Although she had returned to her Jewish name
by then, she nonetheless signed her own deposition with her
Polish name, Irena Dabrowska. Since then, she had devoted her
efforts to gaining recognition for her rescuers, the nuns of Turkowice. She visited Israel and Yad Vashem. Like Maniek, she too
married and had a child. She too is successful in her chosen profession. However, in contrast to Maniek, she found it very difficult for many years to admit that she was Jewish. Maniek was
proud that he had never hidden his Jewish identity.

Both Kasia and Maniek married Polish Christian spouses and
raised Catholic children, a very frequent occurrence. When our
interviewers asked child survivors in Poland why they married
out of their Jewish faith, they almost always replied that there
were not enough Jewish partners. Yet, for almost every Jewish
woman who married a Gentile man, there was a Jewish man who
married a Gentile woman.

It is well known that in 1946 there were pogroms in Poland
and that many Jews emigrated. In 1956 and again after 1968, it
was not safe to disclose one's Jewishness, not for fear of death,
but for fear of losing one's job. There were only a few Jews who
consistently disclosed their Jewish identity and retained important posts. Since then, the atmosphere in Poland has changed.
Poland without Jews began to search for Polish Jewish history
(M. Kestenberg 1985b). Because not enough Jewish scholars
were available, Christian Poles were employed by the Jewish Historical Society in Warsaw. Today, under the guidance of the
Lauder Foundation, sons and daughters of Polish Jews, who often

have just discovered their Jewish origins, can study Judaica and the Jewish laws. Even though Jews have become popular in Poland, it still is not easy for some to make their Jewish voices loud and clear. In many instances, the "hiding" of one's Jewish identity was so successful that even other Jews did not recognize that some of their "Gentile" co-workers were really Jewish. Kasia is right; it was not safe for Jews to come out of the closet after the war.

A Haven Among Gentiles: The Child and the Adult

There is a need in adult survivors who were hidden as children to seek a haven among Gentiles. Untoward circumstances in such countries as Poland and Hungary help explain why so many hidden children grew up to marry Gentiles. Yet it is notable that child survivors' marrying outside their faith was not uncommon in the United States and other Western countries, where it was safe to live among Jews. The story of an American child survivor who was interviewed offers an explanation. Harry was married for some years to a Jewish wife and had two children with her. When his younger child reached the same age Harry had been when he was hidden in an East European country, he left his wife and children to marry a Gentile woman. He could not explain and obviously did not know himself why he felt safer and happier with a Gentile. But as a child, hiding on a farm and playing with Gentile children, he had been happy. He felt safe there and could engage in hide-and-seek games with children who did not know he was really hiding. All he knows now is that he tends to withdraw; his wife, who loves him dearly, feels she cannot reach the "hidden Jewish child" in him. Similarly, a teacher of Jewish studies at a university, a woman who was happy in the convent during her years of hiding, chose a Gentile as a second husband.

Not only in Eastern European countries, but also in countries like the United States, survivors who were hidden as children seldom obtain real security but always seek it. For Maniek, the aunt who married a Gentile was his rescuer, as were "Grandma" and the farmer. What better security could he give his child in Poland than to supply him with bona fide Polish Gentile ancestry?

This split allegiance to Jews and Gentiles in Eastern European countries frequently creates a situation for survivors and their children and grandchildren in which they officially know nothing about their Jewish descent, yet develop symptoms or act out in such a way that their hidden knowledge is revealed to their therapists (Virag 1984). In Western countries too, children who were hunted and hidden continue to hide their past as if it were shameful or dangerous. The fear remains in them; the confrontation with death has never really left. In all the countries in which the former hidden children eventually settled, they tried to blend in with the indigenous population; they quickly lost their accents and became more French than the French, more American than the Americans. For a long time they could not tell their stories, because that would make them different.

It is true that most latency and especially young adolescent children want to be the same as their peers. For the persecuted children, however, this natural tendency was greatly exaggerated. To be a stranger was fraught with peril. It carried the stigma of being condemned to die. Further, this childhood trait did not change in adulthood. When external circumstances reinforced the old fears, hiding and seeking protection among Gentiles became a way of life, rather than simply an avoidance of coping with the past and overcoming the trauma.

Discussion

The confrontation with death and the constant fear of being discovered led some children to further their assimilation into the safe Christian environment, whereas those who had to fend for themselves had no one to coach them on how to pretend successfully.

Child survivors often feel that they grew up prematurely.

A burden was put on them not to behave like children, but like adults. Yet in many ways they remained the children they were. The latency-age children described here wanted very much to be like others and to be part of a group. Youngsters left to their own devices lacked the foresight to protect themselves except on a day-to-day basis. This was especially true of those who were isolated from peers and were not guided by adults. Some regained their childhood after liberation, and most adapted very well to new circumstances, but almost all retained their fear of being persecuted, killed, or discriminated against.

The indelible influence of the experience of being hunted—of being pronounced evil and deserving of extermination—continued after liberation. The hidden children grew up to act out and really hide as adults. It depended on prewar experiences and external circumstances after the war how far this hiding of one's identity would go. There was also the wish to bring up their children as non-Jews in order to protect them from a similar fate. The external upheavals that fostered anti-Semitism in Poland further justified the hiding of one's Jewish identity. Another safeguard against persecution was to marry a Gentile, providing an illusion of protection. In Israel and in Western countries, Judaism was rarely denied, but a great need to be like others led many child survivors to hide their pasts. Underneath these rationalizations, however, there seems to lurk a compulsion to re-create the past.

Germany's Jews deserve special mention, because they differ in one significant respect from Jews in other countries (Biermann 1964): some remained in, and others came back to, the very country that had persecuted them. Why did they do it? It seems likely that both groups were conflicted between wanting their children to assimilate and wanting them to maintain their Jewish identity, yet in returning or staying, they ran the danger of themselves becoming persecutors. It seems that a certain percentage of returnees needed to go back into the lion's mouth so that they could survive once again. For some, returning to a once beloved country comes from the abiding love these families feel for their country of origin. The majority, perhaps, are simply people who, while waiting in displaced persons' camps to emigrate, created a safe nest for themselves and could not leave. As is so frequently the case, these parents expect that their children will undo the harm and immigrate to Israel or the United States.

To survive and run from danger is certainly the safest thing to do. To survive and stay or even return to danger is proof of one's right to live anywhere. To many, a symbolic return to the site of one's persecution in childhood is an attempt at self-healing, of going back into the danger zone on a trial basis, and of surviving all over again and being able to tell the story.

Superego in Young Child Survivors

Ira Brenner, M.D.
Judith Kestenberg, M.D.

Under Nazi rule, adults and children were subjected to a curious mixture of rules, routines, and sudden changes difficult to understand. As we have seen, conditions were different in various camps and hiding places. Kitty Hart (1983) aptly described life in a block in Birkenau—the confusion between rules, laws of survival, and an inner need to use ego strength to find a way out of the confusion. She pointed out that keeping track of time was impossible. Only one hour of the morning, starting at 4:00 A.M., was memorable, when amid shouting and bullying one had to turn out for roll call. It was equally impossible to keep track of seasonal changes in order to know how long one had been in the camp; one could not rely on changes in vegetation, because there

---

Revised from article in *International Journal of Psycho-Analysis* 67:309–316, 1986. Published by Baillier Tindall, London. Used with permission.

was none—only an endless sea of mud. All the time one had to anticipate a new trick; one could not rely on past experience. One could not believe what the overseers said; seemingly good news could be the harbinger of something wicked. Nothing could be believed, and there were no landmarks in external reality to guide one.

Although children suffered even more from such chaotic conditions, they also acquired a premature strength and became little adults (for a more detailed consideration of this phenomenon, see Chapters 2 and 7). The task of adapting to an uncertain environment, to deprivation and potential or actual separation from caretakers, while at the same time negotiating developmental milestones, required the capacity to adhere to several norms. The precocious awareness of the worst possibilities greatly magnified the developmental dangers. The degradation of parents whose values were shattered resulted in confusion over whom to listen to—adult relatives and teachers, the Nazis, or the streetwise older children. The usual pattern of listening to an adult took on a bizarre twist. Obedience could result in getting caught, being deported, or dying; at other times, strict obedience to parents' directions was necessary in order to avoid the same dangers.

Moreover, the parents' admonitions not to lie or steal and to adhere to religious precepts were often transgressed by the parents themselves. Children were systematically taught to pretend to be Christians while preserving Jewish values inside. As discussed in Chapter 2, the younger the children and the less imbued with values by their parents, the more difficult it was for them, at liberation, to abandon their temporary identities as Christians (Donat 1965). The fragmentation of points of view was further compounded by the children's own tenets of self-preservation, based on their own judgment of reality. The child's awesome perception of having the power over life and death in his or her hands was often confirmed by reality. Pain merged with shame and guilt and was experienced with profound intensity. Premature feelings of responsibility for the family merged with inappropriate grandiosity to increase feelings of guilt.

Psychoanalytic Views on
Superego Development

The pleasure principle—in its original form and in its later modification, the reality principle—are both internal laws, each of them valid for specific periods, areas, and concerns of the personality (A. Freud 1975, p. 170). "The caretaking mother," according to Freud, "[is] the first external legislator" (p. 169). She further notes that "the parents' own social ideas . . . are carried from the external into the internal world, where they take root as the child's ideal self and become an important forerunner of the superego" (p. 174).

The maternal caretaker not only controls the time and the locale of the infant's gratification, but she also gives him support to counteract the pull of gravity. However, she herself is governed by both internal and external rules and regulations. She is, further, guided by child-rearing practices typical for her culture. Her anxiety about the infant's safety may make her tense, so that she clutches him and disturbs his breathing. She may even drop his head during nursing because of a kinesthetic memory of her own head being dropped when she was a baby. She may feel most comfortable holding the baby for long periods of time and not letting go of him. The infant reacts in various ways to his caretaker's ministrations. His genetic makeup and physical condition present themselves as an internal law, and the mother's responses are felt as external law (A. Freud 1965). Her own internal laws, based on her drives and ego strength, have been modified by the internalized laws she has acquired in the course of her own development. Rules about child training are based on the organizing influence of the group and are "transmitted to the infant's early bodily experiences and, through them, to the beginnings of his ego" (Erikson 1959, p. 21).

We see in early gratifications and frustrations that which makes a baby feel "good" and "bad," respectively. Feeling "good" as forerunner of self-esteem and feeling "bad" as forerunner of self-deprecation, shame, and guilt integrate the "total instinctive self-regulation of a culture" (Erikson 1959, p. 24) with the infant's inborn preferences for self-regulation (J. S. Kestenberg 1965a, b).

All early rules and routines have an effect on ego development, and they leave their traces in the most archaic and the most advanced structures of the superego (Blum 1985). In transitions from one phase to the next, the regulatory system changes; it requires a reorganization of mother and child that not only includes the old but also integrates it with the new set of rules. Sudden and repeated changes in conditions, which make it impossible for the infant to reorganize her self-regulation, are traumatic. Mothers report that their babies scream in terror and require maternal assistance in reregulation. There may ensue a temporary loss of the infant's trust in the mother and in the infant's own capacity to anticipate that she will wake up and see again the things she knows and can recognize. When her mother does not appear at such times, the infant may take a long time to trust someone again. She needs her mother's physical touch to recapture the sense of sameness that she was in danger of losing. Sameness is a regulation that brings on good feelings and is essential to structure formation. Without the sameness of the laws that guide our actions, the superego becomes split or fragmented (J. S. Kestenberg 1982).

The superego contains rules and regulations, even outlines of routines that are a far cry from adult concepts of morality. The transformation from "feeling good" to feeling good in the moral sense, from "feeling bad" to feeling bad as a self-condemnation, traverses a long road, and perhaps it does not even end when the superego has developed into a cohesive structure. Among the many steps involved in uncovering connections and reconstructing the patient's past, there are those that help him discover the varieties of feeling bad—feeling empty or constricted. Although there is considerable desomatization and differentiation of affects in successive development phases (Krystal 1974; Schur 1955), there always remains—though often hidden—a somatic and psychomotor component to all affects. The efforts of deregulation and increased somatization are particularly striking in survivors (Niederland 1961), and even more so in those who were persecuted in their childhood.

Effects of the Holocaust

A report from a child survivor, born in 1938 in a country occupied in 1940, reveals that even before the invasion, her parents were preoccupied with many refugees who crowded their house. The family and neighbors tended to deny that danger was imminent for them as well, but the doubt and fear were there. After the invasion there followed a series of travels and returns, unsuccessful escapes, and changes of decision that continued with some interruptions. The trust of the child in the traditional protection by the family and the authorities was severely undermined.

Unusual rules were imposed on her. To avoid detection she should not cry; she was not to make demands or betray her identity as a Jewish child. Even though she was dependent on her parents' moment-to-moment changes of rules and decisions, she became responsible for herself and for the parents: it had been said that her Aryan appearance had saved the family. This was a source of pride, but also of guilt. Another source of guilt mixed with anxiety was that she had cried out "mama" when the family was smuggled over the border. She had been told to be completely silent, but had lost control. She understood that she had endangered the whole family.

When she was three years old, two soldiers came to take the family away for deportation to camps. Her mother had the presence of mind to take her by the hand and run away while the soldiers were busy removing other members of the family. After hiding for some time, mother and child returned to the now empty apartment to get some clothing. In addition, she recovered her doll and a pink pocketbook, a possession of a deported aunt that the child had coveted for some time. A mixture of pain, pleasure, and guilt remained with her in connection with this incident. Pink pocketbooks that she "adored" made her feel horrible. She said, "I know it's an uncomfortable memory." Pink pocketbooks would now make her just want to cry. "My hands would start shaking. It was almost as if I wanted to punish myself. Like I have done something horrible."

Significant in the pocketbook memory is the fact that even though her mother allowed her to take the pocketbook, the child was uncomfortable about it. Elaborated in later life, this child-hood experience evoked a feeling of guilt, but the somatic reaction betrayed the early mixture of anxiety and physical discomfort. The doll she recovered was broken. She remembered, at a later time, asking some men to fix it, but they pushed her away. We venture to guess that the little girl felt broken herself and in need of fixing.

The issue of "stealing" from the dead, as a special type of misdeed, was very prominent in the life of another child, who at the age of five or six witnessed the devastation of empty and littered houses in the ghetto after his family escaped deportation by hiding. He was particularly eager to acquire certain items that fascinated him as he discovered them in the ruins of a house that had belonged to a butcher of the community. The guilt of this deed haunted him. By the time he was nine or ten, he saw a great number of dead soldiers on the road the family traveled on. He took a knife from the pocket of a dead soldier, but he soon began to fear that the dead man would come back for it. Only after he was helped to return the knife and to bury it next to its owner was his fear assuaged. In adulthood he suffered from nightmares about coming close to death. He felt a panic, "as if I had swal-lowed poison," and his chest was constricted. In his mind, taking from the dead was like swallowing poison and a greater sin than stealing food from the living. The purloined things became bridges to the dead (Volkan 1981), who could take a living person with them into their world. Such feelings could make hands shake and chests constrict.

Oliner (1979) felt, when at the age of twelve he was faced with the loss of his entire family, that "something rended and tore loose within me as I sank to the floor. The small childish sobs did not come, instead my chest felt crushed with the mature agony of an entire people" (p. 9).

The feelings of something tearing loose within and of the chest being crushed have their roots in the despair of the infant, who feels he has lost part of himself when he loses a loved one. Doubling up, he puts his head on his knees, he hides his face on the floor. He may not be able to sob because his chest is constricted and his glottis closed. Later on, broken dolls, for example, come to symbolize the broken inside. Such tears and constrictions have to be repaired. One way to mend them is to take a part of someone, a belonging that becomes a bridge to the lost person. Yet this healing bridge also evokes a guilt over wrongdoing and a fear of dying.

Good memories from a childhood beset by deprivations and disturbances of rules and routines frequently attach themselves to single physical objects that have given the child a good feeling. These encompass a gamut of sensations that symbolize security and relief from fear, distress, and extreme hunger. They are bridges to the child's feeling accepted and to increased self-esteem. (For an extended case discussion of this multisensory bridging, see Chapter 4.)

A four-year-old boy, every night for two weeks, overheard his parents discussing that he would have to be hidden and where. When the time came to leave, he was prepared. Armed with a souvenir from his mother, he walked for a long time until he reached his destination. He remembered very vividly that, upon his arrival, he was given a glass of milk. The milk was a highlight of an experience where everything seemed white and shining. As a result, he mistakenly thought he had been hidden in a hospital, while in reality he found shelter in a brothel, where the occupants accepted the uprooted child.

A two-year-old born in 1940 was given to a farmer for hiding while her parents remained in the ghetto and were subsequently deported. She remembered sitting in a farmer's house for days on end and refusing to eat. When her parents' payments ceased, the farmer's wife threw her out in the street, from which she was taken to a convent. Beleaguered by the Germans, the nuns and their wards walked through the country barefoot in the snow, subsisting on once-a-day rations of soup and bread. They landed in a mountain resort, where their deprivations continued. One day, the survivor remembered, a lady came with a horse and buggy and took her and four other Jewish children with her. When they arrived at a Jewish orphanage, they were given sugar cubes.

This screen memory (a memory that concealed much of the underlying trauma) is part of a true story, described in a book by Lena Kichler (1961). After the war, she collected wild, starving, and sick children, returned from camps or from hiding in convents, in forests, and in closets, and took them to a mountain resort (Zakopane), where they became socialized and where their fears and their starvation illnesses gradually subsided. When Kichler then discovered that in a remote convent in the mountains there were additional Jewish children, she had to work hard to get them released, because the nuns wanted to rescue their souls through Christianity. Finally, however, they did go by horse and buggy to join the others in Zakopane. They had shaven heads, had colds and were incontinent, were clothed in rags, and looked like skin and bones. Crying constantly, they were scared of horses, dogs, cats, and people. The children already in the orphanage took care of them, fed them, carried them around, and rocked them until they recovered.

Our informant remembered the lady in the horse and buggy, but for her all the good things she received in the orphanage were symbolized by the sugar cubes. Like the milk for the boy, the sugar was the highlight of her experience. Later on, when her mother found her and she had to leave the orphanage, to which she had formed new bonds, she was so angry that she ripped apart the only toy she had ever had, a doll given her by her mother.

It is rather striking how often broken-doll symbols come up in histories of child survivors. Here we must distinguish between the use of symbols to facilitate memories of affects, the use of metaphors (Grubrich-Simitis 1984), and physical pain that merges with mental pain in a "physical memory." The younger the traumatized child, the greater the trauma and the more it is relived in the form of physical sensations. Pain condenses memories of hunger, cold, toxic states, and the feeling of loss that no one came to take away the pain.

The complexity of the way pain can be experienced—as a mental anguish, as a metaphor, and as a hunger pain—was revealed by a patient who, after she lost her mother, complained, "Why do I always have to have that pain?" As a child she had been hidden with her mother. She was told that both she and her mother had been swollen from hunger, but she did not remember the feeling of hunger. After numerous sessions in which she repeated the above question, the therapist asked her where the pain was located. In a flash, she pointed to her esophageal region. She realized that she had hunger pain, which subsided after she ate. She had been chronically hungry but did not know it. She disregarded hunger signals (J. S. Kestenberg 1982); instead she felt deprived by her mother. Being hungry for food intertwined with being "hungry" for her mother, who had not fed her. Her mother's death had left her with no one real to blame for her pain. After liberation, the patient's anger, pain, and excessive clinging to the "bad" mother did not allow her to forgive her mother, to identify with her as a mother who gave her good feelings, and finally to accept her loss.

The disruption of routines, the irregularity of need satisfaction, the severity of deprivation—physical and mental—the vacillation of rules, and the example of cruel enemies as lawgivers provided a base for a fragmentation of the superego in many survivors. It is remarkable how, under those circumstances, the ego was saved from disintegration so that the analysis of the superego deformation could liberate the ego's capacity to adapt and form or rebuild object ties. Underneath the severe guilt (Niederland 1961) we discover in such a survivor an appraisal of the body as broken, empty, numb, or missing an essential part. States based on such early feelings, leading to self-deprecation, must not be confused with advanced feelings of guilt. The latter are a signal that a transgression is planned or has been committed that demands renunciation or atonement. In many child survivors, feeling bad, broken, or empty underlies a somatized superego. On the other hand, good feelings, symbolized in objects such as sugar or milk, give rise to a healing of the body image, forming a base for rehumanization and regularization of structures contained in the superego. Feeling good underlies the peace we feel when we resolve a conflict and look upon ourselves as good, moral persons. Many survivors, even those born in the Holocaust, convey their pain to their children and raise them with high ethical values, often with a mission to propagate goodness in the world. The contribution from such an ego ideal has a healing function, which continues through generations.

The Analysis of a Child Survivor

One of us (JSK) analyzed a forty-year-old man who was born in a ghetto and was deported to a camp at the age of two and a half. His family had to run away from a ghetto in a larger city to a small one, where they lived in constant fear of being deported. When he was about two years old, his older brother was hidden with relatives, and he himself was handed over to a Gentile associate of his father for safekeeping. The rescuer, afraid for his family's own lives, handed the child over to the Germans, who treated him well until he got sick. Put in the hospital, he was in danger of being killed until his father almost miraculously found him and brought him home in a drugged state. When he arrived home, he saw neither his brother nor his mother. She had been deported in his absence. From now on he was shunted back and forth and left with strange women to be cared for while his father went out to find food to feed him and to pay for his upkeep. He and his father were constantly on the run until they were deported to a camp.

Here he could stay all the time with his father and his older brother. It was so cold that he had to stay in bed with his brother. In his mind, however, camp was a safe place, where he was never left alone or with strangers. After liberation, his brother went to school and his father to work. Eventually, he was placed in an orphanage, where he continuously longed to be back with his brother. The rules of the orphanage were incomprehensible to him; he only knew the arbitrary rules imposed by his father, which had depended on the father's fears and needs. In his adulthood, it was difficult for him to understand rules or routines, including simple analytic rules. He disregarded not only external but also internal rules, ignoring such signals as hunger and bowel pressure. He never knew what and when to eat, sometimes experiencing hunger for hours without becoming aware of it. He also disregarded traffic rules, so he was in constant danger of an accident. Rules of grammar escaped him too, and the meanings of words did not seem fixed. He used words differently from other people, but he insisted that it would not be his fault if people did not understand him. Superimposed upon this dysfunction, which made communication very difficult, was a desire to outwit the rule makers of the world, who had the power to change codes at will.

When a mother feeds a baby on demand, she finds out after some weeks that the baby has put himself on a schedule. By responding to his cues and allowing him to respond to hers, she facilitates the development of a trusting and trustworthy little individual. Thus mother and child can create a system of regulations that is to their mutual benefit—a system that is also at the core of the therapeutic alliance. As far as this patient was concerned, however, he was in analysis to be helped, and the analyst had no rights of her own. Rules, which were created to accommodate the analyst, seemed alien to him. He did not understand the simplest courtesies, such as respecting the analyst's property or respecting the difference between being a patient and being a family friend. When these breaches were pointed out to him, he behaved in the same way as he had with his teachers in school, asking what he had done to make the analyst "angry." Such a confrontation would increase his acting out to a point at which he was finally told that he could not be helped if the analyst had to be busy defending her rights to privacy.

He took this statement as a threat of abandonment. It was then possible to show him that by disregarding rules, he provoked people—a process that he would continue until punished, thereby making himself into an innocent victim. It became increasingly clear that he exploited various rules masochistically, obeying them only if it were a matter of life and death. It must be remembered that abandonment, which he dreaded, was synonymous with death. It seemed quite likely that as a child he could disregard external rules because his crying in frustration would endanger the adults, who therefore had to pacify him. On the other hand, when he had to run for his life, obedience to adult rules was mandatory. One of his screen memories was playing in a forbidden place from which only the threat of a rifle pointed at him would chase him away.

At first it seemed as if he had an ego deficit, and organic damage (perhaps because of undernourishment in infancy) was considered the basis for his disorder. The analysis of his identification with the Nazis, with his confused and frightened father, and with his rigid brother revealed the nature of the conflicting and confused rules and routines under which he had been brought up. This process then enabled him to think more clearly. His concrete thinking gave way to a newly acquired or liberated ability to generalize what was right and what was wrong. However, now, when he could muster good feelings toward his father and his children, his intrinsic feeling of being "bad" came to the foreground. In the midst of a bout of depression, his father died, and his feelings of "badness" increased. Hour after hour he lamented his desolate feelings of panic and pain. He cried like a small child, demanding that his diffuse, nagging discomfort be taken away from him. From time to time, he broke into very loud sobs, exclaiming, "I am bad, I am bad." It was difficult for him to differentiate between the pervasive bad feelings, the many times his father and his teachers had called him bad, and his own feeling of worthlessness. He treated the feelings and the ideas associated with them as if they were a bad thing that had been put into him and needed to be removed. This was part of an intrinsic belief that he had been taken away from his mother because he was bad and that he was responsible for her death. Only when he could find her would he feel good again. Yet he could assuage his "bad" feelings by the realization that in the last year of his father's life he had begun to understand his father rather than just condemn him.

Surrounded by victims and persecutors, he had experienced victimization by an idealized father whose power he had overestimated and depreciated at the same time. On examining higher aspects of his superego, we saw a contradiction in values and a split between his ego ideal and the punitive aspects of his superego. He wanted to be good and moral, obeying the laws of the community in which he lived. He was grateful to his father for having rescued him from the Nazis and to the United States for having admitted him and given him a chance to survive in freedom. Yet he cheated his associates and transgressed rules of authorities. He invited victimization by exaggerated trust in and unrealistic expectations of care from his wife, his children, and his employees. By a rule of reciprocity, he then felt free to victimize his would-be persecutors. He seemed to change his values as he saw fit, giving charity to some and cheating others. Sometimes rules of fairness did not exist; they were ignored or repressed. At the same time, he aspired to being a deeply religious and law-abiding man. This constellation of feelings and attitudes seemed to be the result of a split in the superego, which overlaid the uncertainty and lack of routine he had experienced in babyhood and early childhood. Not only was his infancy disrupted by separations from caretakers, by hunger, and by physical neglect, but the people who did take care of him were in such dire circumstances themselves that they would convey their anxiety without being able to account for it. He "knew" that there was something they could do to alleviate his anxiety, but he could not pinpoint what it was.

As his analysis progressed, it became more and more apparent that whenever his superego functioned without clashes and he gained self-confidence, his ego showed an unexpected strength. His ego's capacity to attend to a matter, to plan, to think things through, to conceptualize a problem, and to anticipate consequences of actions had been severely curtailed by the superego's conflicting directions. He could never be sure that he could predict anything, because every rule he knew could change at any moment and all his planning would come to naught. He longed for omnipotence, thinking that if he were in charge of all the rules, he would be safe. This conviction enhanced the defense of identification with omnipotent aggressors and with benevolent yet arbitrary "rule makers." Yet one was struck by his persistence, by his ability to pull himself out of the doldrums and start anew, by his resilience, and by his faith, which led him to pursue intensive treatment. His frustration tolerance was much higher than initially expected, and his capacity to be confronted with what seemed to him his own shortcomings was surprisingly good.

His capacity to mourn had been severely curtailed. It became possible for him to mourn only after he had realized and worked through the idea that he had incorporated many conflicting regulations, imposed by different people and by the same people at different times. His own standards revealed themselves to be of the five-year-old-child variety, in which there were good guys and bad guys and you could play either side. This formulation was dependent on the way he felt physically and affectively. In contemplating with the analyst the idea that other people—his father, his children—felt bad as well and needed help, he began to dissociate feeling bad and panicky from being a bad person. He desperately wanted to become a good father and a good son. These aspirations had a healing effect on his ego, and they finally overrode all other conflicting rules. Only then could he begin to forgive wrongdoers and mourn his dead.

Conclusion

Data from several sources have been presented to elucidate the following thesis: the disruption of rules and regulations in the lives of infants and children born during the Holocaust leaves as an aftermath a recurring affectomotor or somatic state of *feeling* bad that is conceptualized as *being* bad. The younger the child, the more likely he or she is later in life to reexperience trauma as feeling bad, whereas feelings of emotional relief are remembered by things that made the child feel good, such as milk or sugar.

The superego that is built to a great extent on feelings of comfort and discomfort, of pain and pleasure, that come and go unaccountably can become fragmented. In analysis an ego strength is revealed that has been masked by a split in the superego. The ego of the child survivor can be quite resilient and flexible.

Children and adults suffered from a disintegration of the superego when their values were shattered in the extreme demoralization of a society of persecutors and victims. The parental fragmentation of the superego served survival, but it compounded the lack of integration of the superego precursors in children. As former child survivors regained as adults a feeling of worth and could reestablish their old values and rebuild their superegos, their children were greatly helped in integrating their own. Parenthood raised the survivors' aspirations and helped them to heal the rift in the superego.

Multisensory Bridges in Response to Object Loss

Ira Brenner, M.D.

Children who survived the Holocaust often experienced traumatic separations from their parents, disruptions of rules and routines (as seen in Chapter 3), and the need to acquire new identities. Amid the chaos and life-threatening turmoil, they discovered ways to maintain a sense of contact and continuity with all that was lost. Some acquired souvenirs, mementos, relics, and personal belongings from a variety of sources, which have remained highly cherished even to this day, some fifty years after liberation. In addition to such magical inanimate objects (Volkan 1981), living

Reprinted in revised form from *Psychoanalytic Review* 75:573–587, 1988. Published by the National Psychological Association for Psychoanalysis. Used with permission.

animals were also used by these children (Green 1958; Levinson 1967). They re-created their families through creative and artistic expression, which kept their loved ones with them in fantasy (Pollock 1977, 1978, 1982). For some it was even possible to conjure up memories of early sensory experiences that themselves became bridges to lost objects.

Such bridges to lost objects may occur developmentally or in response to trauma. Winnicott (1953) observed that transitional objects, which often appeal to the senses of touch and smell, provide an "intermediate area of experience . . . between oral eroticism and true object relationship" (p. 89). These prized possessions include elements of past, present, and future. J. S. Kestenberg (1975a), on the other hand, described the importance of food and body products, considering them intermediate objects. In addition, her emphasis on the body parts themselves, as "organ objects," furthered the understanding of how unity between mother and child was maintained through phase-specific erogenous zone stimulation by the mother.

My hypothesis is that in response to traumatic loss such as that experienced by children during the Holocaust, early, developmentally appropriate sensory experiences were revived in memory and organized. Thus, these experiences became available as building blocks or components of object relationships. Some children, possibly because of their psychological and cognitive plasticity, were then able to re-create the illusion of being with their lost loved ones. This adaptive capacity required creativity and ingenuity, which aided in survival. The following is the account of a child survivor who exemplified this capability, using both inanimate and animate objects in her attempt to bridge the separation from her parents.

Alice: A Case Report

When Alice was five years old, she was stripped abruptly of her past. Her last memory of her parents was seeing them, hands in the air, being led off by a soldier in a black uniform with a red bandanna. Mother made momentary eye contact with her, and though no words were exchanged, this glance made her feel safe and protected. She had then been entrusted to a young Gentile woman, who sent her to a farm in the Polish countryside, and Alice had been instructed to keep her Jewish identity a secret and not to talk to anyone. Because she was so young, and an only child, the separation from her parents and her placement in a large, strange, rural family was bewildering. She felt very much alone. Her soft, refined, dainty clothing was taken from her, and she was given a typically rough linen dress to wear so as not to look conspicuous. She vividly remembered the difference in texture on her skin as she longingly recalled her soft white rabbit jacket.

By smelling the food, the rich, heavy aroma of chicken soup, she could conjure up the illusion of being with her parents. Though she could not visualize the image of her parents, she could re-create the feeling of being home through her sense of smell and touch. As she described this experience to me, her profound sense of longing and sadness was replaced by euphoria and bliss.

Living like a young Gentile farm girl, Alice was responsible for a cow, even though, since she was afraid of all the animals, it was obvious that she did not belong on the farm. However, even though she was frightened, was very cautious, and kept to herself, the elderly farm woman took a liking to her and cared for her.

Alice spent her days in the fields with the cow, holding on to the heavy cord tied around its neck. After a while she began to feel safe and secure and thus was reminded of how she had felt with her mother. She recalled this feeling the first time she had eye contact with the cow. When the cow licked her with its rough, abrasive tongue, she welcomed the sensation and felt comforted. She would sleep alongside her cow, feeling its warmth and strength. Her mission in life became to take very good care of the cow and to find the best food around for it. The cow was "someone that I could touch . . . and I related to the cow . . . more than a pet. She was a mother." She knew that her time with this affectionate cow was limited, however, when she saw soldiers in green uniforms come and take the smaller animals away. She cried until her eyes were red, but for the time being she still had her cow. She even had affectionate names for the cow—which in later life she would use with her husband and son. A year later, however, Alice, her caretaker, and other local peasants were rounded up by the Germans in the middle of the night and transported to a large city. Alice never saw her cow again—another traumatic separation for her.

She was then sent to a camp and issued a rough, hairy blanket and a mess kit, along with a small steel comb with tiny sharp teeth. This comb became a treasured possession, which she tied to a string and wore all the time. While at this camp, eating soup, Alice would imagine herself back home, eating her mother's soup and taking in the smell. She would linger with the spoon in her mouth and feel protected. Again, while describing this memory, she exuded an air of bliss. She recalled that she had developed an itchy, inflamed skin rash and remembered how good it felt to scratch herself with her comb. Her blanket and comb came to represent her cow, which provided warmth with its rough hairy body and affection with its sharp tongue scratching her skin.

After several months, Alice was transported to a factory in Germany. Her first frightening memories there were of soldiers in green uniforms with their metal helmets. She felt that if she got bumped, "I would fall apart." She was finally allowed to take a shower with soap, which made her skin feel good and clean. She received a work uniform and again hid her Jewish identity. Then, owing to her so-called Aryan looks, she was instantly "adopted" by a Gentile woman.

Alice's job at the factory was to empty the wastebaskets and water the plants. Again she felt safe; she became known as the "little one," because she was the smallest child there. This distinction made her feel special and protected: "I was powerful . . . like a bundle of energy. . . . Inside I was dead . . . [but] from everywhere I had someone always helping me."

Her two favorite plants, which she watered dutifully and talked to regularly, came to represent her parents. She encouraged these plants not to turn yellow and die. She let the leaves caress her cheeks, reminding her of the cow once again, making her feel protected and fearless. The plants, her comb, her blanket, and the smells of the soup gave her the illusion that she was safely protected by her parents back home.

When the Allied bombers approached, the sirens shrieked, and a dense choking fog was released to hide the factory; however, for her, these noxious stimuli were a welcome sign. She felt a surge of hope—somebody actually did care about her. During one such air raid, she ran into a forbidden area and fell into a trap that mangled her leg. She awoke in an infirmary, her leg in splints and severely infected; she then underwent an operation, begging the doctors not to amputate her leg. She pretended that her good leg was a stronger, older sister who could look after and protect her sick, younger sister, the damaged leg. Comforted by her comb and blanket, she endured excruciating pain, but she eventually returned to the factory on crutches, still with both legs. After liberation, she was sent to a sanatorium to convalesce and once again felt safe and protected. After she recovered, she was returned to her native country, was placed in a series of orphanages, and finally came to the United States, where at the age of fifteen she was adopted.

During the transatlantic boat trip, Alice recalled how she distributed lollipops to all the children but had none left for herself. The children were so grateful that they wanted her to have a lick of each of their lollipops. Interestingly, she noted how her own tongue became enlarged and swollen after she affectionately licked these lollipops, reminding her of her licking, maternal cow.

After the war, she received a doll with long hair, which she treated like her own baby. It never left her side, day or night. However, the doll eventually was damaged and was discarded by her adoptive mother. Alice became infuriated with her new mother's insensitivity and felt like "I could kill her for this." This rare expression of anger was fleeting, but very intense.

She lived with her adopted family until she married a fellow survivor and began her own family. Struggling to integrate her Holocaust experience into the continuity of her life, she kept some of her possessions from the orphanage, and also her comb, which was never used, but stored in a secret place. Nearly forty years later, after the Washington Gathering of Holocaust Survivors, she finally took the comb out of its hiding place, looked at it, and was flooded with feelings and memories.

She felt "destroyed" after this reunion, and in an attempt to repair herself and place her own experience in perspective, she sought out her little steel comb. Both she and her comb had survived, but her parents had not:

> I had nobody. All of our friends have somebody. I did acquire a family . . . and I am clinging to them, but when I want[ed] to go deep, I was thinking of my father . . . he was not touchable to me . . . my mother was touchable, but completely faceless. Once upon a time I had like a shadow image [of her].

Discussion

Alice's early childhood, ravaged by war, was experienced as a series of losses and subsequent attempts to return to the tranquillity with mother that existed before the Holocaust. Her memory from age five—the traumatic separation from her parents—is visual: black uniforms, red bandannas, and parents with their hands held up. The eye contact with her mother provided a visual bridge to her. This unspoken good-bye had a profound impact on the child, reinforcing her feelings of omnipotence through the visual bridge to her image of an all-protecting mother, who would return some day. She could look but could not get close enough to touch. Her visual memory of her mother then faded, and other senses became primary in re-creating the feeling of being with her mother. Comforting tactile memories of the confiscated soft clothing reminded her of being at home with her mother and wearing her fur coat, and the rich aroma of the chicken soup and the taste of the food further represented a bridge to her mother.

The understanding of *organ object imagery* provides a basis for viewing this food as a bridge between the child's mouth and the mother's breast. When this concept is expanded to include the multisensory aspects of nursing, it becomes evident that taste, smell, and touch are also integral aspects of the experience. Thus the original mouth-breast unit of infancy is the early basis of later sensory memory links in the form of vestiges, displacements, condensations, or elaborations of this early nursing.

For example, one may speculate that when Alice found her cow, early sense-organ object memories were revived and coalesced into this new object. Thus the cow served as accessory object and was imbued with the importance of her mother.

Pets have long been known to serve a replacement function (Levinson 1967), but the relationship this little girl had with her cow went far beyond what would be expected with a pet. Little has been written about the kind of use of a living animal that is seen in this case: "I belonged to her and she belonged to me." The warmth and holding function of the mother were important, as were the cleaning and grooming duplicated by the cow's licking. I speculate that vestiges of her rooting reflex were revived when her cheeks were licked, renewing the bliss of the neonatal period. Indeed, her wish to feed the cow "the best food" reflected her own wish to have been fed in the same way—"all good" mother's milk.

This reenactment was then interrupted by soldiers in green uniforms. Her memory of the Germans' transferring all peasants from the village, which parallels her memory of her parents' deportation, is visual; the colors of the uniforms are remembered. Her speaking of never seeing her cow again similarly reflects her use of vision as a means of coping with the separation from her objects. This time, however, there was no exchange of eye contact, and her cow was lost forever. She was deprived of a last look at her cow, which could have developed a visual bridge, so she needed another means of staving off grief. This time, it was through identification with her lost cow, as she let the food linger in her mouth as though she were chewing her cud.

While at the work camp, her hairy blanket and small steel

comb became magical links to the cow. Tying the sharp-toothed comb to a string and attaching it to her waist provided symbolic reunion with the cow, whose tongue had felt like the comb and whom she had held by the rope. The tethered cow and then the tethered comb had sequentially come to replace Mother as a soothing, touching, ever-present object. It seems that just as the umbilical cord appears to be the original anatomic prototype of the transitional object, the cords here provide important linkages to the maternal representations. In addition, the lingering smells and tastes of the food, which she longingly savored in her nostrils, lungs, and mouth, brought back imagery of Mother cooking and nurturing. The texture of the blanket, the scratching of the comb over her body, the cooking aromas, and the taste of the food provided a mosaic of sensory memories that helped rebuild the fantasy of being protected by mother. In recalling the importance of a mother, she solemnly declared that "a mother could die for you."

Her penchant for living transitional objects then resulted in her "adopting" two plants as her parents. Given the ever-present threat to her survival and the growing doubt about her own parents' welfare, it is no wonder that she valued life as a characteristic of her objects. She fed the plants well, just as she had fed her cow, and she enjoyed the touch of the leaves on her cheeks.

During the hospitalization, when she was weak and unable to walk, she anthropomorphized her legs, making them sisters. In this case, a part of her body was used to create a family member who could care for and protect the younger, weaker one. Fortified by her comb and blanket, she maintained symbolic contact with her cow and her mother while she used her legs as children often use toys, symbolizing both imaginary sisters and aspects of herself: weak self/strong self, as opposed to weak sister/strong sister. This symbolic play demonstrates a shift toward playing with children instead of her mother. Later on, when her tongue became swollen after licking the children's lollipops during the ocean crossing, her tongue became the link between herself, the cow, her mother, and the children.

After liberation, her doll became her new transitional object, but it did not withstand the rigors of time. Like her own self-image, it became damaged and could not heal. Like her real parents, it got "deported" by her adopted mother, never to be seen again. The rage that was stimulated in her by losing her doll recapitulated her feelings about the loss of her parents. At the actual time of loss, she had not reacted emotionally, which made the loss of her doll all the more charged.

These memories themselves served a transitional function, linking her childhood with her adulthood. Her use with her husband of the loving pet names she had given the cow demonstrates the contribution of this period in her life to her sexuality. Furthermore, when she later became a mother herself, she used similar names when talking to her babies. Her projective identification with the maternal fantasies of the cow had a healing effect on her, as she had projected an idealized image of the good mother, which she in turn internalized.

Her steel comb, no longer used as a comb, was put away in a safe, secret storage place and became a linking object (Volkan 1981) available for emergencies. It was not discarded—indeed Alice made sure of its whereabouts throughout the years, keeping it "under control" but more or less stored away. As such, it was called out of suspended animation after the survivors' reunion. Confronted with the Holocaust and the inevitability of her parents' death, she became depressed and grief stricken, unleashing her many years of pent-up sadness and rage. The comfort that she got by reuniting with her little steel comb, therefore, could be understood from several levels. First, as a transitional object persisting into adulthood (Coppolillo 1967; Kahne 1967), it was a bridge to her mother in the form of a soothing, grooming caretaker. Second, it represented the displaced maternal object, the cow—an accessory object, whose abrasive tongue was like the sharp-toothed comb. Thus the comb also served as a linking object, which interfered with her mourning. By maintaining the illusion of never having been separated from Mother, she could believe that Mother was still alive. This illusion was perpetuated by her "new identity" with her adoptive family, in that her parents were replaced, thus further postponing her mourning (Wolfenstein 1966).

The comb also provided a sense of continuity to her life, bridging her early childhood and her adulthood. This indestructible little piece of steel survived the war—as she did. Looking at it—as she looked at her mother for the last time—provided a bond between herself and an everlasting, omnipotent mother. She identified with the comb-mother, herself becoming an indestructible little piece of steel: "I was powerful . . . like a bundle of energy." When she viewed the comb again, after so many years, it flooded her with her incomprehensible ordeal, her losses, and her desperate attempts at reparation. What had provided solace during the war was sought again to comfort her.

Thus, through the creative rearrangement of memories, along with the use of inanimate and animate objects, a child survivor forestalled mourning and adapted to extremely harsh conditions. Her mourning remained incomplete throughout adulthood, however, as her lost loved ones remained fragmented, in a state of suspended animation.

Diary of an Adolescent Girl

Judith S. Kestenberg, M.D.

Diaries of adolescents ages thirteen and older have been a rich source of Holocaust research (Cahn 1988b; Dalsimer 1982; Van Dam 1992, 1993). This chapter is a reflection on the writing of Donia Hapon between the ages of fifteen and eighteen years, the time of mid-adolescence, characterized by growth and differentiation (J. S. Kestenberg 1975/1995). In Donia's case, there also appears to be an eating disorder, quite possibly anorexia nervosa (Bruch 1991; Risen 1982), a condition that can develop during this period.

The works of Dalsimer and Van Dam pertain to the old and new diaries of Anne Frank (Barnouw and von der Stroom 1989); Cahn's (1988b) pertains to a girl who grew up in the Cracow

Authors Kestenberg and Brenner are grateful to Ewa Kurek for having given them this diary.
The name of the diarist and all those mentioned in her diary are changed to preserve anonymity.

ghetto. The diary presented here also pertains to Cracow but includes the time before the ghetto too. Donia could not take her diary when she escaped to avoid deportation. The diary was found thirty-seven years later, transcribed on the occasion of a competition in the Year of the Child 1979, and sent to the Museum of Majdanek by Tadeusz Kusczkal.

The Diary

The diary, which describes the period before and during which Donia's eating disorder developed, begins when she was fifteen and a half. The diary ends when she was just over eighteen years old. A first phase of the diary covers the period from January to May 1940. The family sojourned in Przemysl when she was fifteen years, seven months old, then had to prepare for a move from Cracow. A second period of entries in the diary lasted about nine months, until March 1941, when she was sixteen years, seven months old. At that point she developed symptoms and stopped eating. A third phase of the diary ends with Donia's intention to hide with a friend on August 18, 1942, when she was barely eighteen. During the period when she wrote the second and third sections of the diary, the family was living in Niepolomice, and Donia was without any friends.

January–May 1940

The diary begins on January 7, 1940, and is prefaced by the following quotation from Cara, the author's love object: "Saddest are the moments in which we recall good times when things are bad."

Donia had gone to see her grandmother in Przemysl when the war broke out in 1939. A few days later, the family went further on to Delatyn, where she met a nice, intelligent boy named Harry. This was the first boy she went out with, and she thought she had fallen in love with him. Her two girlfriends, whom she met at the gymnasium (the high school) at Przemysl, were in love with other boys. This was her first love, but nothing surpassed the love for her girlfriends, Julie and especially Cara, that fills the diary.

Donia's father, a physician, was in the Polish military, and the family did not see him until they reached Lwow. Then they all proceeded to Przemysl, where she became enamored of Cara, with whom she studied and took long walks to the fortress. All three—Donia, Cara, and Julie—loved one another, not ever imagining that a time might come when they would have to separate.

A homosexual love affair developed between Donia and Cara, who dreamed of being together all the time. Everything was mutual, exaggerated, and sheltered in what seemed like a never-ending love affair. "We imagine," Donia writes, "that our husbands will be as good friends as we are with each other. We sat for a while and then we kissed on the eyes, noses, lips, foreheads, cheeks, and even our hands while whistling a song: Ah, how I long for those moments!"

This interlude was followed by the sad fact that she could no longer go to school, "because Jews should not study." She had to wear an armband and ride in the rear of the tram. She also was not allowed to go to certain parts of the city. But worst of all was the dread that the Nazis would confiscate everything the family owned and take whoever they wanted for forced labor. The family feared that her father would be sent to Lublin to care for infectious patients.

The girls were together until the end of April 1940. Then—perhaps as a sign of things to come—Cara's sister, who had been sick, died. During the funeral her mother screamed and her father wrung his hands in despair. They then went to the headstone of Donia's paternal uncle and adorned his and others' graves with pine branches.

This fifteen-year-old girl writes in succession about death and love: tears were flowing when the two girls said good-bye to each other after the funeral. Their love is described as sexual love would be described. They went through a doorway, kissed, and then cried terribly. "It is always like that," Donia reflects in her diary, "that fate must separate people who love each other; our love was and still is as great as the love of a husband for a wife."

Finally Donia and her parents got to Cracow, where they shared an apartment with two other families. Donia's family had one room, where she slept in her mother's bed and her father slept alone. (Przemysl, which they had left, was occupied by the Russians. The family had spent a night in a large dirty room and slept on the floor.) Donia felt very weak from the twelve-hour journey to Cracow, so her parents let her sit in the corridor of the apartment building, where it was quieter and there was room to stretch out. From then on, she rarely left home because she was so afraid.

In the midst of this upheaval, she recalls that Cara and she have agreed that when they look at a certain star, they will know that the other is looking as well. She recalls talking to Cara about meeting in America many years later, when they will be grown up and married. However, they both regard marriage as "great piggery."

Though Donia was fifteen, she appears to have been still in prepuberty, judging by the lack of organization and certain lapses in her thinking (J. S. Kestenberg 1975/1995). Is it possible that the dread she experienced made her regress, looking upon sex between her parents as piggery, while she kisses and loves her girlfriend? Is this regression fostered by her sharing her mother's bed?

In the diary Donia complains about the monotony of life. Donia worked with Hanka, whom she and her schoolmates did not like anymore. Hanka was considered a "crazy" girl who took offense at everything; "because of that, they [people at school] annoy her." Here we see another prepubertal trait, the tendency to become sadistic toward people who are considered "crazy." Unexpectedly and perhaps unconsciously, Donia generalizes the theme of sadism as her thoughts turn to the severe political situation: "People treat others worse than animals." She asks whether anyone will remain whole after this war and wonders, "How long will this war last?"

In the next entry, she comments on missing her Cara and Julie: "I did not imagine that I could live without them. I long so much for them." Despite the war, she never laughed so much as when she was with them. The three of them did not fully appreciate this happiness at the time, but now she does. For some reason, she reminds herself of her grandmother, who was a terrible person. Then she abruptly notes that it is raining outside and that she is angry because she told her mother about ruining her stockings: "I felt very bad; I shouldn't have told her that." When her mother yelled at her, she cried. She then describes her lessons with a teacher, who is very demanding in the correction of her essays. After a long discourse about various teachers, she turns back to the rain, remarking facetiously that Cracow has become Venice, and she is expecting to ride in a gondola. She ends by wondering what her two friends are doing, and then comments about Harry: "I am terribly stupid, an idiot, and a cretin, because I am interested in an idiot. But it seems to me that I like him very much. It is difficult to deal with the amorous donkey, it does not want to go away."

Donia has a conflict between her love for her girlfriends and for the boy. She is alone with her thoughts, as she does not hear from any of them. Again, as in prepuberty, she does not seem to discriminate between boys and girls. She then describes how she met Harry. That story in itself, which unfolded as she was fleeing the Germans, is a study in young adolescent courtship during wartime.

"Thursday was our unhappy day," she writes. "We always run away on Thursday." In Przemysl there was continuous bombardment as the German army advanced. After a sad good-bye to her father, who could not leave because he was in the army, three cars left town. One car took her mother and her, and the one at the rear took Harry. The chauffeurs were afraid of the bombardment and wanted to avoid Lwow. She did not feel well and had vomited. As they arrived in Doliny, there was an air alarm, and they were told to go to the apartment of a Mr. W; Harry came in and said he would show her the garden. He called her Miss, which made her laugh. She had not known any other boys—at least, since she was a young girl, but "that does not count." She and Harry ate fruit and threw the unripe apples against a wall. By the time they went back inside, his parents had left, so they were alone. Being alone in the apartment, she was a little afraid. When their mothers returned, she lay down on Harry's bed and fell asleep.

They moved on again and stopped at a lawyer's house. Everybody went to another room, but she stayed in the first room with Harry. They played cards and he asked her if he could call her "ty" (you), a word used to address children and familiars, and she of course agreed. Every morning after that, they went out together, and Harry and Mr. B taught her how to ride a bicycle. Once she fell into a hole, but "this is not important." They met several boys and girls and went out dancing, which was her first time with boys.

When the Soviets invaded, Donia and Harry were unable to see each other for an entire day. After that, for a week, Harry sang "Bei Mir Bist Du Schoen" ("I Think You're Beautiful") almost all the time. Once, when they returned from dancing, he told her he loved her, which made her feel so funny she pretended not to understand. When Harry had to leave, he was happy until he looked at her. After saying good-bye, he said, "I'll see you again," and then, "For sure, I will see you again." But he never did. Her mother wrote the family several times but did not receive an answer.

At the next entry, there is no more mention of Harry, and she writes about learning English. She of course expected that Harry would write, but when he did not, she called him "an idiot," and herself an idiot for still being interested. She could not see how her pretending not to understand his saying he loved her might be taken as a rejection. That is the way boys and girls react to a first encounter. She wrote him a letter from Lwow but never got an answer. After that, notes about him rarely occur in the diary. In contrast to her constant worry over Cara, these feelings for a man go underground and seem to be a deep-seated secret.

Then comes one of her repetitive ideas: she is bored and

angry. Mama is always dissatisfied with her, and there is no word from Cara or Julie. She then casually mentions her menstruation, which she probably has had for some time. She is so nervous, surely she will get the "paka" (bundle of rags or pads). Despite her being able to menstruate, one wonders if these were anovulatory periods. She does not progress to the growth phase of adolescence (J. S. Kestenberg 1975b), at which time fertility occurs.

The day before her mother's birthday, she was arrogant to her and got yelled at. A defensive description of Cara and Julie, whom she has all but lost, then follows. Next there is a renewed criticism of two of her new friends: Fryda is odd and comical, and Lala met her with coldness. Finally, her thoughts turn to reality: Paris has been taken. There is a criticism of the French for having let this happen. Everybody is afraid, and they are resettling the Jews from Cracow. The Germans are happy and ring the bells. She asks, "When will I be able to be glad when they leave?"

There is an alternation between her inner conflicts and a horrible reality in which Jews are uncertain what will happen. At that point, they were only afraid of resettlement, not of deportation to a ghetto or a camp. Sometimes there is an interweaving of ideas, as in the following sequence: "The Germans seized two forts in Verdun. I no longer believe in our victory. I have not heard from Julie or Cara yet. The French occupied Turin in Italy [this is historically incorrect]. The Russians entered Lithuania. Altogether, there is a great mess. One does not know who fights with whom. The Italians surrendered and Mussolini has hidden himself but that would be too beautiful" [also incorrect]. The veering from one subject to another continues without transition, as one might expect in prepubertal diffusion of thinking (J. S. Kestenberg 1975a).

In France, she writes, the government is Red. Léon Blum is in Moscow. They take revenge on Jews. Daddy did not allow her to go on the street. We also hear that she has very bad skin, probably severe acne, for which there is no remedy. She describes what was done during her visit to a Gentile skin specialist and how the electricity hurt her.

June 1940—March 1941

As her sixteenth birthday approaches, she would like to be happy, but does not know how without Cara. She hates cities, but she likes green areas, mountains, villages, and water. But Jews are not allowed to swim or go to the park. She ends the entry by noting that she went to the park without her armband and it was very nice. She studied English words there. She observed the German army: how wonderful they look—involuntarily, one has to admire them. No one knows where they are going, or for what purpose.

Today, it is amazing how children at that time liked the Germans' clean, self-aggrandizing appearance. This is not the first time that such a view has been described. There was something imposing in the Nazis' self-esteem, which most people called arrogance. This was the height of their triumph in Europe. It was July 1940.

At last Donia has heard from Cara, but she is afraid to answer for fear of reprisals. But her heart aches for her two girlfriends, especially Cara. On her birthday, July 25, she notes that in Russia it is very bad because people get deported to Siberia. There is a rumor that on August 15, her family and others will be resettled from Cracow. Everybody is worried. She bemoans their coming to Cracow when they could have stayed in Przemysl. "It is so terrible and ghastly that one cannot describe it. Where to go?"

Her writing style changes, and she may have entered the "growthsome stage," where everything is exaggerated, but her integration still lags behind. The uncertainty of the situation and her worry about her family's future make her look away from her inner longing for the pre-oedipal mother, for whom her girlfriend is a substitute. She then returns to a worry about her two girlfriends, whom she fears will be sent to Siberia. At the same time, her father forbids her to go out in the street lest she be taken for hard labor. Her worry continues, this time for her aunt, about whom she has heard nothing. Sick again and vomiting, Donia stays in bed, but her heart longs for her "wonderful beloved Cara."

The Polish Gentiles enjoy what is happening to the Jews but

do not acknowledge that it is happening. All military officers (including her father) are to be registered, and they are very much afraid. Frank, the gauleiter (Nazi district political officer) of the Cracow region, has said that the Polish intelligentsia must be destroyed. He has also said that there will be no more Poland and that the Jews will be sent away from all of Europe. The Austrians are as bad and vile as the Germans. Her father is examining Jews, who are supposed to report for hard labor. Those he thinks cannot handle it are then examined by a German.

At that point, her family reserves a room in Niepolomice, where her parents have already gone. There she thinks about her future, and her thoughts shift to Cara. She longs for her, but she cannot count on Julie.

Donia begins a new era: she starts to work at a pharmacy, which helps her organize herself, and she is also much more politically preoccupied. She does not trust England. On September 1, she notes that it is the first anniversary of the beginning of the German-Polish war. Already there has been a year of misery and suffering, which has affected all of Europe and shaken the world. But the world does not seem to remember the destruction and barbarism the Germans inflicted on Europe. Here the diary then becomes more organized, as Donia stays with her themes. When she writes about Cara, it does not interrupt her thoughts. She dreams about her, longs for her, and worries about her.

She repeats what Cara has written her. Julie is estranged from them both, and Donia does not know what to think of her anymore. She tried to love them equally, and she now sees that she is stupid, but she is not an idiot. The name *Cara* evokes a wonderful feeling in her mind, and she says, "I am simply in love with her. Maybe it is funny, but that's how it is." In her relationship to men, she knows what to do. When a son of friends of the family treated her to ice cream, she wanted to pay—it felt disagreeable otherwise.

Standing in the doorway at work, she sees many German soldiers passing by. It is September 18, 1940, and people are talking about a war with Russia. The Germans are terrible

cheats: they put a Red Cross sign on their fence and store ammunition behind it. After a long discourse about politics, she
then writes a new paragraph about Cara, having received a postcard from her "wonderful, dearest" Cara.

Then a regression occurs in her writing: it becomes less coherent and organized. It is all about bombs falling on Berlin, receiving
her first paycheck, and her longing for Cara. She and Cara could
not have imagined even one day apart, and now it is so many
months. But there is still hope, and thanks to that, she does not
break down. At this point, she has no friends her own age.

The importance of peer relationships in adolescence is well
known; these relationships help the loosening of parental ties.
Here, apparently, Donia needs to think of her ego-syntonic
homosexual love in order to distract herself from her attraction
to her mother, with whom she sleeps every night.

Her father punctures his own leg in order to drain fluid from
it after a war injury. They both keep the problem from Donia's
mother so as not to aggravate her, even though her father is in
pain. When this happens again, she writes of it, blending it together with the fact that she got a letter from Cara. Once more,
she deflects her envy of Cara's school experience, which she
misses herself, by saying she envies everybody who is with Cara.

In the midst of nature, love, and longing for Cara, she has
an accident, burning her eyelashes and a bit of her hair. She was
very frightened when the crazy apparatus in the bathroom, the
one that opens the gas, exploded. Her mother scolded her. She
also broke a glass, but these things did not spoil her pleasure
when she received three cards from Cara.

Here her superego may be playing tricks: happiness on hearing from her girlfriend is counterbalanced by her carelessness,
and closeness to her girlfriend correlates with fights with her
mother. There is a togetherness with Cara as she writes how
much she longs for her. She is sure that her girlfriend feels the
same as she does. She feels what Cara feels because she knows
all about suffering. When Cara writes about her school, it is very
good for Donia, because she feels she is right there with her. She
asks whether Cara feels funny studying by herself now, because

they always did it together. Does she also miss the walks they took together? Donia then mentions that she saw Harry when he was riding the tram, a long time ago. The girls know each other's thoughts, but they also know they are far apart. Work is good, but she thinks about her lost girlfriend all the time and kisses her hands and her lips in fantasy.

Perhaps the burning of her hair and eyelashes unconsciously punishes her for the sin of transferring her love from her mother to Cara. The mentioning of her "boyfriend" may also mitigate the guilt.

Later on, she is very upset about not receiving any mail from Cara. She is afraid that something, God forbid, has happened to her. Or perhaps the Russians just don't let her write. She is very worried about it. She then does not write to Cara, because she is afraid of endangering her. She longs for her so much she cannot stand it. She quotes Adam Mickiewicz, who wrote about his fatherland, Lithuania: "How much one has to value it, only one knows who lost it." But no, she says, she has not lost Cara, even though there is a wide space between them and the ugly border. Their feelings are congruent, and they are always in each other's thoughts. People do not believe that one can love a person of the same gender as much as she does; her mother says that it will pass, but she does not understand her. Donia knows that she cannot love anyone else that much, even though they have already been separated half a year. She suddenly turns to a lost pen, which has been replaced, but that does not cheer her up. What is she living for? Only for Cara, and she is so far away.

Here is the sort of love that only an adolescent bereft of friends can experience. Her love increases with the distance, and even the new pen is not enough to make her happy. In contrast to her deep love for Cara, she hates the owner of the drugstore, who is abominable and ungrateful. These expressions of disgust are equal in intensity to the endearing terms she reserves for Cara. But then she becomes equally jealous of Cara when the latter writes that Julie does not allow her to write to Donia.

She asks if this is the end of their communications. It would be terrible, since she longs for her so much. Cara's cards always bring her relief, but only temporarily. It seems that Cara is not as far away when she, Donia, can kiss her writing.

There comes a time, however, when even the cards from Cara do not help. The Germans have become enraged, and they catch Jews on the street, demanding to see their papers. Those without papers are imprisoned and deported to Debica. They maltreat the Jews terribly. Those who have come back are bleeding. "Pretty life," Donia laments.

The news overwhelms her inner feelings when she writes, "It is better to die than to be witness to such a kind of sadism and bestiality. It is not possible to describe it in words."

She then describes what she just saw in front of the pharmacy. A car full of gendarmes stopped to talk to a Jew who was mentally ill and poorly clad. They had begun to ask him questions when he suddenly started to run away, and they shot him in the side. He stopped and spread his arms helplessly. Then they beat him and pushed him against the car with their carbines. When the gendarmes raised their carbines to shoot him, Donia wanted to scream, but something choked her and she lost her voice. People stood pale and silent. What she has seen cannot be erased from memory. What does one live for? To suffer? Hitler said that if America entered the war, he would kill all the Jews. She will not survive it. "I have the impression," she says, "that Jews will not live to see better times. They die slowly. Why didn't we stay in Russia?"

After this traumatic experience, she is very worried that they will not be able to stay in Cracow, and she does not know what to do. Where will they go next? Here we see the loss of trust in her parents: they usually make such decisions, but she sees that Jews are at the mercy of the Germans.

She envies Cara, who is in Russia, where Jews are not pointed at or humiliated. She is terribly afraid because she hears that those terrible Germans separate parents from children. On top of that, her English teacher would not come, just as she was learning so well. There is no word from Cara, whose family cannot escape deportation to Siberia.

Finally, she dreams about the cemetery, but it is on the main alley and it has a beautiful black nameplate. She thinks that when people dream about cemeteries, it is a sign of impending disaster. The Germans have not stopped going crazy, and people leave Cracow in droves. She has gone with her father for an examination, and the doctor declared her well, but it is a pity she is Jewish. She had a success, because a man in the next room looked at her and laughed all the time. An idiot! They have deported four physicians. People run away in droves. She would like to unburden herself, but to whom? Everybody laughs at her—they tell her it will pass—but is there a purer love than hers?

Jews are being taken away and killed in the midst of the disaster, which consumes all her thoughts. She becomes her father's keeper and does not allow him to leave the house. At 4:30 A.M. one day, she says, she came to his bed and told him to lie on her divan in her little room behind the curtain. She then left the house and went to the pharmacy, where she phoned home to tell him it was safe to go out.

It is again alarming when she writes, "All the forces have conspired against us. It is sixteen degrees. We now hear about the fate of those who were deported. They were let go and were trying to come back, but they were beaten."

She now turns to the question of Jewish identity and intellectualizes, "On the whole now, I see human emptiness; a being created for suffering. I feel terrible morally, even though the political news is very good. What is there from it for us? A Jew will always remain a neglected individual. And really, in this war, I see how repulsive Jews are."

This entry is interrupted by the realization that she has forgotten to send her card to Cara; it is followed by an apotheosis of her beloved, to whom (because of censorship) she cannot reveal her suffering. But she knows that Cara feels what she feels, because Cara loves her too.

A few days later, at the end of the month, an elegant man comes to see their apartment. Nobody can sleep that night, fearing they will lose the roof over their heads. She had a very bad dream of being with Cara in Przemysl, but she was so angry that she woke up.

When the New Year arrived, she says, they were invited over

by Mr. B. She liked him very much, as he was like her daddy, who embraced communism. He could have been registered as a Volksdeutscher (a native German), but he did not want to sign the list. Then he became poor and had to send his wife and children to Germany. All he wanted was humanity and a future for his children. He called her daddy his brother and said that "we are all Poles."

A new exaggeration follows: there is a terrifying snow. One can drown in it. One day (January 7, 1941) she came to the pharmacy in wet shoes. Then she records jokes about the Nazis, followed by a typical mid-adolescent depression: "I am terribly sad. I don't know what to think. Life is nothing and a person is an empty being. Only Cara is able to break my views."

She feels hampered like a dog on a leash and is terribly sad. Her thoughts turn to her employer, Mrs. C, who is ugly and gossips to Mr. D about her.

The Polish Gentiles come to the pharmacy and use a lot of mean words, which hurt a lot. She doesn't know, really—she feels so broken. Even the thought of Cara does not make her feel better.

There is a rumor that in Oswiecim (Auschwitz) people were so plagued that from despair, without thinking of the consequences, they killed the commandant. How long will this last?

Her bad mood continues. She is very sad, and tears come to her eyes whenever she thinks of Cara or about her own mental suffering. Mrs. C is terrible; Donia cannot stand her. She is crazy about cleanliness, and she created a riot because a Jew stole $30.00. She does not give Donia any peace.

Cara has sent a letter which contains an important aphorism: "The true heroism consists of being on a higher level, above the suffering of this world."

She wonders about high-minded things and is sad, longing for Cara even more than usual. She could have escaped like one of her relatives, who will try to help her family come to the United States. She should be happy, but she is sad instead, because it is so bad here. "I am very much afraid that the roads of our life will part and I will never see Cara again. This would be terrible. Life would lose its meaning for me. But even now,

I feel the worthlessness of my existence."

Her self-esteem drops further, and her anxiety consumes her. She fears losing her job, which, disagreeable as it is, has its advantages, since it allows her to escape from her home. She feels very humiliated. Mrs. C is ugly, and she cannot stand her.

She writes that on February 14, her family received the order to resettle. Daddy was terribly nervous. Perhaps something can be done about it. Mommy was very, very nervous. Donia laughed, biting her lips and fingers because of her nervousness. On Sunday her mother packed things while Donia stood on the steps and watched. Then after two letters from Cara, Father came and said that he had gotten permission to practice in Niepolomice. Mrs. C told Mr. D that she could not imagine that Donia's father had such an ugly daughter, with so many pimples. Donia writes, "I know I am ugly, but there is nothing one can do about it."

Then her mother came and told her that they had received an extension to stay in Cracow. She was "horribly happy." There follows a passage about hating a man who came to visit: "I hate him because he is an idiot, a four-flusher, and altogether a horrible type."

One can see from the use of "horrible" that it can be used positively or negatively, but it is hard to conceive that anyone could be "horribly happy," if not for the mid-adolescent's lack of differentiation between good and bad (J. S. Kestenberg 1975b). There seems to be a transition to the next subphase of differentiation.

Although she rarely writes about him, Donia is still attached to Harry. The verse she dedicates to Harry is

> You shall feel a mother's sorrow
> I shall feel a lasting grief
> You forgetting on the morrow
> I too mourn with no relief.

It is very clear that she misses him and feels he does not reciprocate. The next day she gets a card from her "beautiful, dearest Cara." Cara is very sad at this time.

Donia has also heard that several professors from Cracow

have been released from Dachau, where they suffered very much. Today they resettled people again. On February 27, there were horrible scenes on the street. She stayed home and packed linen because her parents were afraid to go out.

Her hatred for Mrs. C increases, and Donia tells many stories about her misbehavior. This seems to ease her a bit. Her last entry in February lists Mrs. C's misdemeanors toward Mr. D and ends with this sentence: "Mommy and Daddy are terribly nervous."

On March 1, she says, she spent two hours in the pharmacy. Her successor is ugly, and she does not like him. He ordered her around, but she had to show him everything. She seems to sweeten her departure by becoming aggressive toward him. The next day, a Sunday, they all take the train to Niepolomice. While riding, she writes about her complete isolation from anyone her age, associated with her removal from work and from school. There is boredom and eventually illness. On March 3, they are in "this cursed Niepolomice."

"I wished I was never born rather than come here. This is an ugly, sunken hole and there are a great many army people. Each Jew has to greet a soldier. We made a great stupid mistake moving our furniture." Their apartment is "a large room that is supposed to serve as a sleeping area, eating room, the office, and the bathroom for all." Donia does not even want to write her new address because she has no intention of staying. When and if Father tells Mother he has gotten a Kennkarte (a card issued by the Nazi authorities to legitimize oneself), she will persuade her mother to go back. That night, she writes, they slept on their beds with their linen. Mother was upset all the time.

"I long for Cara terribly. Every blade of grass reminds me of her. The sun cries, 'Donia! Cara is very near and yet so far.'"

Donia has to turn from her mother to Cara because it is almost impossible to face her mother, who is so upset about wanting to return to the Cracow ghetto. Like a small child, Donia describes her new abode in detail, turning her attention away from her mother's sorrow. Eventually, she writes, "I will waste away here. What I have learned in school, I have forgotten. In

Cracow, at least I went to the drugstore. What will I do here? Such an existence is pointless for anyone who has no profession, who has nothing. One empty shell is life. All my occupation is to eat and sleep." Her one consolation was being able to go with her father to the forest. It was wonderful, but her heart longed for Cara!

Another disappointment: Father had to go to the Judenrat.[1] These ugly Jews! Daddy had to give them 100 zlotys, which is very little. However, Mother is very unhappy, and because of her, Daddy is also unhappy. In their house there is misery.

April 1941—August 1942

There is nowhere for her to turn, except to Cara and to her books. In the meantime, she and Father are worrying about Mother. It is not as bad for them as Mommy says. Father is being called to help, and he medicates the poor for no cost. Daddy is worried that mother will become diabetic. Meanwhile, Donia's stomach is disturbed, and she eats very little. Thus, a period of time begins in which Donia is the sick one and her mother does not get as much attention as before. In addition, Donia loses her period and starts taking medicine for it.

Instead of worrying about her mother, Donia worries about Cara. Donia writes that her mother, crying, reproached herself for leaving Cracow. In response, Donia wrote to her mother's sister and asked her to help her mother stop worrying, since the aunt had a lot of influence over her. In her next entry, however, Donia is once again complaining that her stomach has been hurting for a long time and she cannot eat. Her parents become increasingly concerned about her weight loss and inability to eat.

She begins to express her own anti-Semitism at seeing a Jewish woman standing in the middle of a street full of Germans,

----

[1] The council of Jewish representatives set up in communities and ghettos under the Nazis to carry out their instructions.

flirting with a chauffeur, while the Polish Gentiles stood around and gnashed their teeth. She also has some bad words for her grandparents, who had been mean to their grandchild, Julek, whom she loves very much, and who has brought himself up, living in the street. How much shame this poor child has endured! His mother had a mental or emotional breakdown before the war and ran away from home, and Julek remained in Przemysl with his father and grandparents. Julek implored his father to run away too, but his father did not want to, especially because the grandparents did not want to leave. The grandparents then cursed Julek and threw him out. His father always sat around in a cafe while poor Julek wandered on the street. The grandparents then sent Julek to Lwow for studies, but they did not pay his school bill. Donia does not love them anymore, even though she once idealized them. She says that in her father's family there is no feeling of belonging. Instead there is envy among brothers.

Her stomach continues to bother her. She feels distention, cannot eat, and still does not get her menses. Do these symptoms have a psychophysiological basis, and are they signs of a pseudo-pregnancy?

Donia worries about Cara and all her loved ones in Russia. It looks as if the Germans will attack them. She is terribly bored here, and she does not know what to do with herself. Help arrived on April 4, however, when she got her first English lesson. At the end of this entry, she writes, "Thoughts really come to me as if I had a depression. Mother still does not sleep at night and regrets that she came here."

Is Donia's depression connected with boredom or with worries about her mother? It is hard to tell. Whereas in normal times she would have started to differentiate and separate from her parents, it is not possible here. She has nothing to do and has no peers to share her thoughts with, except through the open postcards of her correspondence.

Recalling the stomach pain, she adds that Mommy and Daddy worry all the time about her. Eventually she takes over helping at home: she washes the pots, goes to get milk, and cleans the house. Like an adult, she is afraid that her aunt will be resettled. She ends the entry by saying that the ghetto in Cracow has been closed, and Mother should thank God she is not there—the Nazis make Jews suffer in a sadistic way. Mother has quieted down a little, but not altogether.

In April, she writes that she has been very nervous, thinking about Cara all the time and longing for her. Tears come to her eyes spontaneously, and she does not know what to say anymore if someone asks her a question.

She then writes about how people who have to move all the time get ruined. A few days later, she is very nervous again. She cannot eat; she even cried over something stupid. She longs for Cara terribly, but she cannot write to her. In Cracow they dig ditches and use blackouts. Why? Altogether, human life is worse than a dog's life, worse than an animal's. She quotes from a Tarzan movie: "He knew the right to fight, which the animals taught him. He did not know the right to falsehood—because he learned from animals."

There follows a spate of information about her aunt and her father's competitors. It is difficult for her to live in these circumstances, and she is slowly but surely breaking down. They are trying to send her to Cracow for X rays, but this has to wait. Her father gave her the first injection to get her menstruation back. She was afraid, but her squawking was unnecessary, because it did not hurt.

She does not eat and loses weight progressively. She feels guilty because the family does not have the money for oranges, but her parents bought them for her.

On the first of May, Donia writes, she got a card from Cara, who is now in Lwow and has been accepted at the school there. Donia's worries increase, however. The ghetto walls in Cracow have been made in the shape of tombstones, which is very demoralizing for the people. She is still learning English, but she does not know for what. She thinks of Cara day and night, and the longing makes her heart ache. A black despair envelops her when she thinks that the war may last for several years. Donia does not know when she will ever see Cara, who by then will be educated and have a profession whereas she will be a nobody, an unnecessary being. A few days later, she talks about looking forward to meeting with Cara and studying with her, but her stomach burns and she is very, very nervous. The pressure and burning in her stomach makes her suffer. She loves her studies, and she has written a letter to Cara that is all mixed up.

A regression occurs again. She reflects upon what she normally would have been doing in the eighth grade, but she is very sick, both emotionally and physically.

On June 22, she writes that the war with Russia has erupted and she has attacks of crying, thinking about Cara and what must be happening to her. She does not know what "they" want from her—she has had enough. She did not want to go to Cracow for an X ray, but she had to go just the same. Dr. Lapinski, a Polish Gentile, examined her and told her that her stomach had shrunk. He said that she must get fatter, so he wrote for injections and ugly medications. But since this morning (while still in Cracow), she feels much better.

It is hard for her to look at the walls of the ghetto. She sees now that she really loves Cracow, because she has an appetite and eats a lot each time she goes there. Her mother left her for a while in Cracow, and she enjoys nature. The world is beautiful, but not for "us Jews"—it is changeable, false, and bad. The Catholics from Niepolomice registered a complaint about the Jews, saying they should be incarcerated because they deal on the black market. One hundred and twenty people have to register for Debica, where conditions are very bad. On Tuesday there will be shooting in Cracow and in Tarnow, and people are not allowed to leave the house. "I don't know what that means; I am terribly worried about Cara," she writes. Once more, we see a shift in Donia's thoughts from present-day worries to Cara.

She writes that she finally got her period, after not feeling well, and happily went to the forest to gather flowers with a peer. It may be that with the coming of her period, her gathering flowers is symbolic of her happiness at being a woman again. There is a regression in her thinking, as again she mixes things up as she did when she was fifteen and a half.

On May 25, she writes that she does not feel well and she

longs for Cara. Yesterday she went to the forest, and it was pleasant. The next day she writes, "Misery, Hunger, and Illness! We live under the sign of these three stars. Shamelessly the beautiful May sun looks up."

She is learning English, but otherwise she does not know what to do with her time. All of her life is suffering, a terrible suffering of the moral kind, and in addition there is no word from Cara. She loves her teacher, who also instructs her in physics, mythology, and Latin. Yesterday there was a blackout.

She is very upset: at this minute, she has just come back from town. There is spotted and abdominal typhus. She is terribly afraid that something will happen to her daddy. On the other side of the courthouse is a placard with the picture of a "Jew's lice"; underneath, it says "spotted typhus." She cannot shake off this impression. All the time, something "bites" her. She is overjoyed because a girl named Basia, who is much younger than she, will come visit her for summer vacation; they will go for walks together. Her need for someone to talk to and walk with is so great that even someone much younger is a source of joy.

She also confides in her teacher, who does not believe that love can persist in the absence of the beloved; she spoke from her own experience. Donia, however, thinks of Cara as more than a girlfriend. She is a being, and she is necessary to Donia's life. Not hearing from her is very disturbing; she does not now want to think. She hopes nothing bad has happened to Cara. She has gone to buy meat but is afraid Mother will throw her out with it. She collected flowers for Mommy. "Today, I have a bad day. I don't want to do anything and I feel weakened."

On July 16, she feels very unhappy and worse off than others. She feels repulsive, and her self-esteem has dropped further: there will be a party for Mr. S, and everybody will be dressed properly, but she will look like Cinderella.

On August 4, she writes that Mommy does not feel well at all; her side hurts, and she suffers. Donia is irritated by her aunt, who has told her that Mother always wants to make money at the aunt's expense.

Back in Cracow, she feels in chaos, not knowing what she wants. Daddy wrote in secret to Mrs. S, telling her where they were staying, in order to give Donia injections, and Donia is indignant and upset about it. She is beginning to eat more while in Cracow, and she goes to the movies without her armband. She finds a lot of things that belong to them, such as a little sword with a red handle from Palestine. Though it is a little bent, she will take it with her, and maybe it will bring her luck. There is also a small box in which she keeps memorabilia from Cara. Then she writes: "Oh, how I long for you, my most beloved, sweet little girl. When will I see you—but I do not know your address."

She plans to write her mother that overall she feels better, but in the meantime she feels oddly full, with a hard and distended belly; she has eaten a lot, and her stomach has gotten distended again. She meets a woman who came from Lwow, who said that Jews should be happy to be here, because they make Jews suffer terribly there. The Nazis put bounties on the Jews, and the Ukrainians kill them en masse. Donia is terribly afraid for Cara because the civilian population is being killed in a bestial way.

Back in Niepolomice, she does not eat, which tortures her mother; she feels bad because she does not help her mother at all. One day she was overjoyed because her teacher was planning to come, but she never arrived. There is nothing one can count on anymore. People disappear. Eating does not give her pleasure. She now awaits her teacher with longing. She has been to a dance party, and although she did dance a few times, generally she does not feel well enough to.

At last, October 15, she receives a postcard from Cara. Her father has a job as an administrator. Cara herself has gone through a lot, but she is well. She has been back in Przemysl for the last two months and has earned 112 zlotys. Her mother is not feeling well, however.

On October 18, Donia was examined, and they found a lot of worms. Daddy gave her an injection so she would gain weight, but she does not know for what purpose. She is going to take medicine for the worms. She longs for Cara so much she cannot stand it. She received an injection and screamed terribly. A few days later, she had another injection of liver. She misbehaved. Mommy and Daddy yell at her because she does not eat, but she does not know why she should.

The painful and distended stomach continues. She feels bad, emotionally and physically. School has started, but not for her. She does not know what has possessed her. She will not eat at all; Mommy cries over this all the time. On top of this inability to eat, she has a high fever and chicken pox. She feels bad that she annoys her parents terribly, but what can she do? She had a terrible night—she could not sleep, it itched her so. Mommy cries about her and Daddy is upset.

She returns to Cracow for X rays. She is morally exhausted when she sees what a terrible problem she has caused her parents, but she really could not eat and was not able to overcome it. She feels a shooting sensation in her head, and she shivers. Mommy came back from the doctor, who said that Donia would have to leave home unless she promised to eat all day and let Daddy give her injections. Donia is so nervous she does not know what to do with herself. She has tried to eat, but something is lying in her stomach and she is very full.

"Something is lying in her stomach" is suggestive of pregnancy fantasies, worms notwithstanding. At the same time, she preempts Mother's time with Father because of her illness and gets much attention.

She went to a doctor who took an X ray but found nothing. Mommy wanted to leave her in a sanatorium, but she will try to let her stay home. A doctor in the Jewish hospital said she had depression and should be placed in a sanatorium. Mommy will take her home for a week's trial. Donia feels badly again; she should not live, because she causes so much trouble for her parents—she does not feel worthy enough to live. She feels oddly senseless, and she does not know how to stand the guilt feelings. Her mommy lost two pounds. Is she, Donia, worth it? What bad things she has done! And yet she does not know why. For a few days, she eats but feels badly; she gets injections, which are very painful. After six days of standing the pain, she writes, she became crazy at dinner, not eating, and causing so much suffering to Mommy. Her aunt yelled at her.

After a few days, she began to eat "terribly much" and "naturally" the spasms returned shortly afterward. She could not eat dinner. Something overwhelmed her and she did not want to eat. She was very crazy and scratched her face. Mommy cried and thought she would go crazy too. From being so nervous, Donia felt she wanted to die, but that's easier said than done.

By not eating, by vomiting, and by scratching her face, she turns her aggression against herself.

She has heard from Cara, who wanted to visit her, and her parents supported it. Donia is terribly angry at those ugly Germans, who made such a trip impossible. She could imagine the moment when she would be able to kiss Cara on her little mouth.

She writes that she then got a postcard from Cara saying that her family's finances had dwindled and that her mother feared for the future. Cara's own pains are terrible, and she has had enough.

Donia is frequently distended and cannot get comfortable, whether standing, sitting, or lying down.

She is terribly pleased that Cara will be able to continue her studies. At least she can forget about her problems. She and her family send packages to her grandparents. They have to go to the ghetto, where it is very expensive, and they are so poor.

Donia feels very bad when she is constipated, but she enjoys her lessons very much. At last there is someone on whom to take out her aggression: a Jewish man who collaborates with the Germans and thinks every girl is in love with him. He is old, red-haired, and altogether very ugly.

On December 12, Donia's family rents a new apartment. The water closet is not hydraulic, but it is under a roof in the corridor, and there is electricity. "Hurrah for civilization."

Her mother is very regretful that she did not leave Donia in a sanatorium; her mother cries all the time, saying Donia looks terrible. Donia is suffering a great deal from distension, feeling pressure and nausea all day long. Her stomach burns her so terribly she can hardly stand it. She worries about her father's not coming home at night.

A new physician has arrived, and he is going to use a new

method of suggestion. He told Donia to lie on the divan, and he directed her the whole time. He told her she was well. It lasted thirty minutes and was intended to help Donia relax her muscles. At the same time, she begins attending a course on cutting materials. The physician gives her an injection one day and treats her with suggestion the next.

In the meantime, new hardships occur. One has to give up one's furs. A new year, 1942, has arrived, and it is very cold. Mommy gets an injection and has quite a few furuncles. Daddy is getting sick too. He does not sleep at night and worries about typhus fever, and he smokes all the time. He suddenly got an attack of very high pulse and was terribly afraid what that could be.

On January 19, Donia had a terrible day. At about two o'clock, without any cause, she experienced terrible distension. After she had eaten, she belched, became nauseated, and had such spasms that she had to lie down. At night the symptoms continued, and Donia was so nervous she did not let anyone sleep. "Poor Daddy runs around in this cold, and what awaits him when he comes home?" On this day she will stay in bed and be on a diet. Daddy has a stone in the salivary duct. She had forgotten to write that all during her sickness, she could not read, not even any easy books. But now she is able to read again.

She reports in the next entry that she went to a revue and liked it very much. At least she laughed a lot. She is eating very well, but her stomach still burns; she hopes the burning will pass.

On February 22, she writes that life is boring, but her appetite is good, even though her stomach "swings" from time to time. She has begun to spend time with Lila, whom she likes very much. She is happy enough to write a few jokes.

On March 9, she complains that life is ugly and monotonous. She has a lot of stomach trouble and wants to vomit all the time. The only ray of hope in her life is a card from Cara, even though she senses sadness in her writing. It is difficult to live in this world! She has heard from Julie that Cara has lost all her things and has nothing to wear. Donia is very sad and resigned, and she has nothing to write. She sits in this damp hole where everything and everyone are ugly. Donia's daddy does not make enough money to support the family.

But one should be glad just to be here, because so far, they have not resettled anyone. One is not sure from minute to minute; these villains shoot Jews without reason. Here there is peace, but in Przemysl they have orgies. Julie writes that they have killed Eda D. In Cracow terrible things are going on. They arrest innocent men and make them suffer, torturing them to death while their wives and children look on.

On her eighteenth birthday, Donia writes, she got candy and flowers, but the times are killing her—the not hearing from Cara, the not knowing what the morning will bring. "Oh Cara, when will we be together again?" She then gets a good-bye letter from Cara. They are deporting people from Przemysl, and Cara does not know what awaits her. Donia despairs and hopes. Maybe there is a kind of haven somewhere. They have sent a telegram to Grandmother, but there is no answer. Donia and her mother have begun work for the military; Mother works from 12:30 to 3:30 and Donia from 7:00 to 12:00. They mend socks, and her eyes hurt her a great deal. She hopes to see Cara and Grandmother still, but she can't write anything—there is such chaos in her head.

On August 14, she gets a letter from Julie: Cara has been deported. It is so very hard. "My hand shivers, I can't cry." She feels weak and stupid because she cannot help Cara. "What to do? What to do? I do not know what will be with us tomorrow, but this does not concern me. I can no longer write, my nerves are tensed up like cords, tensed up to the point of bursting."

The last entry says: "Now they have got to us. Terrible despair. What to do? To go to Wieliczka or hide? It seems to me I will escape with Julie, and you, my little diary, must unfortunately stay here."

Discussion

We do not know what happened to Donia. Did she flee or go into hiding? Did she survive? What we do know is that she left her diary behind, which documents her development during this crucial period in her young life.

Donia's writing illustrates the three phases of adolescence—prepuberty, the growth phase, and the phase of differentiation. There is increasingly more political thinking in her writing, and she becomes old before her time. She worries about what will happen to Cara and to her family. The worry eventually settles in her distended stomach, and she becomes very depressed. Over time, her self-esteem and hopefulness wane.

Although hypnotic suggestion had an effect on her, it was temporary. Her stomach was still distended, and nausea overcame her. Her condition suggests a hysterical syndrome that might have resulted from her being unable to transfer her feeling from her parents to her girlfriends, except in fantasy. The infatuation with Cara is present to the end. That preoccupation allows her not to think of her parents all the time. There is a progressive deterioration in her life due to the persecution of the Holocaust, and she cannot help but deteriorate mentally as well. In a characteristically adolescent way, she regresses and feels bored.

The anorexia and the concomitant symptoms, which appear to have a psychogenic component, cannot be understood completely on the basis of what we are told by the diary. She does not seem to have deeply disturbed feelings toward her mother, but rather normal reactions to her mother's worries and to her own worries about the future. Her adolescence is disturbed and prolonged, and she feels isolated from her peers and has lost faith in her parents' ability to protect her. She then regresses, stops menstruating, and eventually develops other symptoms, which may be based on an unconscious pregnancy fantasy. It has been postulated (Bruch 1991; McDougall 1985) that anorexia nervosa stems from a disturbance in the mother-child relationship in infancy. In Donia's case there is no way to determine the precursors of her illness. It does seem possible, however, that it is both a response to an incomplete separation from her mother and an oedipal fantasy transformed into psychosomatic symptoms. The role of medical pathology, including parasitic infestation, needs to be considered also.

Donia's despair mounts as time passes. As the situation becomes bleaker and bleaker, she clings to the hope of a reunion with Cara. Initially she fears that Cara will become so educated and mature that she will have nothing in common with her anymore. Then Donia receives news of Cara's own deteriorating life and grieves for her. In the end, Cara is deported and all hope is lost. Indeed, Donia's own fate is unclear, as her final entry describes her desperate thinking about her family's imminent "resettlement." But her diary leaves a lasting record of one teenage girl's struggle to survive the external and internal chaos of her life during those dark years from 1940 to 1942.

Child Survivors as Parents and Grandparents

Ira Brenner, M.D.

The effect of the Holocaust on later parenting is difficult to study because of the many factors contributing to the way one raises children. The broad spectrum of experiences in survival makes this important topic even more complex, and we therefore need to be careful in drawing conclusions. A number of trends, however, have become evident. For example, many child-survivor parents appear to be very protective of their children, hoping that the children will avoid the traumas of childhood that were experienced during the war. The parents may even want to block their children's knowledge of the Holocaust itself. They love their children as much as any parents do, and when their children reach the age that these survivors themselves were when they suffered, their worrying increases. The children often become replacements for lost parents or siblings, and role reversals may occur, because survivor parents have a great need to reclaim their own lost childhoods. This need to become a child again is in contrast with their inability to play, a tendency that may interfere with their relationship with their youngsters.

Child-survivor parents may identify with their children, projecting the danger of their own persecution onto them, thus worrying that their children may be in constant danger. Many survivors, having been abandoned by their own parents when they were hidden, relive this fear by worrying about being abandoned by their children.

Child-survivor parents may often give the message that survival is possible, even under the most dire circumstances. Seizing opportunities, adapting to a new environment, achieving success from hard work, and having the chance for a new start were possible for more child survivors than adult survivors. As a result, this optimistic but cautionary set of values has been conveyed to many, but not all, of their children. The unique story of each of their survivals has been transmitted to their children in varied and subtle ways, creating a legacy that has burdened many. In the following sections are described four persons—two brothers (in considerable detail) and two girls—who exemplify child survivors in many of the ways just discussed.

Carl and Otto

Two brothers, four years apart in age, had completely different wartime experiences and reunited after liberation. They emigrated to the same city in the United States, married, and had children. One was a dedicated family man, whereas the other did not even raise his children. Their personality differences notwithstanding, these extremes in parenting might be understood in light of their survival ordeals.

Carl and Otto were born in Germany into a wealthy clothing manufacturing family in the mid-1920s. Their father was the eldest of five brothers, who were born in Poland and moved to a large German city in the early 1900s. There they developed a successful business and lived a well-to-do, Orthodox Jewish life. Their mother was also the eldest of a large family born in Poland who moved to Germany. The parents' marriage might have been described as typical for their day in that it was patriarchal. Together they had four children, three of whom survived the war.

The father was described as strict and businesslike, but with a gentle side. His diversions were raising birds and playing cards, which he pursued with a passion. The mother was described as beautiful and loving, but with an argumentative streak. Carl fondly recalled how his mother was outraged to hear that he was struck by the school principal in an effort to discipline him. She immediately took her son back to the school and confronted the man, hitting him with her umbrella in retaliation. The principal, completely taken aback by her assault, left her son alone afterward. This protectiveness would serve two of her children well during the war.

Carl's bar mitzvah occurred after Hitler had come to power and the restrictions on Jews had already begun. He was quite aware of the changes in his life and of the fear he began to feel in public places. He was harassed in parks and on the streets, and his life became more constricted. Otto too, though younger, felt that their lives were changing despite their father's insistence that everything would be all right. Carl was interested in joining a youth group and emigrating to Palestine, where he thought it would be safer for Jews, but his father forbade it. Disobeying the word of his father was unthinkable, because his father's authority and honor were still intact at that time. Carl could not have imagined the degradation that awaited him and his father. As the head of the family business, with important customers, the father felt assured of their safety as long as they could ride out the vandalism of the brown-shirted Nazis, who delighted in destruction.

November 9, 1939, Kristallnacht, the night of the shattered glass, the national pogrom in Germany, dispelled any myths about their future. The family business was looted, set afire, and destroyed, and their home was defaced with swastikas. The next year was one of uncertainty, fear, and mounting despair about their lives. By this time, many members of the extended family had fled Germany, some going to Shanghai, others to South America and the United States. One night the boys' sister—the rebellious middle sister, who was thirteen at the time and who could not stand the daily pressures of confinement—ventured out to a dance against everyone's better judgment. She never returned. The family was panicked, but helpless to do anything to determine her whereabouts, fearing the worst. It was discovered after the war that indeed she was apprehended in a roundup and eventually died in Birkenau. Despair and desperation mounted in the family until one early morning, on the day before the Jewish New Year in 1939, when Carl and his father were arrested by the Gestapo and sent to the Dachau concentration camp. Their nightmare had just begun. Only one would return.

Otto, his mother, and his surviving sister, who was just a toddler, were left to fend for themselves. Not knowing how soon the Gestapo would come back for them, his mother decided to go into hiding. Her resourcefulness was put to the test as she made arrangements with a Gentile man to help them hide in the surrounding countryside. She had hidden whatever jewelry had not already been stolen, and she paid the man in gold to protect them. It was thought that it would be safer if the three split up, so Otto went to the home of a Gentile woman whose husband was a soldier fighting at the front. His mother and little sister hid nearby at a farm. They maintained regular contact with each other throughout this ordeal, and they changed location frequently, staying just ahead of the Gestapo, who were looking for Jews in hiding. They lived in constant fear of getting caught and being murdered.

Otto became sexually involved with his older woman caretaker, and as he moved around, he found himself in this position several times. His puberty was spent in hiding with a series of lonely German women who protected him in exchange for sex. Toward the end of the war he was caught by the Nazis at one of these women's houses and sent by truck to the railway station for deportation "to the east." He managed to jump out of the truck during a bit of confusion on the highway and escaped into the woods, where he eventually found his way back to his mother. He then went back to the home of the first German woman and stayed there until the end of the war. His secretiveness, alertness, and successful hiding saved his life.

Carl, on the other hand, went to a series of concentration camps over the next six years until he was liberated by the American army after surviving the death march from Auschwitz. He and his father found themselves in the surreal world of the lager (death camp), where the German master, with his machine gun and guard dog, had absolute control over their lives. Humiliating uniforms, pitiful rations, exhausting work details, sadistic punishments, and capricious executions were designed to dehumanize them and break their spirits. Carl's father, by then a man in his forties who was not physically fit, was simply not prepared. Carl protected him as best as he could, staying near him as much as possible and sharing his food with him, which was a crime. He recalled receiving a savage beating with a lead-tipped cat-o'-nine-tails for being caught giving his father a stale crust of bread. Such beatings took weeks to heal, and the grueling work details did not allow much recuperation.

Carl was also incarcerated with several of his boyhood friends from the neighborhood, who all tried to stick together. Carl described how he held onto one of his friends who tried to attack the guards as they were about to hang his brother for some trivial offense. The friend's brother was clearly doomed, and the friend would have been shot immediately if he had made any attempt to move toward the hanging. Carl's world changed bizarrely as he and his friends from the soccer field were violently thrust into the camps. But within their "organization" of friends and family, they could preserve trust, respect, and human dignity amid the indescribable degradation that constantly threatened their lives.

Miraculously, Carl's father survived for three years, until 1942, when he was simply too weak to report for the daily roll call. He was never seen again. At that time, Carl and his father were in separate barracks at the Monowitz camp in Auschwitz (Czech 1990). This camp was to supply the massive synthetic-rubber manufacturing complex owned by I. G. Farben with slave labor in order to support the German war effort (Ferencz 1979).

Carl could not think anymore, but he dragged on by instinct. By this time, he had become a veteran slave laborer, having survived by virtue of his youth, endurance, cunning, and luck. He was appointed kapo, or supervisor, of a work detail involving construction of the complex. One of his friends, Bruno, had befriended a Gentile woman during their earlier excursions to the work site, and a plan for their escape started to develop. They knew that the chances for success were very small and that anyone caught or thought to be involved in the conspiracy would be tortured and executed. Lots were drawn, and Carl got the short one, so he had to stay behind. On the designated day he feigned illness and went to the infirmary, which in and of itself was a life-threatening decision, because selections for the gas chambers were regularly made from workers who were too sick to be useful anymore. Carl's assistant, Bruno, was then appointed kapo that day. At the agreed-upon time, Bruno's girlfriend Elsa took Bruno and a third friend to a nearby farmhouse, where they hid. Carl did not know the fate of his dear friends until their reunion long after the war, and he could only hope that he had been more successful in saving them than in saving his father. He was interrogated by the SS about the escape, but because he had been sick that day, incredibly, he was not held responsible.

Carl was evacuated from Auschwitz in advance of the Russian army and survived the death march in the brutal winter of 1944–1945. By the time he was liberated at a munitions factory near Buchenwald, he was an eighty-pound living skeleton. He convalesced at a nearby hospital, needing to be fed with a dropper for weeks until he was able to eat normally again. Once strong enough, he was discharged, and he found his way back home in order to look for his family. With the help of other survivors, he was reunited with his mother, brother, and younger sister. It was next to impossible for him to explain what had happened to his father. Despite the joy of the reunion, the horror and grief of their individual ordeals was an unspoken barrier that was never breached.

A relative who had had the foresight to leave Germany in time financed their passage to the United States, where they arrived in 1946. Through a mutual friend, Carl met and married a very religious woman, who took it upon herself to restore his faith and keep him well fed for the rest of his life. Otto, on the other hand, again found a Gentile woman and started living with her, moving around town to a variety of locations until they married. Otto kept in regular contact with his mother during this period, but this time she disapproved of his living with a non-Jew, because it was after the war.

Carl and his wife lived in his mother's house for the first several years of their marriage, where their first child, a son, was born. A miracle of survival and a testimony to Hitler's defeat, his son was named for Carl's dead father, and great things were expected of him. Carl was extremely busy working long hours at a series of manual labor jobs, using the skills acquired at Auschwitz in carpentry and roofing. Though quite intelligent, he was too anxious, preoccupied, and troubled to consider returning to get a high school diploma. Carl's wife worked as a teacher, so their son was essentially raised by his grandmother for two years. Though loving and devoted to her family, she was profoundly depressed and had become somewhat paranoid during the war. The child was therefore alternately overindulged and deprived during this time in his life. What little contact Carl had with his son was terribly important to him, but he could not tolerate much closeness for fear of hurting his fragile offspring. One time, while changing his son's diaper, Carl inadvertently pinned the diaper to the baby's hip, and the child shrieked in pain until Carl realized what he had done. Another time, when making formula for an early-morning feeding, Carl was so anxious that he fell down the steps and aggravated a war injury.

Carl and his new family left his mother's house after the birth of their second child, another son. His wife stopped working to be with the children, and they bought a house. Interestingly, it was in direct view of a huge industrial complex, which Carl later realized reminded him of Auschwitz. He also had limited involvement with his second son, leaving the early infant care exclusively to his tireless wife. As the boys got older and wanted their father to play sports with them, Carl was supportive, but at a total loss in American games. His reminiscences about his own idealized boyhood before Hitler would interfere with his involvement, and he seemed to get lost in thought when the boys wanted to play with him. Similarly, his attitudes at mealtime seemed to reflect those of another era. He ate his food voraciously and made it a sin for anyone to leave any food on the plate. He would regularly announce that there would always be enough to eat, even if there were not enough money for new clothes or luxuries. He conveyed a sense of daily economic uncertainty and impending doom and would then reassure everyone that they would all survive somehow. He seemed oblivious to his own behavior, but he would get irritated if he saw someone eating too quickly, mocking them for acting as if their food might be taken away.

Carl valued his children's education, encouraging them to excel, but he was unable to participate directly in their learning. The subject he knew best was German, his mother tongue. He felt much conflict about his children studying it, conveying his ambivalence about his beloved language, which was also the language of the Nazis. He was generally too busy working to be available and when home would bury himself in a newspaper, consumed by world events and any news pertaining to anti-Semitism. He would watch television with his family, but he could not tolerate graphic war films or frivolous children's programs. He was short-tempered and explosive in his limit setting, requiring obedience, though rarely resorting to corporal punishment. Memories of his own countless beatings flashed through his mind at such times, and he tried to maintain as much control as possible.

Carl was very much concerned about the weather, insisting that his children be well protected from the elements, though he was numb to the cold and rarely wore winter clothing. However, he knew the lifesaving value of a warm coat and a solid pair of shoes. He was also reminded of having "tested" a new type of boot for the Germans while in Dachau during a sadistic twenty-four-hour march which nearly crippled him. Carl tried to shelter his children from the knowledge of his actual experiences in the camps, but his absent-minded references to his starvation and lack of clothing were obvious.

He also had a mysterious pair of black leather boots three sizes too small for him. When the boys discovered them, they were told a story about how Carl had borrowed a coat and these boots from a German soldier after the war. As they got older and the story unfolded, their fantasies about these German boots took on murderous proportions as they wondered how many people their father might have killed in order to survive.

Carl also had a tattoo on his forearm, numbers permanently inscribed when he entered Auschwitz. He would joke that it was his old girlfriend's phone number, hoping that his levity would change the subject. Carl believed that if he did not talk about his experience, his boys would not be affected. The thought of any more victims filled him with despair, and he espoused the philosophy of standing up for one's rights, yet avoiding undue attention while capitalizing on others' mistakes. Though he was opposed to stealing, he would delight in the slightest error in his favor at the cash register in stores, justifying his booty as a result of someone else's stupidity. His ever watchful eye and his readiness to put one over on anyone seen in any role of authority was a survival lesson he taught without realizing it.

Carl was fanatical about disease, hygiene, and safety. He preached incessantly about not putting things around the neck or climbing into boxes or tight spaces for fear of suffocation. He had claustrophobia, refusing to use elevators and becoming highly anxious if he had to wear a necktie or even if he experienced nasal congestion. He had been buried alive overnight for not moving fast enough at Auschwitz, and he blanched at the thought of his loved ones being in the same situation as he. The outbreak of infectious disease, the daily filth of the camps, and his nauseating latrine duty punishments reinforced his obsessional tendencies to be extra clean. He avoided hospitals and did not visit sick people. He could not tolerate his young children's accidents in toilet training, so he remained uninvolved.

Interestingly, Carl noted a subtle change in his ability to be a parent when his third and fourth children, both girls, were born. He was older, more financially secure, and less identified with the girls then the boys. He felt less rivalry and ambivalence toward his daughters, who idealized him as an invincible, immortal superman. He tried to provide them with all the material comforts that had been taken from him, and he strove to give them a painless existence. Though he was essentially uninvolved in the daily routine of their lives, he insisted on knowing their whereabouts at all times, a trait that continued even after they had grown up and left home.

Regarding his attitude toward religion, Carl had witnessed too much to have any illusions about life, death, or salvation. He had been forced to watch the humiliation, torture, and death of many religious leaders, whose beards were cut off and who were then subjected to all types of sadism. For example, he had seen the SS kill a famous rabbi by taking a hose, inserting it in his rectum, and filling him with water until he ruptured. As a result, Carl's cynicism and rage at God left him feeling disillusioned and betrayed. He believed that the most religious had been least prepared to take care of themselves and subject to worse treatment than the others. He developed great contempt for the passive, pious ones who did nothing but pray for deliverance and adhere to their rituals.

He would get anxious about going to the synagogue with his family, which resulted in considerable tension. Though he had been raised in a very observant family, his experience had taught him that religiousness was a liability, and he wanted no part of it after liberation. Yet he married into a very religious family. He therefore made a deal with his wife before they married that she could keep a kosher home and raise the children in an Orthodox way as long as he could eat whatever he wanted when out of the house. As a result, he was the exception who was permitted to break the Jewish dietary rules while his wife and children had to comply. The resulting confusion and double standard transmitted Carl's religious conflict to the children, who, as a sign of coming of age, would conspire with him to sneak nonkosher food behind their mother's back. He would take great delight at these times, showing a rare mischievous and playful side of himself. In so doing, Carl defied another authority, breaking the rules of an institution that had once had meaning for him. Interestingly, Carl's little transgressions with his children forged a special closeness with them as they came under his protection and shared a little secret with him. Though he was often brooding and distant, these forays endeared him to them, because he opened up and included them in his world of survival. He could not play their games, but they learned to play his games, feeling his love for them at these times.

In contrast, Otto had two children who were not raised in his home. His first child, a girl, was named for his sister Clara, who had never returned from the dance. This Clara, for his mother, was a replacement child; she unofficially adopted the infant and essentially raised her. (By this time, Carl and his family had moved to their new home, leaving an emotional void in the grandmother, whose emptiness was filled by her new grand-daughter.) Otto took a passive role in his parenting, essentially abdicating his fatherhood and continuing his secretive, nomadic life with his Gentile wife. When he would visit his mother, he would superficially play with the baby, who grew up quite con-fused about both her identity and her relationship to her parents. Otto's wife quarreled in vain with her mother-in-law over the child and ambivalently let the arrangement continue. When Clara was five, she even lived with Carl's family, but she was so gullible and naive that she was teased by Carl's children, who sensed how different she was.

Clara was not sure whether she was Jewish or not, and she was not even sure who her mother was. As she got older and talked about her early years, she recalled how her grandmother would scream and hide under the bed whenever she heard sirens or loud noises, fearing that the Nazis were coming for her. Clara would tease her and complain to her father, but he also seemed to be reliving the horrors of World War II. Clara therefore re-signed herself to this life, for which in return she received many material things and a very special role in the tattered remains of the extended family.

Otto's dependence on his mother and brother resulted in a plan for a new family business, a clothing store. In an effort to revive the success of their father and his brothers, Carl and Otto embarked on the venture (an ill-fated one, as it turned out) with their mother's blessing. Carl remembered that as a child, Otto had been very stubborn and had always wanted his toys, so Carl had some misgivings about working with him. But they had essentially been strangers since the war, and they hoped to become closer once again. Unfortunately, Otto's preexisting sense of entitlement, reinforced by his years in hiding, made it difficult to resist temptation. As a result he took clothing and cash from the store regularly, refusing to acknowledge it and becoming indignant about being accused. The business went bankrupt, and each blamed the other for its failure.

The brothers went their separate ways once again, but Otto could not keep a job because of petty thievery, for which he was inevitably caught. Consequently, he was unemployed when his wife gave birth to their second child, a son. He felt he could not take care of this child either, so arrangements were made for the infant to be raised on a farm on the outskirts of town. He and his wife saw their son infrequently but heard of his welfare indirectly through a mutual friend. Otto then drifted apart from his wife and got divorced. As the boy grew up, he had little sense of family or Jewish identity; his life as a farm boy was isolated and provincial. His contact with his father lessened further as he became a teenager, and after the boy joined the service, he was rarely heard from again. Before he disappeared, however, he wreaked some havoc. He had a very troubled adolescence, abusing drugs and joining an unsavory motorcycle gang that wore German helmets and Nazi regalia. This behavior terrified and enraged his father. The boy showed the ultimate in disrespect and vengeance in response to his own feelings of rejection, becoming a little Hitler who had contempt for all authority and structure. It was hoped that the military would straighten him out.

Otto's daughter, on the other hand, desperately tried to stay connected with her grandmother and parents, but there was continuous fighting over where she belonged. Eventually Otto re-married, but he was divorced from his second wife; because this left him penniless, he had no choice but to move back with his mother and daughter. Tensions escalated in this triangle, and the daughter moved out to live with her boyfriend, who was a Gentile. She married him at an early age against everyone's advice, and as an adult she never felt accepted by her family. She then moved away but continued to maintain contact with her father through her grandmother. When her grandmother died, however, Otto's daughter too disappeared after receiving her share of the estate.

In contrast, Carl's relationships with his children improved as they grew older. Feeling alienated from his own brother, sister, and mother, Carl felt more and more that his children were the only real family that he had. He seemed to be able to relate to them better when they became adults, after they too felt bur-dened by the responsibilities of life instead of being fun-loving children. Carl could not help but be reminded of the tragedies in his own life when his children became the same ages that he had been during his persecution. For example, when his sons were bar mitzvahed, he was reminded of his own rite of passage into manhood as the Third Reich's policy against the Jews inten-sified. When his daughters became old enough to date, Carl tried not to think about what had happened to his sister when she had gone out that night and never returned. Similarly, when his sons graduated from high school, his happiness was tinged with sad-ness over being reminded that he had been in Auschwitz by the time he was their age.

Carl's oldest son could not break away to go to college; he and his father were an inseparable duo. Despite Carl's wishes that his children not work as hard as he had had to, Carl was delighted that his son became his apprentice, joining him in the construction business he had built up over the years. On the way to work, Carl began to open up about his experiences, because to him their jobs were reminiscent of his slave labor under the Nazis. Their bond increased as they seemed to be living in the past and in the present. Carl was constantly commenting on the inhumane conditions, the accidents, the gruesome savagery, and the hopeless odds while he was nailing a piece of wood or climbing a ladder. His son seemed to absorb this experience, because he felt a special closeness to his enigmatic father, but at the same time the son felt trapped and inordinately responsible for his father's welfare. The young man had a deep sense of guilt, thinking that if he were ever to reconsider his future, something horrible would happen to his father.

During the war Carl had had a foot injury from a fall while in Auschwitz, making it difficult for him to walk without considerable pain. Interestingly, his other son became a podiatrist, the professional of the family, who specialized in treating foot pain. Carl was puzzled about the reason his son chose such a field, having hoped for a lawyer in the family, who would have been the mouthpiece for his grievances. He tried not to influence either of his sons' decisions, but he could not avoid registering his disappointment in their lack of greatness. As a result, the boys often felt that they needed to do superhuman things to please their father; they had some vague awareness of their need to make up for his losses and almost to justify his survival.

Carl's daughters were expected to marry rich men, who would take care of them so they could raise large families. One daughter rebelled, preferring an alternative lifestyle and living on a commune. Eventually she became a designer of the rather unusual clothing that was worn by her friends. The other daughter obeyed his dictate, marrying a very Orthodox man and having six children, all of whom loved their grandfather. Carl seemed to have rediscovered his ability to play, and in contrast to his brother, he celebrated the birth of each grandchild as a continued personal triumph.

With his advancing age and the growth of the grandchildren, his awareness of the importance of telling his story increased. In addition, a life-threatening medical illness revived memories of the Holocaust, and he began to speak more freely. He joined a survivors' organization and offered to give interviews. His new openness about his life allowed him to consciously transmit his legacy, but his grandchildren became very sad and protective when they were old enough to comprehend his ordeal. However, it seems as though Carl could now satisfy their curiosity about the tattooed numbers on his forearm—some forty years after liberation—because he had had the time and distance he needed in order to really open up. He even went to Sunday School with them, offering living proof to a new generation that the Holocaust had actually occurred.

Henrietta

The issue of being able to sustain the life of an infant has come up in women survivors, in contrast to men, because the onus of care typically falls on the mother. Henrietta, for example, who survived a Polish ghetto and Auschwitz, was sixteen when she was liberated. She was the only one in her family who survived, partly because she had been working in a bakery the day her family were dragged from their house and shot by the Nazis. She was then transported to Auschwitz, where she worked as a slave laborer until liberation, surviving a year in the camp.

She married several years later and had trouble conceiving. When she finally became pregnant, she was diagnosed as having leukemia, and she was told that she had to make a choice between her life and the baby's. It was thought that not terminating her pregnancy would accelerate her condition to a point where she might not even survive the full term. Confronted with what she felt was a *Sophie's Choice* dilemma—deciding who should live and die—Henrietta became severely depressed as she relived the selection at the ramp of Auschwitz: Dr. Mengele or his associates would send the newly arrived inmates to the left, condemning them to the gas chambers, or to the right—a chance to live—if they appeared capable of working. Therefore, as an adult, Henrietta refused to give up her unborn child, believing that in so doing she was condemning herself to death to give her baby a chance to survive. She knew that she could not live with herself unless she gave her baby a chance—the one she was never given to save her parents from the Nazis.

Henrietta's blood disorder did not progress as expected, and she had an unremarkable labor and delivery. She was then told that she had no more than six months to live; because she could not bear the thought of her child losing its mother, she entrusted its care to a friend, who planned to adopt the infant. Interestingly, her blood disorder resolved—another miracle of survival for her—and she eventually resumed the care of her child. It appeared that Henrietta's mysterious condition, which may have had a psychosomatic component, contributed to her feeling that it would not be possible or appropriate for her to be a mother. She felt that the circumstances would result in deadly consequences, especially because she was warned by persons she saw as authorities. Pregnancy and birth in the ghettos, and most certainly in concentration camps, were often a death sentence for both mother and child.

Henrietta's medical problems during her pregnancy thus revived not only the losses of her parents, but also her fears of becoming pregnant during the Holocaust. This reaction resulted in a postpartum depression, which immobilized her, rendering her unable to care for her newborn. She recovered, and she became a very dedicated and loving mother, who had difficulty tolerating separation from her children. Henrietta, like Carl, could not help but teach her children the lessons of her survival.

Lena

It is significant how the relationships between survivors' children and grandchildren have affected the survivors in coming to terms with their pasts. We have observed two ends of a spectrum: those who were upset that their children were uninvolved and seemingly uninterested in the Holocaust and those who were worried that their children were unduly preoccupied with it. In the former group, this concern has spurred some survivors to become close to their grandchildren in order to pass on the oral history themselves. The need to personally transmit this legacy—having skipped a generation, as it were—seems to have become all the more important for this group. In the other group, some survivors minimized their own suffering to themselves, said little to their children about it, and/or were not involved in survivors' organizational activities because they had become distraught over what was happening to their children. Feeling that it was unhealthy or wrong to dwell on the past, they may have opposed or criticized involvement in Holocaust-related programs. In some cases, the children's involvement promoted the parents' participation, though it was not always smooth.

Such was the case with Lena, a child survivor from France, who was sent to live in hiding with a Gentile family when she was five years old. The family was kind and generous, essentially raising Lena as their own, and they indoctrinated her with Christian dogma in order to make her false identity more authentic. When the war was over three years later, the family grudgingly relinquished Lena to a relative, who as the sole surviving adult of the family found and claimed her. Lena experienced no physical hardships such as starvation, beatings, or daily exposure to death and dying. Because she had been successfully shielded from the grim realities of the war, she knew about the persecution of the Jews only in terms of their not being allowed to play in the parks. Her false identity was never questioned, and she denied ever feeling in danger of being caught or getting hurt. Though the abrupt separation from her parents, whom she never saw again, should not be minimized, Lena's experience was relatively benign. She came to the United States, was lovingly adopted by relatives, was immediately enrolled in school, and became an assimilated American child by the age of ten.

Lena's life was happy, successful, productive, and not traumatic. She married a decent man and had a large family. She even traveled to Europe for the express purpose of finding the couple who hid her, making her pilgrimage back to her roots long before it was in vogue. She felt she had made peace with her past, and because she did not consider herself a Holocaust survivor, she could not relate to the national reunions that came into prominence in the 1980s. As a result, she was bewildered when one of her daughters became very interested in the Holocaust, reading extensively and joining a child-of-survivors support group.

Lena began to worry that her daughter was becoming obsessed, and she advised her to stop thinking about it so much, resulting in a bitter, angry confrontation between them. The daughter apparently felt that her mother was minimizing her ordeal, and in an effort to reconcile, they agreed to attend a conference on the Holocaust. Lena felt very self-conscious and anxious, feeling that she was under observation and had to react in a certain way. Tensions escalated between mother and daughter by the end of the day, and after a verbal explosion they stopped talking to each other for many weeks. Lena's worry about her daughter then evolved into a depressive reaction as she felt she was losing her child.

Lena eventually recognized that the feared loss of her daughter revived long buried and unresolved grief for her parents. Her daughter intuitively knew more about her mother's grief than Lena herself, and efforts to help Lena come to terms with this most painful part of her past were met with great resistance. Lena needed to mourn for her parents in order to let her children grow up and individuate. During her childhood the mourning process had been bypassed, and because of her excellent resilience, Lena initially suffered no sequelae of the war. (See Chapter 4 for a discussion of object loss and how mourning was avoided.) Over time, however, she began to see that she too was a survivor. She came to realize that her daughter had never known her grandparents, aunts, or uncles and so felt very much identified with the Holocaust despite her mother's adjustment.

Discussion

In Carl, Otto, Henrietta, and Lena are seen many of the traits we have found in child survivors who became parents. The Holocaust experience seems to have influenced parenting, whether the losses and traumas were merely repeated or whether there were attempts at mastery and regeneration. Henrietta repeated the trauma in her pregnancy and postpartum period. Lena, on the other hand, did not become symptomatic until her adult daughter emotionally abandoned her after their confrontation. Lena's capacity for regeneration had kept her unresolved grief hidden until then.

Otto appeared to repeat the story of his survival indefinitely. The young brother who enviously looked up to Carl and who survived in hiding with non-Jewish women continued these patterns throughout his life. He lived a nomadic lifestyle in secrecy, maintaining periodic contact with his mother. Infants and young children were a life-threatening liability to people in hiding, because the crying was likely to betray their presence to the Nazis. Consequently, Otto may have unconsciously felt threatened by the presence of his children and thereby been willing to let his mother raise his daughter. His mother had survived in hiding with a young child, so she was already familiar with the risks. Unlike some survivors who did not want to have children for fear of not being able to protect them if another Holocaust were to occur, Otto's solution was essentially to give them away.

His son was a stranger to him, having been sent to a farm on the outskirts of town, a fate similar to Otto's when he went into hiding from the Nazis. The son's aggression had a particular quality to it as he identified with the Nazi persecutors and terrorized his father, contributing to the repetition of Otto's trauma. Otto's daughter seemed to become a resurrection of his murdered sister—not only named for her, but raised by his mother as she too relived the daily fear of living in hiding. The daughter's only hope for psychological survival was to escape with a non-Jew, just as her father had done.

Otto's adaptation to postwar life in a new country seemed to be hampered by his inability to resist the temptation to take what he felt he needed to survive: money, food, and clothing. Though it is difficult to be sure just how much his preexisting character tendencies contributed to his propensity to steal, the circumscribed nature of this behavior had a highly symbolic quality to it. In short, he appeared to be too preoccupied with his mission of survival to be able to parent his children; his dependency and his focus on his own needs predominated. There appeared to be complicity with his wife in this regard as they lived in an isolated, self-contained world. (For further discussion on the effects of hiding, see Chapter 2.)

By comparison, Carl made an enormous effort to normalize his life after liberation despite his years in concentration camps. In contrast to the loneliness, secrecy, and hiding experienced by Otto, Carl's ordeal had been more social. Though he had lived in a most bizarre world, he had been with his father for three years and had had daily contact with trusted friends, providing him with meaningful connections throughout. His mode of survival had left an indelible imprint on his psyche, but his had not been the dyadic experience that his brother had had. Carl's behavior had reflected not only extraordinary determination to survive but also heroic risks and sacrifices to help others.

Because he had been unable to do the impossible, however, he felt bitterness and hatred toward the Germans for the murder of his father. His return home without his father seemed to symbolize the enormous and irrational sense of failure that he felt for not being able to save him. Carl denied any sense of conscious guilt, and indeed he had risked his life regularly to share his pitiful rations with his father. But the nature of the psyche is very complex, and there was evidence that he experienced unconscious survivor guilt. It may be that because of the inherent ambivalence in the father-son relationship, even in an "average expectable environment" (Hartmann 1958), the extraordinary conditions of the Holocaust had exacerbated the developmental conflicts such as the Oedipus complex. As a result, Carl's survival, among other things, may have felt like an unconscious Oedipal victory. Carl's suppressed anger at his father because of his denial of the danger and because of his refusal to let Carl go to Palestine may have intensified Carl's conflict. Furthermore, Carl had then become his own father's failed protector, reversing the parent-child roles. (See Chapter 7 for further discussion about role reversals and aging.) It would therefore follow that Carl's traumas and his limited ability to grieve for all his losses would color his relationships when he became a parent.

Having children became the cornerstone of Carl's new life—as with so many survivors who felt it was their greatest triumph over Hitler's attempt at genocide. Thus he was able to create a new family, reestablish a foundation for his shattered life, and maintain a continuity of the generations. As is the tradition among Ashkenazic Jews (those of European descent), his children were named for deceased relatives, all of whom had perished during the war. As a result, Carl's children became living links (Volkan 1981) to his massive losses, and they grew up with a peculiar sense of carrying an important burden for their father.

Carl's desire to have a family was greater than his fear of bringing up children in a world where a Holocaust could happen again. He was, however, unable to participate in their early care because of his fear of hurting his infants and because of his intolerance of excrement. Although it may not be unusual for fathers to shy away from such responsibilities, it seems that such contact may have been a reminder to Carl of the stench of bodily products and the daily exposure to the fragility of human life in the camps. Carl knew his children were being cared for, so he did not need to worry—consciously at least—that they would die of neglect or starvation. Unlike Henrietta and Lena, he was not expected to care for his newborns, so his issues was transmitted to his children when they were older.

For example, he transmitted his experience of being buried alive, mercilessly beaten, and starved. He also conveyed his having witnessed the torture and senseless execution of others. In addition, he expressed his disillusionment with God and the need to be constantly on the lookout for any lapses on the part of the oppressors, which could be used to his advantage. Such opportunities, which had once yielded a lifesaving crust of bread or a chance to avoid a deadly work detail, were indelibly etched into his superego. (See Chapter 3 on superego formation.) As a result, he was better able to teach his children how to survive in Nazi Europe than to help them negotiate growing up in America in the 1950s and 1960s. Nevertheless, his protectiveness of his family and his complete dedication to them were never questioned.

As mentioned earlier, his children intuitively sensed his pain and his not always being "there." He seemed to get lost in thought, an event that had a dissociative quality. His children—unconsciously, in an effort to restore his losses and somehow give their father's survival some meaning—followed life patterns described in earlier research (Bergmann and Jucovy 1983). For example, the oldest son, who could not break away, became his father's apprentice and right-hand man, a dutiful and protective junior partner who accompanied him on all his dangerous jobs. He was the most identified with his father as they relived his daily survival scenarios (Brenner 1988b). The second son, "the professional," seemed to live out the father's ego ideal, whose own aspirations were never realized. This son not only became what his father could not become, but he also chose a specialty treating the painful foot ailments that his father had incurred during the war. One of his daughters, following the biblical tenet to "be fruitful and multiply," devoted her life to providing grandchildren—which not only perpetuated the family but also attempted to make up for the lost family. The last child, the rebel daughter who lived the alternative lifestyle, also found a bridge to her father. Her designing and making clothing, in her own idiosyncratic way, regenerated the family business destroyed by the Nazis.

In their various ways, Carl's children lived out his aspirations and helped him recoup his losses. As a grandparent, Carl felt a heightened sense of the passage of time, allowing him to be more of his prewar former self. His limited responsibility for the grandchildren's care relieved him, and he could enjoy them more fully. In turn, they helped him tell his story so it could be passed on and not forgotten.

Conclusion

In the four vignettes presented here, the interplay between parent, child, and grandchild was significantly colored by the survival experience. The broad range of Holocaust experience is illustrated by a young girl in hiding with a benign family, a boy who survived in hiding by having sex with female protectors, a girl who was in the ghetto and in the camps, and an adolescent boy in concentration camps for six years. In each of these situations, the importance of lost relatives and the unique lessons of survival came into play during their parenting. Further, it is speculated that survivor mothers transmitted their survival lessons earlier than did survivor fathers. There was a dynamic tension between reliving of the trauma and mastery/regeneration. Difficulty in allowing their children to develop autonomy, because of the survivor parents' fears of new losses, was often present. The children were likely to be intuitively aware of their parents' losses, and they grew up making efforts to repair and restore what could never be replaced. In situations of neglect or abuse where aggression predominated, the child's wish for revenge could take on a Nazi-like quality, perpetuating the parent's persecution. The oral history of the parents' legacy was a central feature of their relationship to their children and grandchildren in the families in which survivors were able to come to terms with their past.

Aging of Children in the Holocaust

Judith S. Kestenberg, M.D.
Milton Kestenberg, Esq.

Demons

I threw my childhood away
I didn't want it anymore
It wasn't any good.
But it came back.

I gave my childhood away
To someone who might need it.
But no one wanted it,
And I had to take it back.

I ran away from my childhood
And hid in faraway places
Pretending to be someone else.
But it followed me.

So here we are at last
My childhood and I
Unable to shake each other off
We will have to find ways to Shalom.

—Francisca Verdoner Kan

Primary aging is intrinsic to the organism, whereas secondary aging refers to problems arising from environmental factors such as trauma (Busse 1989).

Children grow older, but they do not age. They grow up, becoming more mature. They may be precocious, advanced beyond their years, taller than the norm, or functioning above average. But when we speak of children aging, what have we in mind?

We have seen young or middle-aged adults aging overnight, becoming gray or stooped over after an unusual ordeal, but the Holocaust brought us face to face with the phenomenon of aging in children. Our interviewees, who are child survivors ranging in age from forty-seven to seventy-one, speak to us in phrases such as these: "I lost my childhood," "it was stolen from me," or "I became an adult prematurely." Observers of children persecuted during the Holocaust frequently refer to their adult "looks." We therefore speculate that not only adults but also children can undergo an aging process under the influence of massive physical and psychic traumas.

We approach this subject from two major perspectives. First we ask the question, How did persecuted and severely deprived children age physically and psychologically, and in what ways did their aging resemble the aging of the elderly? The sections immediately following include passages from the literature and from our archives that describe children's aging during the Holocaust and their behavior in the period immediately after liberation. Later sections deal with the question, What effect did the severe deprivation and traumatization of children during the Holocaust have on their development and on their subsequent ability to cope with the developmental tasks of adolescence, adulthood, and old age? Again, interviewees recorded in our archives speak of these areas of their lives.

Physical Aging

Several hundred children, from a few months to fourteen years of age, entered the hospital for children in the Warsaw ghetto. At first only infants came—those severely malnourished, who suffered from dystrophy or from more advanced atrophy. At the end of 1940 and in 1941, two five-year-old children entered the hospital, sick from hunger. Later, when the still older children could no longer draw on their fat deposits, the younger children were already dead. By the latter part of 1942, most of the little patients were over eight years old.

The doctors and nurses, themselves starved (as described in Winick 1979), observed atrophy without edema in starved children; they called this form *desiccated destruction*. Although there was no evidence of aging such as cataracts or brain atrophy (Winick, personal communication, March 1991), this phrase indicates a destructive process ending in premature death.

The earliest changes in the hunger disease in children were behavioral: the children became slowed down, apathetic, humorless, irritable, and incapable of playing. Their behavior seemed adult, but their intellectual level was low. When the malnutrition subsided, the psychological development regained its normal level.

In advanced stages of hunger, the children just lay on their sides, legs curled under. Growth was stunted: a nine-year-old would look like a five-year-old. The same is reported about children who grew up in Auschwitz (Strzelecki 1974 and our own archives). However, the stunted growth and retardation of intellectual functions indicative of immaturity was often accompanied by physical changes associated with aging, such as highly pigmented brown spots. The atrophic process affected many organs as the pulse slowed down and the excitability of the autonomous nervous system was reduced.

Although we cannot truly speak of aging when development was inhibited as a result of malnutrition, the descriptions of the starving, sick children who underwent these experiences are highly similar to those of adults' withering in old age. Therefore, not only a psychological but also a physical aging process seemed to be operative in children who were destined to die.

With the Eyes of Adults

Additional information from the Warsaw ghetto comes to us from the compassionate account of Dr. Adina Blady Szwajger (1990). We are grateful to Dr. Henry Fenigstein, who was the pathologist in the Warsaw ghetto hospital, for discussing this issue with us and drawing our attention to Szwajger's book. She writes that toward the end of the existence of the ghetto, there were more and more children emaciated from hunger, "with the eyes of adults." She describes children in the tubercular ward as strange—mature in their knowledge of their inevitable death, yet at the same time cut off from everyday atrocities as if shielded by an invisible wall. She refers to the often-described numb indifference in people under extreme stress. Every day the doctors saw the distended bodies and expressionless faces of the "ageless creatures" four to twelve years old. Their eyes were terribly serious, expressing the "sorrow of two thousand years of Jewish diaspora."

Despite the despair, children kept some childlike, human traits. A boy who was losing the power of his limbs because they were contracted screamed until someone put a pencil between his contracted fingers. He then began to draw from imagination and memory. Again, at one point, a playground was established for the hospital toddlers. They played mama and papa, lighting candles on Friday night. They cooked soup and "real potatoes," all in their imagination.

Yet much of the children's behavior was tainted with the horror of the time. When some of the starving, sick, horrible-looking children began to feel better, they sometimes smiled, but their smiles made the adults' hair stand on end. Eisen (1988) also gives accounts of children playing in the Warsaw ghetto. The toddlers would play what they saw—for instance, razzias (raids) and funerals. When a child dropped dead among them, they continued to play. In concentration camps, children played Blockaeltester (block elder), roll call, caps off, and even gas chambers. They played what they needed to understand, and what they did understand was the horror of an adult world gone mad.

Once Szwajger (1990) overheard the conversation of older children in the hospital. They discussed the adults' play with the toddlers: "They [the adults] think that this is ordinary life and that they are real children." These older children were talking to adults as equals, and they were perhaps even more realistic than the adults, as seen in a conversation with six-year-old Ryfka. This child no longer had a mother, and her three-year-old sister had died in the hospital. She said, "When a person has to do the washing, cleaning and cooking, she hasn't got time, and I never managed to look after the child" (p. 46). This adult-child walked away with the "tired, shuffling step of an old woman" (p. 47).

Szwajger also described children who were not starving and not sick, but were hidden to escape the Nazis. There, other dangers lurked; the hidden children were not allowed to cry (see also J. S. Kestenberg 1991a, 1991b; M. Kestenberg 1994). These children "were already grown up, with that maturity of five [to] six year olds" who understood that they "must not cry, must never talk and that almost all day they had to stay in bed, on a pallet" (p. 137). Lying down all day, children stopped walking; some suffered from rickets, others from the disuse of muscles. The small children forgot how to talk, and some did not know how to play. Quite a few children survived without parents; some begged, others died of starvation or disease. Children sold newspapers and cigarettes, spending their summer nights in dugouts, in gardens, in ruins, or in cemeteries. They mistrusted adults. Szwajger reports that some of these street children, who acted like adults, were children nevertheless. For instance, they moved about in scooters, forgetting to be careful and running into the gendarmes, who brought them to the Germans.

Szwajger tells the story of a five-year-old girl whose mother died in the ghetto. The girl had been shunted from one place to another, passing as a Gentile. After liberation, her foster mother told the child the truth about her Jewish origin. Jasia confessed

that she had known her real name all along but that she had not
thought her foster mother was aware of it. Even though Jasia had
been well treated and loved, she had kept her secret to herself.
Had she been shielding her foster mother, or distrusting her, as
would a cautious adult?

Szwajger herself, a young woman, never thought seriously
that there would be anything for her after the war. She felt very
old. It seemed to her that she had already experienced everything good and important, so the future seemed unimportant.
One of our interviewees, a child survivor, said that she was a mil-
lion years old, judging by how much she had already experienced
in terms of suffering. The "aging" children felt burdened by their
adult responsibilities, and they hardly remembered the good
times of their short pre-Holocaust life. Their Holocaust experiences burdened them, making them feel aged—sometimes for
the rest of their lives.

Another aging effect on children was the development of
a new morality and a new sense of responsibility. Children who
became breadwinners for the family stole and smuggled at the
risk of their lives, and adults welcomed their help. In camps,
children saw that only those who lied and beat others had full
stomachs. Lauscherova (1965) described a girl in Terezin (Theresienstadt) who at the age of eleven did what she pleased and
did not listen to her mother. She lived with girls the same age
and got her food from the canteen; when she had a toothache,
she went to the dentist by herself. When her mother lectured her
about some flaw in her behavior, she did not want to listen to her
"preachings" and answered back, "I am grown up already"
(p. 96). In Terezin particularly, where teachers tried to uphold
moral principles while teaching children clandestinely, the issue
of lawlessness became a topic for discussion. The children knew
that their parents themselves stole food from the kitchen to give
the children some extra nourishment; they knew the adults were
cheating. Identifying with the adults, they too felt like adults
(O. Klein 1965). Many children who took care of themselves
completely during the time they had to hide retained their childlike attitude, which surfaced either when they were caught or

when the danger was over. Such was the case with Maniek, who was described in Chapter 2, on hidden children.

Not all children in hiding showed signs of aging. Some survived by remaining childlike and obeying all orders given them: when Betty was seven years old, she was hidden with a relative who passed for a Gentile and worked with the underground. One day the relative asked Betty to wait for her in a church but never came back. After hours of waiting, Betty found out that her relative and the people she had met had been taken away by the SS. Betty, however, did not become a self-reliant street child, but walked around crying until a nice Polish woman met her and took her home. After that, she was placed in the country, where she was welcome and well taken care of. She maintained her false identity for a long time, but her main survival strategy was unquestioned obedience. Later in life she began to question her persistent obedience, which she had carried to the point that she would do whatever was asked of her.

Precocious Children or Premature Adults?

Lena Kichler wrote a 1963 article, reprinted in Eisenberg's book (Kichler 1982), on surviving children's accounts she had collected after the war. A fourteen-year-old told her a hair-raising story about her sister Helena: when she went down into the sewer to escape from the ghetto, many younger children beseeched her to take them along. They begged, kissed her hands, and assured her, "I shall not cry! I shall behave well. I want to live too!" They were too small and would have drowned in the sewer. Helena marveled how "clever" these tiny children were. They knew that they had been sentenced to death, and they were terribly afraid to die by themselves. Were these children adultlike or precocious because their terrible reality did not fit the average expectable environment of a child?

The older children were aware that they had taken on the tasks of adults, frequently reversing roles with them. A ten-year-old girl told her mother to leave the children and save herself (Kammer 1982), and she asked her mother to pray for the daughter's easy death. When the girl was caught by Ukrainian Gentiles and tortured, she did not reveal the whereabouts of her family, thinking that "four lives must not perish on account of me" (p. 193). Eventually she asked to be shot, and her torturers acquiesced.

The helplessness of a mother evoked adultlike responses from children. They seemed to be reality oriented beyond their years, and the internalizing of adult values proceeded through identification with their lost adult protectors. An eyewitness account describes the children sent to the camp at Drancy in France (Levy and Tillard 1976). The bigger children immediately took the smaller by the hand and carried them up the stairs. They never quarreled and were consistently helpful to each other. They exhibited an unusual affection for their younger siblings.

The younger the children, the more precocious they became in their appraisal of reality. The longer they lived in the "Holocaust culture" (J. S. Kestenberg and Gampel 1983), the more they became prematurely adult, protective of their families, and capable of reacting quickly to a variety of dangers. However, it seemed, in all developmental phases beyond infancy, that underneath the restrained, scared adultlike child there lived almost independently a normal growing child whose fantasies and impulses were ready to erupt from captivity when the opportunity presented itself.

By the time children were twelve to fourteen years old, many took on adult tasks and were able to make their own decisions. Perhaps as adolescents they became more daring than their elders. In many camps, young boys served as runners, housekeepers, and sexual partners of kapos (prisoners who were supervisors of work details). Many of these boys, called piepels, identified with the Nazi masters and emulated their cruelty to the prisoners. In some instances they were induced to hang their own parents. They lorded it over persecuted adults, pretending to be in charge. Their "adulthood" equaled that of the adult persecutors who demeaned or tortured their Jewish parents. But not all piepels were evil. "They matured before their age and developed resourcefulness as adults. Their roles were changed" (Shtrigler 1946/1982). One of them brought food to his despondent father. He came every day and always " . . . talked to his father as a father would to a helpless 'little son.'" In this instance, the adult type of behavior resulted from the internalizing of parental values, which persisted despite the Nazi indoctrination and despite the prestige these piepels achieved in the camps.

Most of the youngsters who lost their parents, older relatives, or rescuers were forced to assume adult responsibilities. However, quite a few children realized that their parents were degraded and could not defend themselves. The younger the child and the more he or she idealized a parent, the more traumatic it was to see the parent's humiliation. A moving example (Kichler 1982) is that of a nine-year-old boy who lowered his eyes in shame when he witnessed his father obediently lie on the floor to be beaten and kicked by an SS man. He reported, "I could not look at his face" (p. 119). Was this his courageous father, who had guided him all his life? The father seemed to recognize his son's silent mortification. He got up, looking straight at his son, and defied the enraged German, who beat and stamped on the father until he died. The boy was helpless but proud: his father has shown him how to die with honor. His death represented a pledge they had made to each other not to bow before the German murderers. Left all alone, the child fled to the forest and, under the guidance of his father's friend, became the youngest partisan in their group. The father left him the legacy that he defend himself and, if need be, die with dignity.

Many parents who were debased in front of their children reversed roles and were protected by their children (Wiesel 1969). Some, however, were able to preserve the ideal image of a parent, which allowed their children to keep their childhood trust and to seek protection from other adults. This was also the case with many girls who, separated from their fathers for a long time, never stopped hoping for their return. They looked to father substitutes to protect them. A story of a five-year-old girl who was rescued by being placed in a soup kettle illustrates this point. She had suffered a great deal and "like the rest of the children" dumbly accepted being placed in a greasy pot. When she was taken to a safe spot, she asked her rescuer, "Where shall I go?" He could not help her and told her to run (Shappell 1982, pp. 244–246). Did this child then find helpful Gentile rescuers who appreciated her obedience, or did she join the ranks of begging young children—those who became prematurely adult, having lost their faith in adults?

It seems that precociousness exhibits itself in the child's early recognition of harsh reality. Aging psychologically is based on the recognition of the loss of adult protection. There are also varieties of adjustments—from identification with the aggressor to identification with the lost protector to becoming prematurely independent and distrusting adults.

After Liberation

Liberation gave children moments of joy and exhilaration, but the joy was overshadowed by not finding parents, siblings, or other relatives. The younger the children who lost trust or never learned to trust, the less able they were to adapt to new circumstances. They behaved as if they still lived in terror of their lives—intimidated, all too quiet, and exhibiting robotlike obedience.

A train with two hundred little children (none older than four) arrived in Jerusalem after the war. Many of them had been born in concentration camps. They were obviously disciplined not to cry. They had learned that only total silence would save them. On seeing them, an adult exclaimed, "How adultlike the newcomers are!" She felt that adults could learn self-discipline from these little ones.

Despite attempts to speak to them in their native languages, they never uttered a sound, including times when they were inoculated. Even when left alone, they never broke their silence, like frightened little animals. (We note here the double-edged description of these tots: like adults, yet like frightened little animals.) When the children were invited to light candles for the

Sabbath, a four-year-old girl volunteered, breaking her silence. She knew the blessing and recited it like a Jewish woman who had suffered a great deal. After this ceremony she gave a speech to the children which sounded even more adult and sophisticated as she explained her view about the Sabbath (Lazar 1982).

The seriousness and restraint of these young children were interpreted as a continuation of their adultlike adjustment to their previous life-threatening conditions. To us, it also seems like an extension of the silent stranger anxiety of terrified babies or toddlers. Once a ritual familiar to at least some of them was introduced, a little girl immediately identified with her lost mother and behaved like her. Obviously this was not play, but it had all the characteristics of a child imitating an adult in play, not only in its form, but also in its content. We see here a complex combination of regression, precociousness, and adultlike behavior.

Although the youngsters gradually regained strength and were less afraid, the tragedy did not come to an end. It deepened, because they became more aware of their losses and suffered from survivor guilt—a feeling they shared with many adult survivors. A loyalty conflict then arose for a great many children who had found refuge in convents or in devout Christian families (Hogman 1988). Their new caretakers in Israel had a hard time with children who wore crosses and knelt to pray. This was aggravated by the fact that many other Jewish children were angry and upset at the sight of the ritual of crossing oneself, which had become a symbol of their oppression, evoking painful memories.

A poignant explanation for the prolonged use of the cross came from a woman who surveyed Jewish institutions in Rome (Cohen 1982). Talking about Leah, one of the children there, she explained, "The cross she wears takes the place of father and mother" (p. 326). In psychoanalytic language, the cross became a transitional object, a link between the lost parents and the child (Brenner 1988a; Volkan 1981; also see Chapter 4, on multisensory bridges). This is especially significant because the Holy Family (Mary, Joseph, and Jesus) often replaced the degraded and lost Jewish family. Children who were protected by Christianity, by passing as Polish or French Christians while remaining Jewish in their hearts, did not need to grow up prematurely. They had learned not to trust Jews, yet the feeling of belonging to Polish or French Christians was a displacement of the longing for their lost Jewish family bonds.

Frequently, a child who had already assumed adult responsibility welcomed the care offered by a convent. The conflict between Christianity and Jewishness was then colored by wanting to be a Christian child so as not to have to assume the role of the suffering adult. Leah[1] became an adult at the age of eleven. In the absence of caretaking adults, she put her two younger siblings in bed to hide from the Germans. When they were all discovered by the Germans, Leah used a subterfuge to escape. Still, she was shot twice and once lay in a grave. When Leah recovered, she could recall the Jewish words of her mother, who told her that she, Leah, would outlive the enemy. In the convent her classmates suspected that she was Jewish. She had to avoid them and yet sing anti-Semitic songs with them. Still she turned to the Jewish God, asking that He not punish her for it. She wanted to be Marysia, not Leah, and she yearned for the protection of the nuns and their God, but the Jewish God remained in her. Being safe in the convent revived her childhood; her immediate past had been a premature adulthood.

After the war, educators tried to introduce the joy of childhood into the life of the young survivors. As Nelly Wolfheim (1966) put it, play eases the child's life. In play the child can work through traumatic experiences. She turns from passivity to activity, from helplessness to control, mixing fantasy and reality in such a way that a too-harsh experience can be mastered. Playing the role of the adult is also an important factor, one that makes children understand the behavior of adults. During and after the war, adults wanted children to play, learn, study, and ignore or forget what happened. Still, we have never heard of surviving

---

[1] Leah's story is one of the interviews in the archives of the International Study of Organized Persecution of Children.

children playing out their past persecutions spontaneously, without adult encouragement. Perhaps, after years of continuous trauma, playing out what happened lost its curative value because it too, like memory, became a source of pain. If children indeed lost their capacity to play, it is a most significant indicator of premature aging. Like adults, instead of playing out traumatic experiences, they behaved as if the danger were still there—*acting* out the past, not *playing* it out.

In a transitional center for child survivors in England, the Windermere (Wolfheim 1966), physicians found that almost all children were physically affected, even though they had gained weight beforehand, during a three-month stay in Czechoslovakia. Physical improvement occurred very quickly, but psychic disequilibrium was much harder to overcome, especially for the younger ones. They were very small, had shaved heads, had skin problems, and screamed constantly. They were animal-like creatures who grabbed toys from each other, ran around randomly, and were continuously irritated. Little by little, however, they learned to communicate. After they had been permanently placed, they would sometimes speak about their experiences— some with bravado, others anxiously. A nine-year-old boy spoke about killing and mistreating as if it were an adventure. Another child who had come to Windermere when he was four was described at the age of six as very sensitive to noise and physically retarded. He was afraid of being shot, talking a lot about death and God. He would ask, "Do you know that my parents were shot and killed?" A seven-year-old girl had the posture of an old woman. She related a dream of her mother admonishing her to care for her siblings. Quite a few of the children were burdened by problems like these. References to their past were sporadic; many children did not want to speak about their past at all.

The six three-year-olds cared for by Anna Freud's staff in Bulldogs Bank (Freud and Dann 1951) were distrustful of adults and very unruly. However, their concern for one another engendered a community spirit much more mature than is usual for toddlers. In Windermere the children from Theresienstadt were afraid that everything would be taken away from them, be it food or toys. When people left, they were not expected to come back, which meant they were dead. A new house meant a place where they would be murdered.

Children had lost trust in people; they didn't expect the adults to keep their promises (Wolfheim 1966). Many Buchenwald children were very unruly; to them, freedom meant abuse of power. They were destructive and totally disobedient (Hemmendinger 1986a) until they could be tamed. The adolescents behaved like the adults they had seen controlling the camp. But when opportunity presented itself, perhaps in memory of the few teachers in the camps, children wanted to study and advance (Albertus 1989). It was important for them to have benign teachers, and many progressed rapidly, even under trying circumstances. Later, when they emigrated, quite a few learned new languages quickly. They were all-too-serious students, but at the same time they just wanted to be like all the other children.

Wolfheim wondered whether the children found it difficult to bridge the chasm between advancing into the future and remembering the past. The present seemed to be a transition into an uncertain future. This attitude, she said, was unchildlike and too great a burden on the children. The sections that follow examine the effects of the severe deprivation and traumatization of children during the Holocaust on their later development and on their subsequent ability to cope with the developmental tasks of adolescence, adulthood, and old age.

Developmental Effects of Massive and Repeated Persecution

Babies and preverbal toddlers were largely unable to withstand starvation and illness. Those few who did survive had to deal with their mother's anxiety, depression, and physical deterioration. Separation from Mother without a nurturing person to replace her brought about early forms of depression, to which Spitz (1946) referred as anaclitic. Separation combined with hunger and lack of care brought about apathy, a refusal to eat and play, and immobility. Subsequent separation from the rescuing care-taker repeated the original trauma. Most of the survivors who were subjected to physical and emotional deprivation from separations in infancy retained what they described to us as an inner emptiness, a nagging discomfort—something akin to physical hunger, but different. Perhaps the least known form of early emotional aging is play deprivation, an interference with movement and exploration. The adult look of these infants is due, at least in part, to a lack of the mimetics characteristic of infancy. Such a baby's immobile face has a serious adult quality.

Toddlers suffered a great deal from immobility and being inhibited from crying or loud vocalizing. One two- to three-year-old who was hidden under a table made up stories for herself. When she felt like bursting, she was taken to another room, where there was sometimes a corpse. This did not seem to disturb her as long as she could move, but she lacked children to play with.

If persecution began when children were three to six years of age, they missed the companionship of other children and suffered from exclusion from children's groups. However, the clearer their understanding of danger in the presence of frightened adults, the less toll it took on their development. An important source of burden, which paradoxically contributed to psychological aging, was the secretiveness of the adults. Children who were not prepared or taught to keep secrets learned the hard lessons of life early because they did not understand at first what would betray them.

In some instances, children were not able to keep secrets or inadvertently blurted out significant facts, as did the little two-year-old girl, who, when faced by her Christian rescuers, recited her new Polish name, but also added her Jewish names. Another such case was a four-year-old who had escaped from the ghetto and was brought to a farm, where he played with other children his age. He wanted to be one of them. but when they played church and sang liturgical songs, he remarked musingly, "My grandfather in the ghetto sang different songs." Fortunately he was overheard by an adult and whisked away in time. Adults rightly assumed that children of that age could not be trusted to keep secrets. Yet many young children who had been properly prepared did not betray their origin (Auerhahn and Laub 1984).

Most adults believed that children would not understand what the adults were saying, or that the children were asleep and did not hear. One five-year-old was totally prepared for his secret departure because for two weeks he overheard (while presumably asleep) the adults' discussion of his planned escape and hiding (Auerhahn and Laub 1984).

Not only caution prevented adults from telling children about their plans and worries; they also did not answer the children's questions and kept them in the dark because they wanted to preserve their childhood innocence. The effect of this behavior was to give the children a double message: "know and don't know" (Auerhahn and Laub 1984). This created later learning difficulties and difficulties in remembering what they were forbidden to know: their childhood persecution. The children's natural curiosity was stifled, and many fantasies had to be woven to comprehend, in a child's way, the cruel facts of life.

Children of school age, especially, had a hunger for knowledge that reinforced their curiosity about the reality of their lives. Whereas infants and toddlers needed space to move, explore, exercise, use their muscles, and satisfy their curiosity, school-age children needed to also exercise their brains. They wanted to learn and they wanted to help. Deprived of schooling or having only sporadic instruction, they listened with a redoubled interest to adults' talk.

Older school-age children and young adolescents, who became breadwinners of the family, experienced their daring activity as an adventure, while at the same time they fulfilled adult roles and behaved like adults. In some instances, especially in older adolescents, the need to overcome danger and survive became embedded in a survivor's personality until adulthood or even older age. Henri, a fifteen-year-old who was selected for the gas chamber, saved himself and some of his comrades by telling them, "Let's pick up the corpses," as if this had been their order. Having thus outwitted their adult persecutors, they lifted the heavy corpses, marched away, and mingled with those who were

not selected. Later in life, Henri sought out dangerous neigh-
borhoods to live in and was very proud of himself when he survived attacks on his life.

Although many interviewees assure us that, as youngsters,
they were too preoccupied with surviving to think of sex or were
underdeveloped for their age, quite a few relate sexual activities
during the time of persecution (Edelbaum 1980; Nir 1989). The
desire to experience sex before their death prompted many of
them to engage prematurely in intercourse. After the war, premature marriages and early parenthood were frequent. A relationship based on shared past ordeals of a similar kind
counteracted loneliness, ensured acceptance, and replaced lost
families. A young marriage partner, himself a survivor, could listen compassionately, understand, and believe. Child survivors
who divorced their spouses later in life frequently explained that
they had been too young to get married and assume an adult's
responsibility in marriage. In many cases, both partners needed
to be mothered and had difficulty with the parental role. Many
women complained that they were too young to care for children,
implying that they were children themselves and should not have
engaged in adult responsibilities. They had not learned to care
for babies and did not know how to play with children. They
wanted to recapture the feeling of being a child, but they still
assumed a burden that later became too difficult for them. Instead of working through adolescent gains in a phase of preadult
consolidation (J. S. Kestenberg 1975/1995), child survivors
sometimes remained in prolonged adolescence. How this can be
reconciled with premature aging is exemplified by a man who
had witnessed his father's arrest. Recalling this time of his life,
he remarked that he had then grown several years in six weeks,
but he had never grown since.

Depression often ensued when child survivors were unable
to fulfill the role of spouse and parent to their satisfaction. Depression sometimes originated from failing to meet the obliga-
tion to perpetuate the family, a frequent motivation for early
marriage (J. S. Kestenberg 1972). These young parents had difficulty in fulfilling the tasks of Erikson's generative stage (1959).

Interestingly enough, their mothers, who had not been deprived of care during infancy and childhood, could care for and play with their grandchildren. (For further discussion, see Chapter 6, on parents and grandparents.)

Child Survivors and the Milestones of Life

Almost every turn of a decade brings about a change of attitudes and new reflections about the past and the future. What has been done? What can still be changed? What does the future bring?

How do people deal with their "stolen childhood" in transitions toward aging?

With few exceptions, reaching the age of fifty is an important landmark. Another is menopause, still another the prospect of retiring in one's sixties. The loss of a loved spouse and chronic illness with advancing age are others.

Ida,[2] a fifty-two-year-old married woman, became depressed when she reached fifty. She was unable to reconcile herself with the fact that she was no longer a precocious child. She did not see herself as one who had aged prematurely, but rather as a happy, friendly child who had learned to survive and looked forward to a future. At the age of fifty she was in shock, feeling that she had not had enough time to plan and no longer had a future.

Edith, a fifty-five-year-old married woman who had recently completed menopause, complained that she had not had enough years to play. She missed play and toys even before her deportation at the age of five. As an adult she studied early childhood education and was aware that she didn't know how children play. She made it a point to observe in a nursery before she graduated. At age fifty-five, she declared that she was glad not

---

[2] The stories of the seven people in these paragraphs are from interviews in the archives of the International Study of Organized Persecution of Children.

to have her period anymore. It was perhaps the happiest time in her life, now that she had retired from teaching and was taking care of her grandchildren part time. She had more time for herself and less responsibility. As she talked and laughed, however, her eyes betrayed her sadness. Asked about it, she cried, though she then protested that she was a very playful person, even when she didn't play with young children. Whereas Ida, who was in treatment, reconciled herself to being an adult, Edith still wanted to recapture her lost childhood.

Barbara, fifty-two, had been in hiding with her mother from infancy until liberation. She had always been alone and had no playmates until, at the age of six, she stayed in a displaced persons' camp. Her childhood seemed to have begun when she was in school. She later became an inspiring early elementary school teacher, and her students loved her, but in her adolescence she was severely depressed and suicidal. She married early and soon found that she could not play with her young children. She marveled that her mother, who had had to work for the Nazis and had not been able to play with Barbara when she was a preschooler, did enjoy playing with Barbara's children.

Lorna said that she had lost her adolescence and added, "In some way I became an adult, something in between"—not quite an adult and not quite a teenager. Her loss could never be replaced. Erna said, "I feel the same way; I lost out on friends." Rebecca said that she had been robbed of her childhood and become adult prematurely. She thought that she had not really lived, because she had been cheated doubly—of her childhood and again when she began to age. When she was eleven years old, she lost her mother, who was then forty. When she herself reached the age of forty-five, her own daughter was eleven. She felt then that her life was coming to an end. Her daughter could not understand what was going on, yet felt it.

Arno looked forward to his retirement, eagerly anticipating the time when he would be able to play with tin soldiers again. When the Nazis had come to his country and he could not play with other children, he had found solace in playing with his tin soldiers. He had had various colors of armies—French, English, and German—and he would "shoot" each soldier until every one fell down—he had had no favorite soldiers. All his life he had wanted to "play war." When asked whether he would make war on the Nazis, however, he was stunned. It became obvious that he wanted to pick up where he had left off as a child, when he had been shielded from the knowledge of the danger the family was in. As an adult, he could again replace his missing playmates with tin soldiers. Perhaps retirement meant a new isolation, with which he wanted to cope by playing with tin soldiers.

Gloria had been near death as a child. She used to think that "that's how things are"—death was an expected occurrence. When, in adulthood, she lost her son in an accident, it brought back her childhood feeling that death should be borne without tears. She was not supposed to cry. When her husband of many years became seriously ill, she bore that too, but she made sure that, unlike her parents, he would not die alone. She still keeps vigil with dying patients whom she does not know, and she feels privileged to be with them. She was not afraid to die alone, but she felt her present aloneness as a great burden. Not unlike other aging people, child survivors fear helplessness and loss of function in old age. They fear being dependent on their children and caretakers and thus being reduced to the status of children.

Tessie, a social worker, was one of the few people who escaped from Treblinka. She graciously permitted us to discuss a talk she had given to the Miami child survivors' meeting about aging child survivors. Tessie equated the loss of function in old age with the losses experienced in childhood. Cancer with approaching old age is particularly threatening, she said, because—just as in the Holocaust—one does not know whether one will live another day. During her childhood persecution, she used psychic numbing and closing off, which are functional and adaptive in extreme stress. She later used the same mechanism to endure the stress of cancer. She saw a further parallel: between the technology devised for the institutionalized aged by the current medical establishment and the dehumanization and powerlessness experienced at the hands of Nazi technocrats. Progressive illness with an uncertain outcome, which has an aging effect, evoked associations for her with death in ghettos and camps: an inmate who became sick was "useless" and was killed, deported, or gassed.

At times, child survivors deny that they aged in childhood or that aging has a special meaning for them. Underneath the feeling of needing to be a child rather than an adult may lie a deep-seated, "deadly" conviction that adulthood inevitably brings death. In the following account, we see how Ida at first denied, then understood, that she had dreaded the adult "deadness" in herself and preferred to be a "precocious child."

Ida did not think in terms of an alternative between childhood and adulthood, but between living and not living. Her family had fled to Russia when she was nine months old and been deported to Siberia when she was three. In this process she had lost her nursemaid and her uncle. However, she had become attached to a grandfather who, in contrast to her depressed parents, had let her be a playful, boisterous child and taught her how to prepare herself for her future. She said that a child has a present and a future. When asked whether that meant that an adult has no future, she fell silent and was visibly moved.

For a whole year, while the family was starving, she had never known whether her father would come home or not. As a child and up to the present, she had felt indestructible, while at the same time she suffered from a concealed inner "deadness," which she equated with terror (but which may have been related to the emptiness of her stomach). She had no idea who she was, yet she needed to do what had to be done to survive. She always felt that the present did not count, only the future. When her beloved grandfather died, he too disappeared. She was told he had gone to heaven, and she waited in vain for his return. Perhaps his disappearance and the possible loss of her father created a latent depression, felt as deadness. To counteract the deadness, equated with adulthood, she continued to feel like a happy-go-lucky, precocious child. When in her analysis she was able to accept being an adult in her early fifties, she no longer dreaded her future and became more successful in her work.

In contrast to Ida, Aron did not think that he wanted to be a child, but he also had no memory of feeling he had aged in his childhood. He was able to play with other children until he was deported to a camp at the age of fourteen. It was important there to be "adult," because children were gassed as a matter of principle. He was always able to seek out people and groups who offered him some degree of security. For a few days after liberation, he felt forlorn, not knowing where to turn. Soon, however, he found himself in a Zionist group, and he regained his composure. Similarly, he was happy in the Israeli army but lonely afterward. Up to the time of our interview, he was happier in groups than at home, where he did not let his hair down. He felt tired and burdened by things he had to do. It pained him that he was unable to play ball or engage in sports with his son.

He did not understand that he was acting like an old man who withdraws from a vibrant family. When he thought of the mandatory retirement he would face in a few years, he had the same feeling as during liberation: What would he do with himself? Although he had not worked in Auschwitz, he seemed to keep to the camp doctrine: "You must work or die." Leisure, to which others look forward, appeared too dangerous, and "playing" was permissible only in groups.

Many child survivors who felt abandoned, "thrown out," when they were sent into hiding look upon their surviving parents' death as a new abandonment, which is equated with their own death. Rhoda, fifty-two years old, had not forgiven her parents for leaving her in front of a convent. She was depressed and suicidal. When she thought of her aging mother's death, she felt that she could not live without her. The fear of being left alone again, combined with anger and guilt feelings, camouflaged a childhood feeling that she would never see her mother again and would herself cease to exist.

When we hide, either we disappear from sight or, in a sense, our identity disappears. For many child survivors, disappearance means death, and aging is a road to it. When child survivors speak of their lost childhood, they tell us that the world owes them a new life. They feel betrayed once again when they are faced with becoming older without recompense and without having fulfilled themselves. They are lost again.

Sophie didn't remember much of her childhood in hiding. Her transference indicated that she had been very unhappy when she was sent away from home to a place where she was hungry and neglected. She remembered that in the second hiding place, however, she had been happy and contented. As an adult, she never married and seemed independent enough up to the time her mother died. However, a psychosomatic illness and adverse work conditions contributed to a very pessimistic outlook on life. She was worried that she would not have enough money to support herself. At the same time, she became disappointed in her friends and found solace in withdrawing into herself. Although bright and educated, she could no longer find work or people interesting. She acted out the solitude she had experienced as a child, when not only her mother but also the whole world seemed to have left her. She still feels abandoned, like an orphan.

For child survivors, aging is fraught with reminiscences of the Holocaust. Each, in his own way, tries to resolve the problem of aging in accordance with his own experience. Many feel invulnerable, while others must repeat their abandonment, which they equate with death. Still others must keep proving that they are invulnerable by exposing themselves to danger and surviving over and over again. Like all other aging persons, they conjure up the past as they try to cope with getting old and dying. However, theirs is a different kind of aging, a different kind of death. Neither illness nor loss of loved ones nor death is a stranger to them. They were confronted with illness and death from starvation and violence through the better part of their childhood. For some, death will reunite them with the people they have loved and lost; for others, death will deliver them from suffering and bring them peace.

Discussion

The thesis presented here concerns the aging of children who are subjected to extreme stress and deprivation. Many who lived during the Holocaust were starved, lice-ridden, and covered with boils. Their immune systems suffered, and they were prone to many diseases, especially typhus and tuberculosis. Quite a few had to work very hard and were beaten; some in hiding were not allowed to move or utter a sound. One of their supreme deprivations was an often sudden, repeated separation from their mothers at an early age (J. S. Kestenberg 1991a). In addition, demands were made on them to act as if they were adults with adult responsibilities.

Many examples of children presented here impressed adults as aged and as adultlike in appearance and demeanor, with a masklike face and a seriousness unbecoming a child. Subjectively, the majority of those who survived the multiple strain traumas and shock traumas (Kris 1956) complained that they had lost their childhood and had aged prematurely. Many wanted to retrieve the childhood they had lost, and others pretended they were still precocious children.

Our impression is that these physically and psychologically traumatized children were indeed aging, not only in their minds but also in their bodies. Van der Kolk's (1988) intensive research on posttraumatic stress disorder indicated that, as a result of trauma, there are lasting changes in the limbic system, and these changes pertain not only to adults, but to children as well. Studies of starved adults (Winick 1979) and traumatized adults show signs of aging such as decalcification, cataracts, and deterioration of the liver. There are no comparable data on children, but some retrospective interviews disclose a tendency to diseases that are not common in children.

When one examines the posttraumatic stress disorder of children in the Holocaust from the clinical point of view, one finds the following disturbances, which are also common in aging: 1) irritability, 2) proclivity to outbursts of aggression, 3) constriction of the general level of personality functioning, 4) a lowering of baseline functioning that interferes with exploration, memory, integration, and the capacity to symbolize and fantasize, 5) a tendency to depression and psychosomatic disease, 6) disruption of the capacity to modulate physiological arousal as well as the intensity of emotions, 7) a lowering of the capacity to differentiate between stimuli, to scan, to construct space, and to categorize information, 8) anhedonia and psychic numbing, 9) poor affect tolerance, alexithymia (Krystal 1988), and poor modulation of intimacy-dependency expressions, and 10) fear of abandonment and difficulty in forming new attachments.

To this it must be added that child survivors report a decreased power of concentration and a preoccupation with death and feeling dead inside. Similarly, a decrease of vital and intellectual functions in old age makes quite a few old people feel that they are living dead. In regard to feeling dead, child survivors differ from other traumatized children. They were confronted with death for long periods of time, and they were repeatedly separated from their caretakers. Their protests (Bowlby 1973) were stifled, and they succumbed to silent despair, such as has been described in elderly persons (Erikson 1959).

It is almost impossible to integrate these complicated, multifaceted, massive persecutions in one or two generations (J. S. Kestenberg 1989b). In treatment, recuperation hinges on working through the horrible past: not accepting it—as Krystal (1988) suggests—but learning to live with it by discrimination between the past and the present. By remembering and experiencing the affects and fantasies evoked by deprivation and persecution, a child survivor can establish a better continuity in her life, as well as hope for a good future and for a reversal of the premature aging process (Brenner 1991a; M. Kestenberg 1994).

We have presented data that seem to confirm our thesis that severe traumatization and confrontation with death in childhood have the effect of psychological and physical aging in children. The latter must be tested by comparing the neurohormonal changes in aging with those of severely traumatized and deprived children who barely escaped their own deaths in childhood and saw the corpses of many others.

It appears that many child survivors feel the burden of aging at a younger age than do most people. In some cases, child survivors suffer and die from illnesses they acquired during the Holocaust. Although there are extensive studies of illness and age of death in adult survivors, similar studies have not been undertaken for child survivors. The consensus of European investigators is that adult survivors are prone to adult illnesses and premature death more than the average population (Eitinger and Stroem 1973; Krystal 1991). It is perhaps too early to know whether this is true for child survivors as well. It appears, however, that children recuperated from physical illness and starvation much more quickly than adults. Their progressive developmental forces aided their recovery.

The psychological consequences of early aging have influenced the development of surviving children. Although they have gone through the usual developmental phases, their experiences during the Holocaust have had an organizing effect on their post-Holocaust lives. Although they are reaching the stage of life when aging begins to be felt or can be anticipated, they are deeply affected by the fact that they "lost their childhood" without receiving any compensation for it in terms of a prolongation of life. They are subject to more reminiscences from their childhood than are nontraumatized people, and their premature aging in childhood takes on a new dimension at the time when infirmity, loss of loved ones, and abandonment threaten them anew.

8

Integrative Effect of the Research Interview

Ira Brenner, M.D.

Anumber of child survivors with symptoms of depression, anxiety, and posttraumatic stress disorder initially felt that they were not ready to be interviewed for our study. In fact, they were probably too fearful of further regression to confront their pasts actively at that time (Brenner 1991a). One such woman, who is described in detail in this chapter, illustrates the point. She joined a local child survivor group in New England, but she did not want to be interviewed at first. Instead, she appropriately sought treatment. Toward the end of her therapy, she felt prepared to be interviewed and made arrangements. She gave two interviews, each lasting over two hours, in which her improved mental health and increased insight, acquired through therapy, was reflected. Following the termination of her treatment, she was invited to be a guest speaker at an intergenerational workshop; she accepted gladly and presented herself impressively. A review of this woman's experience in individual therapy, in her group involvement, and in her becoming a public speaker provides a unique perspective on the interview's integrative effect, which seemed to catalyze the entire process.

Excerpts from the interview transcript are used to demonstrate how the interview and its repercussions played a central role in this survivor's story of discovering health. Although the actual time spent in the two-part interview was only several hours, the commitment she made in order to prepare for it was impressive. It became a long-term goal she could work toward. Further, the experience of the interview itself was uplifting, cathartic, and healing for her. The aftermath of the interview was extremely important also, as it influenced her psychotherapy and had a continuing impact on her life. It therefore seemed to be an organizing experience for her psyche, as it has been for many other child survivors.

We have noted that part of the beneficial effect of the interview has been the opportunity to put one's life in continuous chronological perspective—for some, perhaps for the first time (J. S. Kestenberg and Brenner 1989). In so doing, many have begun to see their lives as influenced by their childhood experiences. Some child survivors were told that they were too young to remember, so they should not have been affected at all. Others may have forgotten very painful or terrifying events, not realizing their enormous impact. For many, however, the persistent feeling of loss—a lost childhood, loss of familiar surroundings, loss of friends and family—lingers.

Rachel: A Case Report[1]

Rachel was born in a city in Poland in 1928, the oldest of three daughters. She was eleven when the German invasion in 1939 irreparably changed her life.

---

[1] The quotations from Rachel's story, unless otherwise noted, are from the authors' unpublished taped interview with her.

I just entered the fourth grade and I never forget, it was a Saturday I went to school, and the authorities told me to go home. I was forbidden to go to school. The minute I remember I still want to cry.

Her family was required to relocate to the ghetto and wear Star of David armbands.

They took us to a ghetto and we had to leave our possessions. And they took us downtown. . . . They formed a ghetto there. And they were fenced, of course, the ghetto was fenced. We had to be there. I remember it was wintertime when I had to be there. A few of our possessions were taken on a little wagon with a horse, and I was freezing; then my mother told me to go and run after the thing so I can get warmed up, and so I never forget that day.

Rachel was small for her age and quite defiant, so she would often sneak out at night through a hole in the fence in search of food (J. S. Kestenberg and Brenner 1986).

The people were making little holes and I was very little. At my age I was very skinny and little, so I was able to go out occasionally and bring some food through the open holes in the fence. And one day I was walking out, and the Gestapo was standing there, with the—with the—with the gun. And he looked right at me, and I don't know—a miracle happened. Whether something blind[ed] him, or maybe he didn't want to pay attention—to this day, I don't know why he—he—he—what's the word for—well, I was saved, like for the time being—um, that he didn't kill me. There is a word in English I forgot. Spared.

Her father, a shoemaker, was a kind and generous man, whose many favors were returned at this time despite the threat of very serious punishment. Rachel reported a number of situations, which she called miracles, where her life or the life of

a family member was spared. For example, her older sister became very sick with typhus and was hospitalized. Rachel and her
mother had a premonition and tried to convince the doctor to
release her sister. That night the Germans came and shot all the
sick patients in the hospital.

> My mother went to this hospital, at the back door, and stole
> her. Actually took her out in the back street—the back—the
> back street to take her home because she wouldn't be
> alive. . . . Just a while ago, I don't remember, a year ago or
> so, my sister was telling me that while she was in the hospital,
> she was lying with another woman in the same bed and she
> saw blood running on the floor 'cause they were killing peo-
> ple. That was just a while ago, she told me.

When the ghetto was destroyed, the family was sent to an
infamous concentration camp where her father, his extended
family, and her mother's extended family were all eventually
killed.

> They started liquidating the ghetto. I believe it was 1941, or
> '40, and they were sending people to the camps. Of course,
> they were already open then. And they were sending people
> there, and the children; and children, they were taking
> them, and their parents, and nobody knew where they were
> taking them; and their parents were taken separate, and
> I believe they were—they were buried alive.

Rachel, her mother, and her sister, however, survived. Their
story as recounted by Rachel is one of heroism, defiance, extraordinary stamina, and luck. Apparently they were able to escape
the concentration camp and lived separately in the countryside,
scrounging for food at night, doing odd jobs on farms when allowed, and staying barely ahead of the Nazis.

> We were wearing the yellow band, with a Star of David. I for-
> got about it. Yeah. We were wearing it all the time. Well, when

> we walked out from the camp, I took the yellow band off,
> and my mother and my sister. And my mother says to me,
> "We have to go to in different directions." And by then I was
> already, I think, fourteen, close to fourteen. Um, my sister
> was hidden at a Polish family that used to be friends of my
> father for a while. In fact, they were hiding my father for
> a while also, before, and then my sister and I went there but
> they said "I'm sorry, it's too many people. We cannot do
> that." So I went my way. I remember that I had boots which
> my father made for me, he was a shoemaker, and I had to
> take off the boots because my feet were rubbed all red, and
> I had to take them off. I was practically walking barefoot.

She reported a series of unexpected meetings with her father
at this time, which had almost a dreamlike quality, such as the
time she was walking in a field and saw him walking across it.

> I went and I walked and walked and walked, and I see
> a woman, a Polish woman, and I say, "Maybe you know who
> needs a little girl to be a shepherd." And, um, she says, "Yes,
> yes, come with me." And I was there for a while, and she
> says, "No, I cannot keep you." And she says, "Well, go to that
> particular address. Maybe they will need you." While I was
> walking from one place to another, and I don't know what
> happened—I get the chills when I remember—I see my fa-
> ther. Already, he was walking, he—apparently he went out
> from the camp. He was walking and he didn't know where
> to go because he loved the family, and he was lost when he
> was alone, so apparently he was going to go to my mother,
> my sister, wherever they were. I don't even know where they
> were.

Another time, she was riding a bus and saw him walking
along the road, and ran out to be with him.

Eventually she became exhausted and depleted, and the situation became even more desperate. A Gentile woman, a former
tenant of the family, who was having an affair with a local Nazi
official, informed her that her best chance for survival would be

to volunteer for slave labor in Germany. The woman offered documents of deceased relatives to Rachel, her mother, and her sisters, so they were able to pose as Gentiles (Brenner 1990).

> This lady, how did she know? She had an SS boyfriend. SS man, a boyfriend. I was sitting there, she wanted to give me a meal and who comes in? This SS man. And he knew who I was, but because he—he was her friend, he didn't do any-thing to me. Well, she was serving a meal, and I never forget, there were, it was like—bacon, on the top of some kind of—ah, kasha, which is barley, and when I saw this—this bacon on top, I told her I'm sorry, I cannot eat. I was very kosher and my father was an Orthodox. And he was sitting at the table, this man, I don't remember his name, and he said to me, "Look! Look at this meal for the last time. There will come a day, very soon that you gonna look for it, and you will wish you had this in front of you." I still didn't eat that. At that time, she gave me something else, which I don't re-member what it was, and which I ate. Of course, he didn't know that she gave us the birth certificate. This was a secret.

While most Jews were trying to get as far from Germany as possible, this family had the chutzpah to go there! While on the way to get these documents, she reported another miracle of survival in which a local prostitute recognized her as a Jew and harshly denounced her to the Nazi customers with whom she was walking arm in arm. The Nazis, however, were apparently more interested in sex than in catching young Jews at the time, so she escaped; much to her surprise, a young boy, who had also been hateful and anti-Semitic, helped her climb over a fence.

Rachel was devastated that her father would not go to Ger-many because he was convinced that his Jewish looks and his being circumcised would betray the entire family.

> My father says to me, "Listen, you cannot be with me."
> I didn't want to leave him because I loved him tremen-dously. And I always ran after him. Whenever I saw him, I didn't want to go away. So—but he says, "Listen, you cannot

> be with me. You have to go! You have to go and maybe you'll
> survive. It's very difficult for me to survive because I'm
> a man," and of course everybody knew that the minute they
> undress people, which they always did when they took them
> to any camp, the minute when they see a man who was cir-
> cumcised, immediately they shoot him, because you know
> in Poland, it was very different than it is in America.

Rachel had already heard that the Nazis had mutilated the penis of a young Jewish boy who had earlier been in hiding with her at a farmhouse, so she sadly understood. Her last glimpse of her father, which we have noted as having enormous psychological importance in such cases of traumatic loss (J. S. Kestenberg and Brenner 1989), was through the fence at the schoolyard, the point of departure for those volunteering for slave labor. Her mother made brief contact with him, but he motioned to Rachel to keep her distance so as not to reveal her identity.

> I saw my father, and again I run to him, not paying attention
> what's going to happen. I run to him and he saw me run-
> ning. Before I run to the fence, he just waved the hand, to
> go back, and I listened to him. Like an order, I listened to
> him. Not to come close, he just wanted to see us from a dis-
> tance, and that's the last time I saw my father. I had no idea.
> I had no idea. In fact for this moment I forgot that I was in
> danger, I forgot everything, my father meant all to me. All
> in all—the worries went away as I saw him.

The father apparently felt there was nothing to do except return to the camp; there, according to a postcard sent by friends two years later, he died.

So in 1942 Rachel, her mother, and her sisters got on the train headed for Germany. It was so tightly packed she could not sit during the long three-week ride, a ride which took that long because of the Allied bombing damage to the railroad tracks. They were accorded treatment just slightly better than that re-served for known Jews, but they would be beaten or shot at if caught trying to escape. Rachel knew of someone's dying on the train ride, and she was terribly fearful of being identified as a Jew. They were forced to wear different armbands but nevertheless were recognized as Jews by local Gentiles. In one incident, a young girl was called a Jew, and Rachel came to her defense. The crowd then turned on Rachel, who was rescued by another couple claiming to have known her. Rachel's recurrent stories of betrayal and rescue by non-Jews highlighted her recollection of the times.

When they arrived at their destination, a slave labor farm in Germany, conditions further deteriorated. The Nazi boss was brutal and punishing, but he valued good workers.

> As a slave laborer I was treated horribly by the Nazi boss. He was beating me because I didn't know how to do certain things, because I was raised in a city, and I never saw much, you know, except for being a shepherd for a while before I left the city. I didn't know how to work in the fields. So he wouldn't teach me. He would just be expecting for me to know right away. Since I didn't know, he came and beat me.

Once Rachel's mother was overheard speaking Yiddish, and the family was denounced to him, but surprisingly, nothing was done.

> The Nazi was mean to us. He was calling us names—"Polish swine." He didn't say "Jewish swine." He was saying "Polish swine" because we had this Polish certificate. And all kinds of dirty words in German. And he was beating us. But every bad person has something good in him, and he had some good also. When the people came to his office and told him that we're Jews and it had to be written on a paper, he put it in a drawer, and it never came out from that drawer. Yeah. He had this nature that he would say "Get out of my office! I don't want to hear it!" That's the way he was. Right. He wanted to find out on his own. We find out after the war about these things.

Rachel saw herself as a helper, a peacemaker, and one who was liked by everyone. Though she was defiant and broke the rules, she knew how to get away with things in her likable, flirtatious, and sometimes aggressive way. Rachel cited a daring incident where she was shoveling manure with a pitchfork when the boss threatened to punch her in the ribs again. Desperate and exhausted, her obedient manner gave way to a defiant stand against him, and he backed down.

> One winter we had to work every day loading manure from this place onto the wagons. It was very heavy. I was using a big fork and throwing it on the wagon so it would go to the fields. They would then distribute it on the fields. Well, I'm staying there, on one side of this space where this manure is. And he's on the other side and he tells me I do wrong because I'm right-handed. And, certain times, you had to do it to the left, and I just couldn't do it, and he said, "Why don't you do it this way! The other way!" And he says—and he was walking toward me, again, and I had this fork with me—I says to him, "Don't you dare!" As he is walking toward me. "Don't you dare. You see what I'm holding? It's going to be on your head." I took chances, also. Here I'm watching out for the others, but I took chances. So he was afraid. He was—he was a coward in a way, yeah. He didn't come close. And this passed. It passed, because I just scared him, and that's it.

Rachel felt that she had kept her mother alive, but she never felt appreciated or recognized by her. This already troubled relationship further deteriorated along with their living conditions. The mother reportedly was argumentative, provocative, and vengeful, even at the risk of endangering everyone. At least once, in her effort to restore peace and atone for her mother's meanness, Rachel took a big risk.

> My mother, like I said before, was fighting with everybody and anybody. She has a nature, until this day—God bless her, let her live until a hundred and twenty. And she still

causes me trouble. A lot. But anyway, we were going to work one day. That was probably maybe 1943, or -4, I don't remember. On the wagon, all of a sudden, I see my mother fighting with this young, young boy. The one that was a year older than I. He happened to like me, too, at that time. In fact, he thought I'm going to be his girlfriend. She fights with him, and all of a sudden, I see my mother taking his hat. He has a hat, and she throws it on the ground. While the horses were running, and the speed. And this meant a lot of things, because we—people didn't have clothes. He had, you know, one hat, and you didn't get another one. So, he started screaming at my mother, "Jew! Jew! Jew! I'm going to get you!" You know, to the camps and all. What did I do? I jump off the wagon and start running. And I run and got the hat. This wagon didn't stop for me.

I run back. I don't know how I did this. And jump on this wagon, and I gave him back the hat. And I says to him—I gave him some kind of a—maybe I hypnotize him. I don't know. Eh, I—that time I wasn't talking to him for some reason. But when this occurred, my God! I would do anything! So I start talking to him nice, and I said, "Listen"—he always brought me apples. Oh, I loved fruit! All my life. And we didn't have. So he would steal an apple somewhere and he would bring it to me. So I said, "What about another apple?" He didn't have it but I made a joke, and he quieted down.

Despite the bleakness of their existence, the wooden shoes, the lice, the meager rations, the beatings, and the constant threats of being denounced, Rachel maintained her dignity and her compassion for others. She insisted after liberation that she did not want vengeance against the Germans, but just to live in peace. She reported that others were impressed with her self-restraint.

The Americans came, and that was also a day, a day that I never forget. They give us two weeks of freedom. And they told us, "You can go to a German house, or anybody—you can take whatever you want. It's gonna be all right. And you can kill somebody who betrayed you who you think he did you wrong. You let us know, or do it yourself." The American soldiers, I met them, I met them on the main road where tanks were coming in. Of course, there was so much happiness. They were asking me, "Who did you wrong? Please show us. Where is your Nazi boss?" I say, "No, I will not tell you that, to kill him, because in a way he was a good person, and please, let him be free."

Rachel felt that her kindness and generosity always paid, as illustrated by the following story. During these first two weeks after liberation, while the victorious Allies thus supported individual revenge against the wrongdoers, Rachel encountered a woman in a bar who had been cruel and hateful toward Russian POWs. The woman looked sick and sat very still, as she quietly pointed around the room to the Russians who had just raped her in revenge. As a Russian man then approached Rachel in a sexual manner, another intervened and protected her. Rachel's bartering with the Russians, trading her homegrown tobacco for their bread and sugar, had been much appreciated, and they treated her with honor and respect.

That's the day when I went there, during liberation. And came to visit them, because I always run there before, and who do I see? She's sitting on a stool. And they were playing music all over, and she's sitting there. I said, "Why are you sitting? Why don't you go, you know, enjoy yourself like the other people enjoy themselves?" So she said, "I can't move." I said, "What happened?" And at that time I was close to seventeen. And she says, "You see them? Seventy of them? They all raped me." And I knew why. Because they took revenge on her. Okay, now. Here I am, a young girl, being in a camp, full of danger, because she was just raped by seventy of them. And there I—I am not afraid. I don't know why I wasn't afraid. Well, you know, they drink a lot, the Russians, especially after liberation. This, I'll never forget. This man was going toward me. And, you see, the other people were watching each other. He probably wanted to make passes, I don't know. And another person, from the same place, he walked over toward him, and he says in Russian,

"Do not touch her. Because you gonna be killed. You gonna be cut in pieces." Not to touch me. And you know why? I used to help them.

Such close calls with danger and her subsequent rescue by non-Jews, associated with her own bravado and ingenuity, characterized so much of her account that at times it took on a surrealistic quality.

Following their liberation from the slave labor farm, Rachel and her family went to a series of displaced person camps in Germany until splitting up in 1946. Her mother and sisters stayed in Germany three more years, until immigration to the United States was arranged, but Rachel married a young Polish man and returned to their native country, now behind the Iron Curtain. Her years of hiding her Jewish identity enabled her to adapt to a harsh life with an abusive husband, in anti-Semitic postwar Poland, where she had four children. Rachel's deep conflict over her Jewishness and her fear of another Holocaust caused her not to have her son circumcised. She survived another fifteen years under very primitive conditions in Eastern Europe until she left her husband and immigrated to Israel. Coming to the United States to reunite with her mother was actually her goal, so she cleverly arranged a plan so that she had to spend only a few months in Israel before arriving in the United States in the 1970s.

Much to her surprise and dismay, she was received coldly by her mother, whose Orthodox Jewish background and rigid character did not allow her to accept Rachel's marriage or her children. Rachel was utterly devastated when her mother refused to allow them to stay with her, even temporarily. Survivor par excellence that she was, however, Rachel managed to find a kind elderly woman who took them all in and more or less adopted them. The bitterness and enmity between Rachel and her mother persisted, and we can only speculate about what levels of psychic determinants underlay the chasm. And so, reunited with her mother, Rachel felt as distant from her as ever. She made a new life, working at two jobs to support herself.

Rachel experienced depression, panic attacks, flashbacks, and agoraphobia. With an extensive medical history, including rheumatic heart disease after recurrent infections during the war, Rachel was known to many doctors. She sought urgent treatment in emergency rooms for palpitations and hypertensive crises and had become a refractory patient. In addition, she never traveled without food or medicine, carrying plastic bags filled with bread, crackers, juice, herbal tea, and antacids.

Since Rachel had joined a child survivor group, she had begun to experience a sense of belonging once again (M. Kestenberg and J. S. Kestenberg 1988), but eventually she became embroiled in a controversy that replicated the rift with her mother. She wanted to bring a Gentile friend to one of the meetings, and she casually mentioned this plan to another survivor, who became outraged that Rachel would bring a stranger, especially a non-Jew, to such a meeting. An argument ensued in which Rachel once again felt terribly misunderstood and persecuted. She began to feel that the others were talking about her behind her back, and she felt shunned. She did not attend this meeting and dropped out for many months afterward. It was only after she could talk about this problem with her psychiatrist that she gained enough clarity to resume participation eventually in the group.

Therapy

Working with Rachel was, as might be expected, very challenging. She presented with a multitude of psychiatric and medical problems, convinced that no one could really help her. She reported taking many antidepressants and anxiolytics, but she was still suffering. So how could a young psychiatrist come up with the answer for her? Further, Rachel had questions about his ethnicity, which is to be expected from survivors of such trauma (Brenner 1990). In addition, her agoraphobia made it difficult for her to leave the house. It soon became clear that there were many, many hurdles to overcome in order to gain Rachel's trust, but that understanding her Holocaust survival experience was the key to understanding her eccentric and complex behavior.

The first problem, however, was to develop a therapeutic alliance, which required a blend of flexibility, creativity, and empathy. Initially the psychiatrist needed to expand his role to take an active interest in her medical problems, coordinating evaluation and maintaining ongoing communication with her internists. In addition to assuming the role of a primary care physician, he also helped her with problem solving around the transportation issue so she could make her appointments. Needless to say, there were many problems with lateness and missed appointments at first, and much telephone contact was necessary to maintain an empathic bond. Dealing with such here-and-now reality factors constituted the first phase in Rachel's treatment.

But even when she did attend, she focused almost exclusively on her medical and psychosomatic problems. She stymied any attempts at understanding her symptoms psychodynamically, although she had an intuitive sense that her suffering in the war was an important overall factor. She showed little curiosity about transference, denying any interest in her psychiatrist except in the most general and indirect ways. Any attempt to explore transference issues, even as time went on, often resulted in tremendous anxiety and cancellation of the next appointment. It was striking how often she used the same excuse for such cancellations, invoking a necessary appointment with one of her internists, who could see her only at that time. Her need for multiple doctors—seemingly replaceable cogs in the vast machinery of her medical care—belied her underlying fear of becoming too attached or dependent on any one of them, especially her therapist. Any disruption or break in continuity from his end was therefore very disorganizing for Rachel, and she would again cancel appointments in reaction to these unconsciously perceived abandonments.

About a year into treatment, she presented her psychiatrist with a fifteen-page typed eyewitness account of her Holocaust experiences. He was perplexed about how to handle it because

Rachel wanted him only to read it; she was not interested in discussing it with him. So, in the midst of her frustration and intermittent therapy, she gave him a present they could not use. It was as if the Holocaust had descended upon them, but they were not allowed to acknowledge it, as it ominously loomed in the air, blocking her progress in all directions. Her Holocaust experience clearly was not integrated into her psyche, and once again it overwhelmed her to the point of panic and despair.

After several months of cancellations and threats of ending the therapy, Rachel decided that it was time to be interviewed. Although she had needed her psychiatrist's support and help in order to reach this point, she could go no further until she went through the experience of giving her testimony. It seemed to be a long-awaited rite of passage, and she had taken the time she needed in treatment to fortify herself for the ordeal. The sense of pride she felt for being able to contribute to the project, and the relief she felt for being able to unload her feelings, was a moving experience. It was as if her suffering had been validated and could finally be transformed into something of value for posterity. Transcending her individual pain, she opened up, and from then on she began to talk in therapy about her survival.

> When I came home I wanted to talk, and I was even looking for people to talk to. At that time, I guess you could not stop me. I tried to open up when I got to Israel. People were asking me, they wanted me to write books, and they wanted my help, and I refused. I refused it, I just couldn't talk, and I tried to block out everything for many years. I think I did. But the time came, here, and I realized that I better talk or it's going to be buried with me, you know. So, and for myself, it helps me. And talking about nightmares—I probably had nightmares—in fact, I couldn't sleep after we met. The ironic thing is that they were not about what was said, they were like—my youth came back. And another thing, I'm getting older and I'm scared. You know that it's going to be not finished, the job is not going to be finished, and I have children. I would dedicate maybe the tapes, or some writings that I have already, and give it to them, because they know

a little bit, but not much. I would like them to read or listen
to the tapes. Now I have two grandchildren also, and I want
them to know where they are coming from.

Her psychiatrist's consistency and desire to help Rachel was
eventually communicated to her, and much of her earlier acting
out and testing of him diminished. Her blood pressure began to
stabilize, and her trips to the emergency room stopped. She began to talk more about herself as a person, as a woman, and less
as a medical anomaly or experiment, as it were. Trust increased,
although Rachel always seemed to have an escape plan. She
seemed ready for disaster and prepared for the unexpected. As
mentioned earlier, she carried food and liquid with her at all
times, linking it to starvation during the war. She had her medical team on alert at all times with ample sources of free samples
of medication, in case she ran out, just as years ago she had relied
on the kindness of doctors to excuse her from slave labor on the
farm. This pattern was enacted in the transference.

> I was sick a lot. I had the grippe all the time. I had infections
> in my tonsils, on and off, and there was not a cure. You could
> not have medicine at that time, the way it should be, and we
> didn't have much clothes on, and we were catching all kinds
> of things. I used to go to this doctor, the German doctor in
> that little town, when I was very sick. I had to go because the
> doctor gave us a paper that we were allowed to stay home,
> to show to the boss, and this will give us the right to stay
> home as much as the doctor told them. It was the rule like
> that. So, I had luck—many, many, many ways. Many times,
> this German doctor was very good to me. Again, and I told
> him—I could tell him everything this Nazi boss did to me.
> I just happened to remember, I don't think I ever wrote that.
> But I just happened to remember, I think I was—I was going
> there, in a way, like to a psychiatrist.

Rachel then began to discuss her use of two names, linking
it to her survival with false Aryan papers. Her caution and sus-

picion, which had an obvious paranoid flavor, came to be understood by her as having had survival value during the war, then persisting long afterward. Trains, people in uniforms, and any kind of authority became the symbols of Nazi terror, which exploded in Rachel like a time bomb on a very long fuse. Against this backdrop of the Third Reich, Rachel's oedipal loss unfolded. She idealized her father, who she felt had protected her against dangers, including her argumentative and punitive mother. His loss and subsequent death put Rachel at her mother's mercy psychologically and became the insurmountable tragedy of the Holocaust for her. It later became clear that her stories of reunion and her interest in the occult were rooted in a magical wish to find her father, whose death she never fully accepted.

Discussion

In the second of her interviews, which occurred after she terminated therapy, and seven months after the first interview, she noted how important the experience had been for her:

> Well, the reason I called you back was because I was very anxious to continue our conversation. I think it went very well, to my surprise, because you made me feel so calm that I was able to talk. And I don't think I was crying much, if at all—which very, very seldom happens to me. So apparently I am ready to talk, and that's one of the reasons I called again to ask for time and, if possible, to continue.

She repeated that she had had numerous experiences in which she had become convinced that she had found her father in some unlikely place. Each time, however, her hopes were dashed at the last minute, when she would realize that the man was a total stranger.

> I'm going through some very difficult times right now. Right now, you know, my family rejected me, but I'm still trying to have them back and maybe that's why I recall my father, who

I loved so dearly. And he loved me. In fact, I don't know if I ever mentioned that before, but soon after I left home, before the slave labor, which was 1942, in the fall sometime, I left my father behind. At that time he was still alive. When I came to Germany, and I went in the fields working, I saw a person who looked a little like my father. I thought it was my father. I think this was an hallucination I had, and I still have it occasionally. So many years passed, and I still have this terrible feeling when I see a man walking and I still remember him like in front of me. I still have these false thoughts. That's an hallucination. To me he's still alive because that's what I saw last. He was alive. Then I get a palpitation, like a hurt. I realize it's not—it's not real, but I get a hurt in my heart that this man who today I would still need so much—of course, I'm old, but I still would need the support, and only he could always give it to me. I could still use support of a person who loved and cared.

Rachel's unresolved grief for her father had emerged in the therapeutic situation, and she was therefore able to mourn somewhat. But as the importance of her father emerged in the transference, her resistance increased again and led to the termination of therapy. Her medical situation had settled down, and her agoraphobic symptoms had resolved to the point where she was able to use mass transportation once again. Her anger at the child survivors' group had subsided, so that she could participate again, and her relationship with her children was improved. Her self-respect had increased, and she was better able to assert herself, but her alienation from her mother continued. Having achieved considerable symptomatic relief and having given her testimony for the research project, her goals in treatment had essentially been reached in about two years. Consequently, she had expressed her wish to terminate. Her psychiatrist recognized her flight from the transference, but given her progress, her defensiveness, and the likelihood of her resuming treatment if needed, he accepted her wish to stop.

The follow-up interview with her occurred shortly after this termination, and themes around the loss of her father and her inability to reconcile with her mother predominated. She was disappointed in herself for not talking more about the Holocaust, she said, but her parents were more on her mind. In fact, this interview was much more personal, with many fewer historical facts. Instead, she talked more about her feelings, more about her relationships, and about how she was affected by the war. She began talking more about her grief for her father, veering from the subject when it became too painful. She seemed most uncomfortable addressing her disappointment and bitterness over her mother, saying she felt like a misunderstood victim—a persistent theme she recognized all through her life. She was, however, optimistic about her reconciliation with the child survivors' group.

Rachel was enthusiastic about speaking to young people about prejudice and the Holocaust.

> One person who helped to hide me from the Nazis, a Polish man—maybe I should talk about Polish people. Jewish people always talked against Polish people, that they helped to murder so many Jews, which was true. But there are Polish people who helped Jewish people to survive. In fact, if not for them, I wouldn't be alive or my mother and my sisters also. They helped me, and when I hear conversations, I feel like an injustice has been done, because many, many Jewish people who are alive today wouldn't be alive. I wish I could talk about it very freely. Maybe one day I will, because I'm very anxious to do that. I would be anxious to talk in schools. In fact, I called a certain Jewish agency—maybe I did tell you that.

She was on her way to integrating her past, her present, and her future.

Postscript

About five months after the second interview, Rachel was invited to be the speaker at an intergenerational workshop for survivors and children of survivors. She was delighted and accepted without hesitation—a testimony to her sustained physical and mental health—and she presented herself well.

She had planned to focus on the story of her survival. When, however, she casually mentioned that one of her children had brought her to the workshop but didn't stay, the focus quickly changed. Rachel lamented her children's alienation from movement for the children of survivors, and a lively discussion ensued.

Interestingly, her daughter arrived quite early to pick her up, and with a little encouragement she agreed to join the group. Rachel confronted her as soon as she sat down, and the daughter echoed much of her mother's sentiment about not feeling accepted by her own mother. Feeling like an unwanted grandchild compared to her cousins, she cited her non-Jewish father as the reason. Caught between two religions and two cultures, she felt isolated, bitter, and misunderstood. Her identification with her mother was evident, and the transmission of trauma seemed poignantly illustrated. The group reached out to her in a most touching way, conveying a sense of acceptance and compassion.

Both Rachel and her daughter finally found a sense of belonging in the group of survivors and their children, a feeling they both desperately longed for (M. Kestenberg and J. S. Kestenberg 1988). Rachel then felt ready to speak to the world about the evils of hatred, persecution, and war. At a series of intergenerational workshops that occurred as this was being written, nine child survivors spoke to various groups about the Holocaust. Eight of the nine gave their interviews for our project, and Rachel is one of them.

Conclusion

Survivors who give interviews often undergo a personal transformation. The decision to commit their testimony to our archives, where it is permanently recorded, gives them a sense of being an important part of history. They muster up the courage to make important personal contributions, and this enhances their self-esteem. In addition, the therapeutic value of the interview—the catharsis, the chronological ordering of their lives, and the act of being listened to by someone who values and respects what is being told to them—cannot be underestimated. In Rachel's case, and in many others, the interview process was an integrative experience around which other aspects of her life became organized. In too much pain at first to give an interview, she requested therapy. She then reached a point in the therapy at which she needed to proceed with the interview, which in turn put the therapy back on track. This reciprocal relationship between the interview and the therapy helped her overcome a treatment impasse and work toward a successful outcome.

Children Under
the Nazi Yoke

Judith S. Kestenberg, M.D.

Children in war, whether running away from bombs, separated from parents, in hiding, in concentration camps, among partisans, working on farms, or wandering the countryside looking for a piece of bread and a barn to sleep in, all lived in constant fear. Abandoned, alone, sick, and starving, they were confronted with death daily. Abuse of children in its various forms is ubiquitous, occurring in both war and peace (J. S. Kestenberg et al. 1988a). In contrast to cases of severe one-time trauma (Terr 1985), most children living under the Nazi yoke experienced multiple traumas. There were acute assaults and chronic stress, along with

Chapter 9 appeared in two places in slightly different form as "Children Under the Nazi Yoke": in *Mind and Human Interaction* 2:39–45, 1990; and in *British Journal of Psychotherapy* 8:374–390, 1992. A longer version appeared in German: "Kinder unter dem Joch des Nationalsozialismus," in *Jahrbuch der Psychoanalyse* 28:179–209, 1992. Material used with permission.

sudden, repeated abandonments and uprooting.

This chapter examines the effects of the persecution and restrictions on the developing psyche of children. Although generalizations are made here, the preceding chapters have reminded the reader that circumstances varied from country to country and at different times. We must also keep in mind that children of different ages or coming from different backgrounds reacted differently to the same kind of persecution. And even though, for heuristic reasons, the effects of persecution on different parts of the psyche are isolated here, it must be understood that these parts are interrelated and that a disturbance in one influences all the others. Further, many insults affect several mental functions simultaneously.

The Assault on the Body and Its Consequences

Direct assaults on the body of the persecuted child included deprivations, some as severe as starvation, and unhygienic conditions in which typhoid fever was rife and vermin led to scratching, furunculosis, and scabies. Children, some as young as nine, were overworked. In addition, heat was deficient and clothing too flimsy to shelter the child from freezing weather. Because of overcrowding and lack of ventilation, air was stale in ghettos, in camps, and in many hiding places. At times, one or another of these extreme deprivations prevailed, but more frequently they occurred all at once.

Deborah (Rosen 1971), hiding from her persecutors in the Ukraine, wrote "The bitter winter maintained its grip. Danger, cold and hunger were constant threats" (p. 41). Ukrainian gangs allied with the Nazis

> would fall upon innocent people, rob and kill and mutilate the living and the dead. With axes and knives they dismembered bodies: They cut heads off with saws. They fell upon communists and Poles, and everywhere they found them, on

Jews. But now there no longer seemed to be any Jews left. (p. 41)

Left alone and expecting her persecutors to find her at any moment, she felt the fear of death at every sound. She wrote,

> My strength waned and I felt exhausted, ready to die. I fell asleep and dreamed. It was a nightmare in which someone was rushing me into a huge mass grave. A warm mist rose up from the layer of blood covering the bodies. I was drowning in the blood. It flowed into my mouth, my ears, my nose. I almost choked but I was still alive. People were walking past the grave very quietly. I stretched my hand out to them, begging them to save me, and they went by unmoved. They had contempt for me, they did not care to sully their hands. I sank deeper and deeper in the blood. (p. 42)

Deborah lay there a long time, still full of the terror of her nightmare. She trembled from cold and fear. A rat ran across her feet, and she shivered. She thought, "Let the end come quickly" (p. 42). The long moments of waiting for death were unbearable.

Emaciated, cold, terrified of being tortured, and persecuted by her own nightmare, Deborah wanted to die quickly, as did many children. Some just lay down and froze to death. Others, too weak to walk, would stay where they were and die if no one picked them up.

Debilitation and fear of pain destroy the will to live. They deplete the narcissism that serves survival (J. S. Kestenberg and Brenner 1988). The study of people assaulted to the core of their selves, their bodies disintegrating and their minds weakening, confirms Freud's ideas about the death instinct, a silent force that seeks nirvana. The children call it peace.

In our view (J. S. Kestenberg and Borowitz 1990; J. S. Kestenberg and Brenner 1988), primary narcissism arises from the pleasure to be alive that originates in the body. If a person is to overcome pain, fear, and succumbing to the need for rest, the joy of life has to be reawakened—or, at the very least, there has to be a feeling that there is something worth fighting for other than mere physical existence.

Deborah, who hoped that death would come quickly, had only one thought when she heard her persecutors knocking on the door: "God, give me the strength to protect Olena," her devoted old rescuer (p. 44). Even though she was beaten up and thrown from one end of the room to another until she fainted, she did not betray her beloved friend. Her aggression turned outward to the degree that she would not submit to her tormentors.

Janka Herscheles (1946), the young poet of the Lwow ghetto, wanted to die with her mother, who had taken poison but had enjoined her to endure suffering in order to survive. Having no place to go, Janka went to the camp on Janowska Street. Hungry and alone, one day she stood in line to get to a shower. She asked the supervisor to let her in first. The supervisor's kindness and the pleasure of the warm shower reawakened in her the will to live. Her mother's words—that she must survive no matter how much she suffered—stayed with her.

In these passages from Deborah's and Janka's memoirs, we recognize the workings of the death and the life instincts as they manifest themselves in these children's thoughts and wishes. One can rekindle the will to live not only by experiencing small bodily pleasures, by desiring to help one's benefactors or others who helped us, or by remembering parents, but also by having to move or work or by daydreaming about absent gratifications. The will to live wins out over the need for peace, either by an increase of narcissism, a turning of aggression outward, or both.

Starvation, which brings reduced metabolism and often debilitating diarrhea, is extremely painful. It is a nagging sensation that does not go away and does not let its victims sleep or rest. The psychic response is concentrated on wanting something to eat until the organism is so depleted of energy-giving sources that apathy develops and slow death ensues (M. Winick 1979). However, very hungry people in ghettos and camps suffered more from idleness than from overwork. Even though they expended a great deal of energy in working, it revived them to the extent that many could wait for the thin soup or vegetable coffee with a piece of bread that they were given after work. Most striking are the reports of incessant fantasies about food. Starved inmates exchanged recipes, remembered what their mothers had cooked at home, and planned entire menus together. One would think this might increase their hunger, the fantasies stimulating digestive juices, but that was not the case, except for a few who could not allow themselves to even think of food.

A drive does not operate in a vacuum (Freud 1915/1957); it has an aim. The aim is independent of the object, but the object is the source of gratification. Children and adolescents who fantasied about the food their mothers had given them frequently also recalled the home atmosphere—white tablecloths, candles on the table, all the ingredients of the holding environment on which they had depended. No doubt the recollection of the good object within the context of the infant's and the child's holding environment had an effect upon the body that enabled the starved inmates to endure their physical hardships (see Chapter 4). In this atmosphere, the sharing of the reminiscences and fantasies with friends created a new holding environment within the camp.

Illness, skin diseases, and diarrhea, in addition to hunger, made the inmates feel extremely uncomfortable, and crowding and airlessness made them vertiginous and light-headed. Discomfort is a corollary to, and a source of, the depletion of primary narcissism (J. S. Kestenberg 1989a). Yet the diseased and the hungry, whose bones ached from physical toil, would frequently go to work to avoid going to the hospital, which would expose them to the risk of being gassed. Days of idleness in the quarantine barracks were more insufferable than hard work. The activity itself would often invigorate children. Turning the aggression outward, even in the form of work for the Nazis, fostered the wish to survive. If, in addition, they had friends or relatives who helped them to walk or to hide for a short time in a latrine in order to rest, this further increased the wish to live. True friendships also developed that often lasted a lifetime.

Kindness was sorely needed, since the persecuted children

had every right to distrust people. Not only Nazis and their henchmen could rob, hurt, or kill them, but fellow inmates could trample them, steal from them, and inform on them. Quite a few children lost trust even in their own fathers, who, in the children's minds, had allowed themselves to be taken away. Sadly enough, the distrust of parents was sometimes justified, as in the case of a father who ate his children's food ration in a ghetto and a mother who thought only of her own survival and expected her daughter to die. She consoled herself that she was young and could have another child (Kraus 1990).

It has been said that many concentration camp inmates regressed to the status of children (Bettelheim 1979). No doubt the Nazis did reduce the environment under which the ghetto and camp inmates lived to one of deprived infants, but a great many children showed an opposite tendency. Many were instrumental in bringing food into ghettos, and many organized food in camps. They grew up fast and became little adults who cared for others.

Turning their aggression outward, they often engaged in mischief (Kraus 1990) and fought among themselves, sometimes more than the regressed adults did. They became cruel to those who infringed on group rules, and they also engaged in revenge fantasies. Especially boys, but girls too, hoped to do to their guards what these persecutors had done to them and their families. A few adolescents engaged in hitting and spitting at captured SS men, who were brought to them after the war by the Russians and the French, but only one of the many we interviewed had actually killed a Nazi.

Once peace was restored, the adolescents and children looked after their own needs. They took food, linen, bicycles, or horses for personal use, and enjoyed the fact that Germans were afraid of them. However, their own ability to act, rather than submit, mitigated the aggression they had felt while still in danger (see Chapter 8). As adults, most professed that they would never have been able to kill but expected the authorities to punish the culprits.

We have no evidence that the intense suffering increased

masochism. There is to my knowledge only one report of perverse masochistic behavior in an adult survivor (Friedman 1990). We would not expect to get sufficient material about it from interviews, but in treatment, I have seen one instance in which a child survivor has reported having a mildly masochistic fantasy during intercourse. To be sure, aggression had to be turned inward, especially because its outward expression was forbidden under threat of death.

The Impact of Deprivation and Persecution on Ego and Superego Development

Inasmuch as there is communication among body, id, and ego, there is a mutual influence and cooperation among them all through life. The body ego develops when the child can feel boundaries within the surrounding space. As the child incorporates outer space as a kinesphere, a unique self is experienced as surrounded by air, warmth, and an outside area filled with things to see and hear. With the space that separates the self from external objects, the rudiments of a feeling of independence develop.

No doubt babies in ghettos and camps, and with parents on the run, felt a certain amount of security from close body contact. Even older children needed to hold on to the mother, a sibling, or a friend to feel a minimum of security. However, the overcrowding in hiding, in ghettos, and in camps brought about a complete lack of privacy. Other bodies were needed to warm one's own. Yet freedom to move was curtailed until conditions were established reminiscent of infancy or intimacy.

The need to stretch, to maintain one's own kinesphere, one's personal space, is a primary need that serves the development of the body ego. In addition to the loss of personal space, many children were not able to sit or stand or turn at will. Especially at night, they were immobilized and forced to turn when another intertwined body turned. Children were also trampled by masses of adults who surged and stampeded a small area to get to the roll call on time or to reach the cauldron of soup. Thus, these children could not hold themselves up and at least temporarily lost their ability to cope with gravity. Some were so debilitated they could not get up from their bunks or from the floor. It was not unusual for a young child to have forgotten how to walk when he or she left the crowded hiding place. Some children felt secure lying with corpses, because corpses did not move and because no one shot or hit them.

Eva, a seven-year-old, was hidden among corpses in Birkenau. She seem happy and well supported as she fantasized that she was playing with the head of a doll she had wanted.

Irene Hizme, then a five-year-old, hid among the corpses to avoid being shot at. They immobilized her but counteracted her terror, her fear of being killed. As an adult she could not remember the experience, but she had repeated nightmares about it, as described in this poem of hers, written in April 1985:

Recurrent Nightmare

Some nights
transport me back
to a time
where absolute fear
was mine
Like a stone between
dead bodies
I lie
holding my breath
afraid I'll die.
The earth
a cold wet
gritty slime
stiff limbs with
mine intertwine.

> A shiver or twitch
> will
> reveal
> that I am one
> who still can feel.
> I wait with a pounding
> heart
> will the bullets
> split
> it apart?
> I shut my eye
> so they won't see
> the sadness, fear
> inside
> of me.

Time was no longer measured in adult terms, according to the calendar; every day that passed was one more day survived. Time was measured in accordance with the dreaded appell, or roll call, and in accordance with the rigidly scheduled sparse meals.

In hiding, time passed without landmarks except for an occasional leaving of the hiding place at night or in instances when food was brought in. It was dark in the forest, in attics, or in that hole in the ground on a farm. Even the sun would lose its time-specifying significance. The aspect of the ego that adapts to space, weight, and time as the principal ingredients of reality (J. S. Kestenberg and Sossin 1979) was impeded in its development or otherwise infringed upon.

Fear of death and confrontation with death (deWind 1968) left many immobilized children without adaptive resources. To stand this incessant terror, feelings were numbed. The stiffness of immobile limbs was diminished by feeling inanimate, at one with the earth or straw in which one was hidden. Fear of the rats that bit them paralyzed these children even further. Sometimes it took six months or longer for these immobilized children to walk again. A proneness to inhibition and depression of a simple kind, with a lowering of vital energies, remained with them the rest of their lives. Yet, despite this assault on the body ego, the higher ego functions could develop well. (See Chapter 2 for more about hidden children.)

Where at least there was freedom of action, children became adults precociously. Child survivors say they lost their childhood because they were not carefree, having to supply food and solace to adults, along with providing themselves enough nourishment to survive (Berg 1945; Sloan 1974). By becoming caretakers they developed an unusual ego strength, based on an overabundance of adaptive resources.

Children derived solace from associating with other children, as the family no longer provided them security. A fraternalized society ensued, with a necessary depreciation of paternal and maternal authority. With parents debilitated or disoriented, children could assume a vigilance and a hyperattentiveness to external events of a threatening nature. This became even more pronounced when they were left on their own.

Abram,[1] wandering around the countryside looking for food, became a successful vagrant who looked out for himself. But he felt better when in the company of other teenagers (M. Kestenberg 1994). Being in a group, in a children's home or orphanage after the war, was more helpful to these children than being adopted by a family (Papanek 1968). The group sustained them and provided a support network the family no longer gave (Eitinger 1983; Hemmendinger 1984).

Most striking was the deprivation of learning. Children missed being in school, not only because they needed to be with their peers and needed to play, but also because they had a real hunger for knowledge. Having lost years of schooling, many surviving children applied themselves to their schoolwork so assiduously that they became honor students in a short time. They were successful despite the facts that many had an impaired power of

---

[1] From depositions of children taken after the war and stored in the Warsaw Jewish Historical Society Archives.

concentration and that the majority had to begin their schooling in a foreign language.

Many secrets were kept from these children, and they themselves did not want to understand what was going on around them. However, schooling was fostered by the adults, and as a result, although many traumas were forgotten, what was officially learned was fresh in child survivors' minds. Many older children wrote poetry during hiding or while in camps (Klein 1985; Pearlstein, unpublished poems, 1942; Sender 1986). Some of the poems were expressions of despair; others created hope and looked forward to liberation. Reading these poems often raised the morale of the group (Sender 1986). Out of the ashes of the Holocaust there arose a widespread creativity: many child survivors became painters, sculptors, writers, and poets.

Because of the lack of privacy in crowded quarters, adult sexual activity, usually kept secret, was often displayed in front of the children, but it was not discussed. Kraus (1990) describes how children acted when they saw naked women. The girls giggled, and both sexes were curious, but they got used to it and did not talk about it. Only occasionally do we hear about sex play among children (Nir 1989). Most child survivors profess to have been too emaciated even to think of sex. According to Mrs. Oliwa, a woman who took care of children after the war, even three-year-olds who had come out of hiding would open their legs automatically when a doctor examined them (personal communication, July 1986). They explained that the "master" (i.e., the farmer) taught them to do this when they lay down. One child survivor in therapy told of having witnessed her mother's sexual intercourse with the farmer who gave them shelter. She had been resentful, perhaps jealous, even though as an adult she understood that her mother's "betrayal" had served their survival.

We know very little about sex in camps and much more about children's reactions to death (Gampel 1988). Even the youngest were aware that live people of all ages could turn into cold, stiff corpses and were there for them to see and touch. Young children in the Warsaw ghetto played a game of testing whether a person was really dead by feeling for a trace of breath. If there was none, the person was dead. Some children professed that they knew they would have to die. Some asked the teachers, "Why do they want us dead? Why do they hate us?" (Kraus 1990). Even small children who had never mentioned death, upon seeing a large group of dead, naked Hungarian women, asked, "Does it hurt to die?"

Splitting awareness from knowledge, repressing what they knew, ignoring danger, numbing or isolating feelings—all were ways of defending against not only the fear of death but also the wish to die. Some reported that the finality of death and the daily confrontations with corpses increased the survivors' sense of being alive. It heightened their feeling of omnipotence—their feeling that they would never die like the others.

Identification with the aggressor as a means of survival was not uncommon. Children who stole, who lied to kapos (prisoners who were supervisors of work details), to the SS, and to Jew hunters did what the persecutors had done to them and their families. Those who attached themselves to kapos, predominantly boys, were often abused sexually but identified with their protectors, wearing insignia and clothing reminiscent of the SS. They also were cruel to the less privileged children and treated Jewish adults with contempt (Kraus 1990). Quite a few (Kosinski 1978), who admired the tall, clean Nazis with their shiny boots, identified with them by adopting their vilification of Jews.

As described in Chapter 3, it is amazing to see how the earliest traumas inflicted upon infants can become incorporated into the part of the superego that inflicts punishment on the body. For instance, Lydia, born in a ghetto, was hidden in a hole in the wall. So that she would not betray her whereabouts by crying, she was gagged with a handkerchief tied around her mouth. As an adult, she would wake up at night to find that she had covered her mouth with her hand during her sleep.

Separated from their parents and left to fend for themselves, many children whose superegos had begun to be organized regressed. Kraus (1990) describes a seven-year-old boy, Alex, who attached himself to a hunchbacked kapo and became his runner. For days and nights he would be absent from the camp. An orphan, he took care of himself as best he could. He refused to be taught to read, since he considered the skill unimportant for survival. He witnessed the orgies of kapos and without hesitation became a pimp for Jewish women who sold their sexual favors for food. He would come back to the group to play with the other children, and especially to participate in their competitive marble games. He also used his teacher to take part in a poetry competition; Alex was interested only if he won a prize. His ability to use people for his own advantage and his lack of guilt feelings served his "survival at all cost" (Bettelheim 1980). His superego was severely damaged. Since we do not know what it was like before his mother died and can assume that he suffered some years of persecution before he arrived in Birkenau in 1943 or 1944, we cannot be sure that his lack of morals was due simply to the lack of a mother.

Other orphan children attached themselves to caring adults such as the teachers in camp, but even those who were in the camp with their parents suffered greatly from a loosening of moral values. Kraus (1990) writes that the children's dormitory blocks were "an illusion and a lie"; all were destined to die (p. 107). Neither honesty nor the Ten Commandments were meant for concentration camp inmates (p. 108). When a teacher read stories to these latency-age children, they took the wrong side, identifying with the witch or the giant rather than the "good guy." Yet they established their own rules, to which they more than scrupulously adhered. They knew that they could survive only in a group (Alex being an exception here). They depended on one another "like the organs of one body" (p. 110). At this camp, they were organized in three teams, which substituted for the family and constituted the only "wholeness in a fragmented universe" (p. 110). Children were loyal to their teams, as gang members are, but they could be cruel and deadly to a boy who stole bread from a friend, cheated in the marble game, or otherwise broke the code of the community. This social structure, a forerunner of the fraternal superego, reminds us of Anna Freud's description of many features of the three-year-old survivors from Theresienstadt (Freud and Dann 1951), except that the young children did not develop a punitive system, but rather defended their friends when adults tried to teach them.

Adolescents who left camps tended to break rules and to behave in a wanton way, as if they had incorporated the lawlessness of their persecutors. To our knowledge, however, only a few resorted to vile cruelty and murder. Where the American occupiers fostered black markets and closed their eyes to some pilfering, adolescents also engaged in black market operations, along with adult survivors who might have been their mentors (Pisar 1979). Once these children returned to homes or were taken to relatives' or adoptive parents' homes, the new adults became models for them. The regression of the superego then receded, and a new set of values was quickly established. For many it became a matter of pride that they would not stoop as low as their persecutors did.

Genocide and the Assault on the Identity of Jewish Children

All children suffer in war. Families are uprooted and disrupted, fathers killed or maimed. There is hunger. There is shooting. Houses fall down. In war, revolutions, and other social upheavals, children suffer most. During the bombardment of London, children were sent away to the country. There they were more affected by the separation from home than by the threat of bombs (Freud and Burlingham 1943).

Children left alone in Shanghai when the Japanese invaded, children in Japanese camps in Indonesia, children in French concentration camps for Spanish Republican fighters (Browner 1946), German children in the correction camps of Möhringen and Ravensbrück—all were traumatized severely. They were threatened because they were enemy children or unwanted refugees, but no genocidal intent was directed against them, as was the case with Jewish children.

The similarity between Nazi treatment of Gypsies, sick or retarded German Gentile children, and Jews is clear. Yet neither Gypsy nor sick German and Polish Gentile children who were "exterminated" were made to feel inferior or tortured, as Jewish children were. (We have not been able to interview Gypsy children; our assumptions are based on the literature.) Even in Birkenau, it seems, the SS treated Gypsy children kindly. The exceptions, perhaps, were the children in German psychiatric institutions, who, because they no longer could be gassed, were starved to death by doctors and nurses.

Allied with the Germans, the Ustashi in Croatia persecuted and mistreated Serbian children (Mrkalj 1980/1990). They threatened them with death and even killed them for any infringement of the rules. Slav Gentiles, especially Poles and Russians, were considered inferior, but unlike the Jews, they had a use. They were to become slaves of the German Herrenmenschen (the born leaders; superior race). The Polish Gentile intelligentsia were slaughtered to that end, and Polish Gentile children forbidden to go further than a few elementary school grades. In specially designed concentration camps for children (Witkowski 1975), and in camps such as Auschwitz or Majdanek (see Poltawska et al. 1966), Polish Gentile children were tortured, beaten, starved, and even drowned. But none was destined to die as a matter of principle. According to the Germans, these were the children of "bandits," Poles who resisted the Germans. These children were proud of their parents, and their identity as Poles was rarely shattered. Polish and Russian Gentile children were at times kidnapped to be Aryanized, and although they were beaten when they spoke their own language, many were adopted by Nazi couples in Germany (Hrabar 1968). Those who did not qualify as Aryans were sent to labor camps rather than being exterminated. Thus, there was some hope for a Russian or Polish Gentile child to become part of the German elite. No such hope existed for Jewish children. What attacked the latter first and foremost was the highly publicized claim that there was something irrevocably wrong with being a Jew. They were a bad seed, as their parents and grandparents were bad, and they had to suffer and die for it.

Using Slavs as slave labor, the Nazis wanted to change the Slavic identity from free to enslaved, from intellectual to uneducated, from a rebellious and heroic people to a docile, conquered people. In contrast, no matter how hard the Jews worked and obeyed, they could do nothing to deserve survival. The onslaught on Jewish identity was total. Jewish genes had to be destroyed, and there was no escape from one's genes. DeWind has reminded us that Jews were confronted with total extinction, but their tradition was not to be victims or masochists; rather, their tradition was survival. Indeed, Jewish children who had a traditional, proud upbringing suffered least from identity crises. Only when they saw their revered fathers deteriorate, perhaps eat pork or stop praying, did they begin to doubt the worth of being a Jew.

The identity of the child is molded within the family and within the holding environment of a group. The external environment and its objects defines the child. Playmates provide a feeling of sameness—of belonging to the group, day after day.

The Jewish child under the Nazi yoke suffered a break in continuity; pride in self and in the extension of self among peers and community was shattered. For survivors, the task was to integrate and rebuild self, family, and all that went into a positive sense of identity. This was a big task, because trust in self, family, religion, and customs was lost, and even God seemed to have withdrawn.

Often children whose families were assimilated or converted did not even know that they were of Jewish origin. Their identity had to be recast, not infrequently in a shocking manner. For instance, five-year-old Franzl, the child of a Social Democrat who had to flee when the Germans occupied his country, was playing on the street with Hansi. They took turns hunting Jews and being the hunted. When Franzl's mother overheard the game, she called him and told him he could not play this game because he was a Jew. In that instant he became one of the hunted, not in a game but in reality.

In school the Jewish child heard how superior Aryans were to Jews. Vicious propaganda was aimed at destroying the self-esteem of Jews and aggrandizing Aryans at their expense. Accustomed to believing their teachers, Jewish children envied the superior Aryan children, who could march, go on outings, and sit on benches reserved for their sort (Aichinger 1948). At the same time there began the expropriation of radios and bicycles and the restriction of freedom of movement. A little boy mentioned in Donat (1965) asked, "Will they take away my rocking horse?" Indeed, many SS men and their henchmen would take Jewish children's toys to give to their own children. Thus was the Jewish child dispossessed, uprooted, humiliated, and left totally unprotected by previously trusted adults.

Older children knew that the assault on Jews was based on lies and on restrictions and punishments unwarranted by anything Jews had done. However, the external pressure and the constant exclusion, the abandonment by peers, all had a tremendous impact on their self-esteem. And once it became clear that all Jews were destined to die, children wished intensely to be someone or even something else: to escape persecution and find peace. In the play *Run, Jacob, Run* (Z. Kanar, unpublished play written, directed, and acted by the author, May 1983), the boy Jacob wanted to be a spider, a dog, a tree, even a German, at least for the duration of the war.

Children in hiding, children who had to pretend to be Christians, the little "fugitives from Nazi justice," had to forsake their identity and pretend they were Polish, French, or Dutch Christians (see Chapter 2). For boys this was a difficult task—they were identifiable by their circumcision—but girls too had to be hidden from sight lest curly hair and black eyes give them away.

Hanna Krall (1983), a famous Polish writer and journalist, was hidden with friends of her mother. She could take short walks, provided she showed no one her black Jewish eyes. She was told to kick a pebble on the street, which would explain why her eyes were always glued to the ground. Whenever someone passed, her mother would scold Hanna for playing with the pebble. The injustice of being so scolded, for something she had done at her mother's instruction, added insult to injury. Living with a Gentile girl her age who attended school only increased Hanna's feeling of being different. In her fantasy she was a child of an old Polish family, and in her house was hidden a Jewish child. Thus she exchanged her identity for a better one. She became the rescuer and the benefactor of the downtrodden. When the Warsaw uprising started, Hanna stayed on the street, unafraid of the falling bombs. Exhilarated by her freedom, she did not mind the danger, so long as it did not single her out as an outcast.

Many children raised in Christian families (Hogman 1988) or hidden in convents (Kurek-Lesik 1989) found solace in the safety of the church, and many wanted to be Christian or even to become nuns or priests. And some of them did. To this day the church remains an attraction to adults persecuted as children, even to some who resumed their Jewish identity. Some are still upset because they were taken away from loving and beloved foster parents, by their own estranged parents or by strangers who claimed to be relatives. Quite a few felt betrayed by their rescuer parents, whom they felt had sold them to the Jews for "thirty pieces of silver." Some, like Miriam, a five-year-old, were indoctrinated by anti-Semitic teachings. She had repressed being Jewish and was frightened by the discovery of her ancestry. She did not want to be one of the "devils who killed Christ" (Kurek-Lesik 1991, p. 12).

Children given away as infants often were shocked when later in life they discovered the truth about their origins. Watching their parents and siblings degraded and murdered, many children felt that something died in them. Some had forgotten the good care they had been given as infants and remembered only the gloom of the Holocaust. Their infancy and childhood were taken away from them. They could not even keep their names, a basic part of a person's core identity from the age of three or four months onward.

In camps, adults and children got numbers and no longer seemed to have names. Many reported that they ceased to exist as people and had instead become numbers, only the yellow triangle distinguishing them from those allowed to live. Their lives were wasted, they felt, because they had missed out on schooling.

Children in hiding often became accustomed to their new names and kept them after liberation, their dual identity expressed in their distinguishing their Polish or Dutch Gentile adoptive mothers from their biological Jewish mothers. Jewish children taken to England on the Kindertransport[2] were frequently placed with, or even adopted by, Protestant families. Many children adopted after the war were enjoined to forget their origins and start their lives anew. Repressing or denying their Jewish identity, perhaps afraid to be abandoned all over again, they became embroiled in a double life, one for the external and one for the internal world. Thus was replicated their past pretense of being Gentile outside while being Jewish inside. As Keilson (1979) has noted, traumatization did not always stop at war's end. Cheerful and well adapted to their new surroundings, these children nonetheless felt that something inside them was dead. As Wiesel (1979, p. 223) observed, "We were all absent. The dead and the living."

There were those who recited prayers in an absentminded way, addressing an absent God on behalf of the absent. The younger the child at the time of uprooting, the more deadness or emptiness the adult would later experience. These individuals may not have shown as much overt anxiety as those who were older during the persecution (Keilson 1979; Poltawska 1989), but a depressive core shadowed all they did and robbed them of a joy that is the birthright of all free people.

The child survivors of the Nazi reign have shown a unique ability to adapt. They have founded their own families, established themselves in their community, pursued their professions and businesses, and done well as long as they were busy reorganizing their lives (see Chapter 6). Only when their children left the nest did they begin to feel abandoned once again and to relive the separation from loved ones. At about the same time, childless survivors, married or single, also began to feel the pressures of getting older.

Most child survivors who were interviewed expressed a need to unburden themselves—to tell the world their stories—and

---

[2] Children's transport, a collective effort from 1938 through 1939 to ship children from various countries to England to escape persecution.

many wrote their autobiographies (see Chapter 8). They recalled how they had felt as children when they came out of camps or hiding and no one wanted to listen. As in the case described by Ayalon (1983) of Israeli children attacked by terrorists, the victims were blamed; the community did not want to hear of their plight. Considering that the postwar world was very difficult for the surviving children, they showed an amazing capacity to adapt to difficult circumstances. Excluded again because their accents, their language, and even their clothing were different, they were shunned in Israel for not having defended themselves. Unacceptable also in some of their home countries, such as Poland and Hungary, because they were Jews, they nonetheless survived these traumas as well. Educated in a tough school of persecution, most yearned to find a new identity wherever they happened to find themselves.

Identified with the downtrodden and with their rescuers, they became altruistic (M. Kestenberg and J. S. Kestenberg 1988). Underneath this excellent adjustment, however, lurked an identity problem that left them feeling shy, excluded, and distrustful. They were ready then to create groups of their peers, to have "new siblings" who could share their feelings and reminisce. Many, intent on remembering their past, suffered from the holes existing in their stories. In interviews, but even more so in treatment, we learned that parents did not want their children to remember traumatic experiences; often the parents fooled themselves into thinking that the children did not suffer because they were too little to understand. One of the most important tasks of treatment, we found, is to help child survivors gain confidence in their memories, thereby fostering a respect for themselves as they were and underpinning a renewed self-esteem.

The Impact of Nazism on the Superego of German Children

Nazism did not arise from nowhere. It was prepared for a long time. Gradually it crept into the souls of children who from the cradle heard such stories as "The Jew in the Thornbush," in fact a non-German tale collected by the Grimm brothers[3]:

> A loyal and industrious farmhand had a clean heart and a simple mind. He wished for a fiddle that would make everybody dance while he played, and his wish was fulfilled. He also received an unfailingly accurate shooting implement and was endowed with a power so no one could refuse his request. As he walked with his magic possessions, he met an old Jew. He wished that the Jew land in a thornbush, and at that point he began to play the fiddle, which made the Jew dance. The thorns tore his clothing and wounded him so that he was bleeding all over. The Jew begged the farmhand to stop playing, appealing to God and asking what he had done to be thus punished. The joyous farmhand thought, "You have done enough exploiting of the people. It serves you right," and he increased the tempo of his tune. The Jew offered him money, but the farmhand accepted it only if the Jew gave all he had. The farmhand took the money and stopped playing. Peaceful and joyful, he proceeded further while the Jew, half-naked and wretched, tore himself away from the thornbush. Sued in court by the Jew, the farmhand threatened to continue playing his fiddle if the Jew would not confess that he had stolen the money. The frightened Jew exclaimed that he had stolen the money and the farmhand had earned it honestly. The farmhand gave up playing, and the Jewish scoundrel was hanged for him on the gallows.

As a preamble to National Socialism, the German described by Grimm was both simple and treacherous. The Jew was pronounced a scoundrel and killed, even though the farmhand had tortured and robbed him and then extorted a false confession (Eckstaedt 1980). From this tale, published 118 years before Hitler came to power, we are given an inkling of what lay in store

---

[3] I am grateful to Dr. Gertrud Hardtmann, who gave me a copy of the original story and discussed its meaning with me.

for Nazi youth. They were simple, jolly, very powerful youngsters; they had no scruples and could induce the courts to hang a Jew and keep the money extorted from him. They had no empathy for the oppressed and were cheerful while Jews suffered. The ideal was not to be superior in any moral sense. Rather, superiority lay in their ability to cheat, to lie, and to be omnipotent because of their magic possession—their Aryan genes. If anyone ever wondered where the Nazis learned the game of having rabbis dance for them in the ghettos, here is the answer. Evidently, they simply followed the scenario scripted by the Brothers Grimm (J. S. Kestenberg et al. 1988b). German children under the Nazis were taught to torture Jews. Tales of Jews' despoiling the German people and being warmongers were publicized without any proof. All guilt for sadistic behavior was projected onto Jews, whereas German children were extolled as omnipotent, responsible to neither parental nor church teachings (Wangh 1963). The "godhead Hitler" encouraged them to feel superior and to degrade others. However, Hitler was not the sole culprit. He was but the embodiment of a long-standing strain in German culture whereby a grandiose ego ideal and a corrupt superego were transmitted down the generations.

The ego ideal of Nazi youth was to please the Führer. The individual superego disappeared, and in its place arose a corrupt conscience that allowed Germans to become the sadistic conquerors of the world (J. S. Kestenberg et al. 1988b). But at what price? At the height of Hitler's influence, he and his henchmen taught the children that they must sacrifice their lives for Germany and the Führer. Their death was glorified. Engaged in endless Hitler Youth competitions, they were treated without compassion and were encouraged to hurt the losers and to jeer them. It was clear that these children were being reared to be cruel to their own (Hellfeld and Klone 1985; Hannsmann 1984).

Many of the postwar-generation Germans analyzed by Gertrude Hardtmann (1982) told her that they had been their parents' "Jews"—bad, hated, and exploited. In many instances they knew it even at the time. When bombs fell on German cities, whole classes were sent east with their teachers. When the Russians invaded these areas, many of the teachers deserted their students and fled, leaving the children to find their own way home. And quite often there was no home to come back to. Carloads of children returning from previously safe areas were provided no heat, and entire groups of children are known to have frozen to death.

Conclusion

It is our hypothesis that the destruction and sacrifice of Jewish children to "pagan gods" served to camouflage the Nazis' wish to kill their own children (J. S. Kestenberg et al. 1988b). Indeed, long before they began to kill Jews, they openly killed those who were infirm and sick. As so often happens, the repressed wish here to kill their own children in time reentered consciousness. Unwanted babies were starved to death, and some of the Lebensborn nurseries, where German children were bred by the SS, were deserted as the war wound down. Children were destined to die, and a new crop of children had been bred as cannon fodder. At the end of the war, Hitler demanded that all Germans kill themselves rather than live defeated. Whole classes of high school junior and senior students were sent to the front in the last stages of the war, and a great many were killed. Deserters were hanged (Hartl 1980; Heck 1985). For the sake of victory over an enemy, these children were themselves sacrificed. When children are used to kill others, they end up themselves as victims. And this pattern may then be transmitted to later generations. Children who felt their parents wanted to kill them will treat their own children the same way. The abundant history of child killing (DeMause 1974) is not yet over. Each generation, it seems, must replay the story of Isaac and must stay the hand that would wield the sacrificial blade. To prevent another Holocaust, we must help these child warriors and their descendants—biological or spiritual, German or non-German—to understand that it is they who are the ultimate victims.

Bibliography

Aichinger I: Die grossere Hoffnung. Frankfurt, Fischer Taschenbuch Verlag, 1948

Albertus H: Das Leben von Kindern und Jugendlichen im KZ Buchenwald unter dem Terrorregime der SS. Buchenwaldheft 12:9–21, 1989

Auerhan NC, Laub D: Annihilation and restoration: Post-traumatic memory as pathway and obstacle to recovery. International Review of Psychoanalysis (NIM) 11:327–344, 1984

Avital M: Liberated after living through the hell of nine camps, in The Lost Generation: Children in the Holocaust. Edited by Eisenberg A. New York, Pilgrim Press, 1982

Ayalon O: Children facing terrorists: Can they be helped? in The Holocaust and Its Perseverance. Edited by Ayalon O, Eitinger L, Lansen J, et al. Assen, Netherlands, Van Gorcum, 1983

Ballard JG: Empire of the Sun. New York, Pocket Books, 1985

Barocas H, Barocas C: Wounds of the fathers: The new generation of Holocaust victims. International Review of Psychoanalysis (NIM) 6:331, 1979

Barnouw D, von der Stroom G (eds): The Diary of Anne Frank: The Critical Edition. New York, Doubleday, 1989

Bass-Wichelhaus H: The interviewer as witness: Counter-transference, reactions, and techniques, in Children During the Nazi Reign: Psychological Perspectives on the Interview Process. Edited by Kestenberg JS, Fogelman E. Westport, CT, Greenwood, 1994

Begley L: Wartime Lies. New York, Knopf, 1991

Berg M: Warsaw Ghetto: A Diary. New York, LB Fischer, 1945

Bergmann MS, Jucovy ME (eds): Generations of the Holocaust. New York, Basic Books, 1982

Bettelheim B: Surviving and Other Essays. New York, Knopf, 1979

Bettelheim B: Surviving. New York, Vintage Books, 1980

Biermann G: Identitäts Problem judischer Kinder und Jugendlicher in Deutschland. Praxis Kinderpsychologie, 13:213, 1964

Blum HP: Superego formation, adolescent transformation and the adult neurosis. J Am Psychoanal Assoc 33:887–910, 1985

Bowlby J: Grief and mourning in infancy and early childhood. Psychoanal Study Child 15:9–52, 1960

Bowlby J: Attachment and Loss, Vol 2: Separation. New York, Basic Books, 1973

Braunner A: Les enfants ont vécu la guerre. Paris, les Editions Sociales Françaises, 1946

Brenner I: Multisensory bridges in response to object loss during the Holocaust. Psychoanal Rev 75:573–587, 1988a

Brenner I: Unconscious fantasies of the "selection" in children of Holocaust survivors. Paper presented at the First Jerusalem International Conference of Children of Holocaust Survivors, Jerusalem, Israel, December 1988b

Brenner I: Dilemmas in identification for the post Nazi generation. Formal discussion presented at the winter meeting of the American Psychoanalytic Association, Miami Beach, FL, December 1990

Brenner I: Integrative effect of the interview on a child survivor. Paper presented at panel, The Effect of Retrospective Interviews on Child Survivors, at the 14th annual convention of the International Psychohistorical Association, New York, June 1991a

Brenner I: On confronting the truth about the Third Reich. Journal of Mind and Human Interaction 2:97–100, 1991b

Brenner I, Kestenberg J: The Superego in Young Child Survivors. Psychoanal Rev 75:573–587, 1988

Bruch H: The sleeping beauty: escape from change, in The Course of Life, Vol 4: Adolescence. Edited by Greenspan SI, Pollock GH. Adelphi, MD, National Institute of Mental Health, 1991, pp 313–331

Busse EW: The myth, history, and science of aging, in Geriatric Psychiatry. Edited by Busse EW, Blazer DG. Washington, DC, American Psychiatric Press, 1989, pp 3–34

Cahn TI: Book review of Herscheles J: Through the Eyes of a 12-Year-Old Girl. Psychoanal Rev 75:658–660, 1988a

Cahn TI: The diary of an adolescent girl: a study of age-specific reactions to the Holocaust. Psychoanal Rev 75:589–617, 1988b

Classen E: Ich: Die Steri. Bonn, Psychiatrie Verlag, 1987

Cohen D: Ditta Cohen: a story with a dramatic happy ending, in The Lost Generation: Children in the Holocaust. Edited by Eisenberg A. New York, Pilgrim Press, 1982, pp 326–328

Coppolillo HP: Maturational aspects of the transitional phenomenon. Int J Psychoanal 48:237–246, 1967

Czech D: Auschwitz Chronicle 1939–1945. New York, Henry Holt, 1990

Dalsimer K: Female adolescent development: A study of The Diary of Anne Frank. Psychoanal Study Child 37:487–522, 1982

Danieli Y: The aging survivor of the Holocaust: Discussion: On the achievement of integration in aging survivors of the Nazi Holocaust. J Geriatr Psychiatry 14:191–210, 1981

DeMause L: The History of Childhood. New York, The Psychohistory Press, 1974

Deutsch H: Absence of grief. Psychoanal Q 6:12–22, 1937

de Wind E: The confrontation with death: Symposium on psychic traumatization through social catastrophe. Int J Psychoanal 49:302–305, 1968

de Wind E: Diskussion, in Spätschaden nach Extrembelastungen. Edited by Herberg HJ. Herford, Germany, Nicolaische Verlagsbuchhandlung, 1971, pp 236–237

Donat A: Holocaust Kingdom. New York, Holt, Rinehart & Winston, 1965

Doormann L: Letzte Rede an einen Sterbenden, in Vater und Ich (My Father and I). Edited by Häsing H, Mues I. Frankfurt am Main, Fischer Verlag, 1993, pp 45–56

Dwork D: Children With a Star: Jewish Youth in Nazi Europe. New Haven, CT, Yale University Press, 1991

Eckstaedt A, Klüwer R (eds): Zeit allein heilt keine Wunden (Time Alone Does Not Heal Wounds). Frankfurt am Main, Suhrkamp Verlag, 1980

Edelbaum B: Growing Up in the Holocaust. Kansas City, MO [no publisher listed], 1980

Eisen G: Children and Play in the Holocaust. Amherst, MA, The University of Massachusetts Press, 1988

Eisenberg A: The Lost Generation: Children in the Holocaust. New York, The Pilgrim Press, 1982

Eitinger L, Stroem A: Mortality and Morbidity of Excessive Stress. New York, Humanities Press, 1973

Erikson EH: Identity and the Life Cycle. New York, International Universities Press, 1959

Faimberg H: The telescoping of generations. Contemporary Psychoanalysis 24:99–118, 1988

Ferencz B: Less Than Slaves. Cambridge, MA, Harvard University Press, 1979

Fischer-Rosenthal W: Uber-lebensgeschichte. Psychosozial 15:17–26, 1992

Fogelman E: Intergenerational group therapy: child survivors of the Holocaust and offspring of survivors. Psychoanal Rev 75:619–640, 1988

Fogelman E: The psychology behind being a hidden child, in The Hidden Children: The Secret Survivors of the Holocaust. Edited by Marks J. New York, Fawcett Columbine, 1993

Fogelman E: Effects of interviews with rescued child survivors, in Children During the Nazi Reign: Psychological Perspectives on the Interview Process. Edited by Kestenberg JS, Fogelman E. Westport, CT, Greenwood, 1994

Fogelman E, Hogman F: A follow up study: child survivors of the Nazi Holocaust reflect on being interviewed, in Children During the Nazi Reign: Psychological Perspectives on the Interview Process. Edited by Kestenberg JS, Fogelman E. Westport, CT, Greenwood, 1994

Freud A: Discussion of Dr. John Bowlby's paper. Psychoanal Study Child 15:53–62, 1960

Freud A: Normality and Pathology in Childhood. New York, International Universities Press, 1965

Freud A: About losing and being lost. Psychoanal Study Child 22:9–19, 1967

Freud A, Burlingham DT: War and Children. New York, Medical War Books, 1943

Freud A, Dann S: An experiment in group upbringing. Psychoanal Study Child 6:127–168, 1951

Freud S: Instincts and their vicissitudes (1915), in Standard Edition of the Complete Psychological Works of Sigmund Freud, Vol 14. Translated and edited by Strachey J. London, Hogarth Press, 1957, pp 109–140

Friedman G: Book review: Edelstein DB: Worlds Torn Asunder. Psychoanal Rev 75:660–662, 1988

Friedman IR: The Other Victims. Boston, Houghton Mifflin, 1990

Furman E: A Child's Parent Dies. New Haven, CT, Yale University Press, 1974

Gampel Y: Facing war, murder, torture, and death in latency. Psychoanal Rev 75:499–509, 1988

Gampel Y: In search of the lost love object. Sichot 4:11–16, 1989

Gampel Y: I was a Shoah child. British Journal of Psychotherapy 8:391–399, 1992

Gampel Y, Mazor A: The effects of interviews on child survivors and on the interviewers in Israel, in Children During the Nazi Reign: Psychological Perspectives on the Interview Process. Edited by Kestenberg JS, Fogelman E. Westport, CT, Greenwood, 1994, pp 161–174

Green VA: The role of a vicarious object in the adaptation to object loss. Psychosomatic Med 20:344–350, 1958

Grubrich-Simitis I: Vom Konkretismus zur Metaphorik: Gedanken zur psychoanalytischen Arbeit mit Nackommen der Holocaust-Generation-Anlasslich einer Neurscheinung. Psyche 38:1–28, 1984

Haber C: The analysis of a latency-age survivor of the Holocaust. Psychoanal Rev 75:641–651, 1988

Hannsmann M: Der helle Tag bricht an ein Kind wird Nazi. Munich, Deutscher Taschenbuch Verlag, 1984

Hardtmann G: Spuren der Verfolgung. Gerlingen, Germany, Bleicher Verlag, 1992

Hardtmann G: The Shadows of the Past, in Generations of the Holocaust. Edited by Bergmann MS, Jucovy ME. New York, Basic Books, 1982

Hart K: Return to Auschwitz. New York, Atheneum, 1983

Hartl G: Frisches Gras auf verbrannter Erde. Vienna, Verlag Styria, 1980

Hartmann H: Ego psychology and the problem of adaptation. Translation by Rapaport D. New York, International Universities Press, 1958

Hau Th F: Psychische und psychosomatische Spätfolgen bei im Kriege geborenen Jugendlichen, in Spätschaden nach Extrembelastungen. Edited by Herberg HJ. Herford, Germany, Nicolaische Verlagsbuchhandlung, 1971, pp 263–265

Heck A: A Child of Hitler. New York, Renaissance House, 1985

Heer H: Als ich 9 Jahre alt war, kam der Krieg (When I Was 9 Years Old, the War Came). Köln, Germany, Prometh Verlag, 1983

Hellfeld M, Klone A: Die betrogene Generation: Jugend im Faschismus. Köln, Germany: Pahl-Rugenstein, 1985

Hemmendinger J: Les Enfants de Buchenwald. Paris, Pierre-Marcel Favre, 1986a

Hemmendinger J: Survivors: Children of the Holocaust. Bethesda, MD, National Press, 1986b

Herberg HJ: Spätschaden nach Extrembelastungen (Late Damages After Extreme Burdens). Herford, Germany, Nicolaische Verlagsbuchhandlung, 1971

Herscheles J: Oczyma 12–13 Tniej Dziewczynki (Through the Eyes of a 12-Year-Old Girl). Cracow, Wojewodzka Komisja Historyczna, 1946

Herzka HS: Erfahrungsbericht, in Ein Ast bei Nacht kein Ast. Edited by Wiesse J, Olbrich E. Göttingen, Germany, Vandenhoeck & Ruprecht, 1994, pp 116–128

Herzog J: World beyond metaphor: thoughts on the transmission of trauma, in Generations of the Holocaust. Edited by Bergmann MS, Jucovy ME. New York, Basic Books, 1982

Hogman F: Displaced Jewish children during WWII: how they coped. Journal of Humanistic Psychology 23:51–66, 1983

Hogman F: The role of memories in the lives of WWII infants. J Am Acad Child Psychiatry 24:390–396, 1985

Hogman F: The experience of Catholicism of Jewish children during World War II. Psychoanal Rev 75:511–532, 1988

Hrabar R: Na Rozkaz I bez Rozkazu (To Order or Without Order). Katowice, Poland, Wydawnictwo Slask, 1968

Jucovy S: Book reviews: Friedlander S: When Memory Comes; Minsky Sender R: The Cage. Psychoanal Rev 75:653–658, 1988

Kahn C: Interviewing: the crossroad between research and therapy, in Children During the Nazi Reign: Psychological Perspectives on the Interview Process. Edited by Kestenberg JS, Fogelman E. Westport, CT, Greenwood, 1994, pp 91–108

Kahne MJ: On the persistence of transitional phenomena into adult life. Int J Psychoanal 48:247–258, 1967

Kammer F: Winter in the forest, in The Lost Generation: Children in the Holocaust. Edited by Eisenberg A. New York, Pilgrim Press, 1982, pp 192–194

Keilson H: Sequentielle Traumatisierung bei Kindern. Stuttgart, Ferdinand Enke Verlag, 1979

Keilson H: Sequentielle Traumatisierung bei Kindern: Ergebnisse einer Follow Up Untersuchung, in Schicksale der Verfolgten (Fates of the Persecuted). Edited by Stoffels H. Berlin, Springer-Verlag, 1991, pp 98–109

Keilson H: Sequential Traumatization in Children. Jerusalem, The Magnes Press, 1992

Keilson H: Abschied, Erinnerung und Trauer (Leave-taking, memory and mourning), in Ein Ast bei Nacht kein Ast. Edited by Wiesse J, Olbrich E. Göttingen, Germany, Vandenhoeck & Ruprecht, 1994, pp 11–20

Kelin O: Young people in Terezin, in Terezin. Prague, The Council of Jewish Communities in the Czech Lands, 1965, pp 74–85

Kestenberg JS: The role of movement patterns in development, I: rhythms of movement. Psychoanal Q 34:1–36, 1965a

Kestenberg JS: The role of movement patterns in development, II: flow of tension and effort. Psychoanal Q 34:517–563, 1965b

Kestenberg JS: Psychoanalytic contributions to the problems of children of survivors from Nazi persecution. Israel Annals of Psychiatry and Related Disciplines 10:311–25, 1972

Kestenberg JS: From organ-object imagery to self and self representations, in Children and Parents. New York, Jason Aronson, 1975a, pp 215–234

Kestenberg JS: Phases of adolescence with suggestions for a correlation of psychic and hormonal organizations, I: antecedents of adolescent organization in childhood, in Children and Parents. New York, Jason Aronson, 1975b, pp 215–234

Kestenberg JS: Children and Parents. New York, Jason Aronson, 1975. Reprinted as Sexuality, Body Movement, and the Rhythms of Development. Northvale, NJ, Jason Aronson, 1995

Kestenberg JS: Psychoanalyses of children of Holocaust survivors. J Am Psychoanal Assoc 28:775–804, 1980

Kestenberg JS: A metapsychological assessment based on an analysis of a survivor's child, in Generations of the Holocaust. Edited by Bergmann MS, Jucovy ME. New York, Basic Books, 1982

Kestenberg JS: Editorial: Child survivors of the Holocaust 40 years later. J Am Acad Child Psychiatry 24:408–412, 1985a

Kestenberg JS: The flow of empathy and trust between mother and child, in Parental Influences: In Health and Disease. Edited by Anthony J, Pollock GH. Boston, Little, Brown, 1985b, pp 137–163

Kestenberg JS: The development of the ego-ideal: its structure in Nazi youth and in persecuted Jewish children. Issues in Ego Psychology 10:22–34, 1987a

Kestenberg JS: Imagining and remembering. Isr J Psychiatry Relat Sci 24:229–241, 1987b

Kestenberg JS (Ed): Child survivors of the Holocaust. Psychoanal Rev 75:495–662, 1988a

Kestenberg JS: Memories from early childhood. Pychoanal Rev 75:561–571, 1988b

Kestenberg JS: Coping with losses and survival, in The Problems of Loss and Mourning: New Psychoanalytic Perspectives. Edited by Dietrich DR, Shabad PC. Madison, CT, International Universities Press, 1989a, pp 381–403

Kestenberg JS: Transposition revisited: clinical, therapeutic and developmental considerations, in Healing Their Wounds: Psychotherapy with Holocaust Survivors and Their Families. Edited by Marcus P, Rosenberg A. New York, Praeger, 1989b, pp 67–82

Kestenberg JS: Children in hiding in different countries, I: where did they hide, what did they hide, are they still hiding? Paper presented at panel Psychological Impact of Being Hidden as a Child, at the meeting of the Hidden Child, New York, May 26, 1991a

Kestenberg JS: Children in hiding in different countries, II: hidden children: latency age during the Holocaust. Paper presented at the symposium Verfolgte Kinder und die Kinder der Verfolgten (Persecuted Children and the Children of the Persecuted), University of Erlangen-Nürnberg, October 1991b

Kestenberg JS: Kinder von Uberlebenden und Uberlebende Kinder, in Schicksale der Verfolgten. Edited by Stoffels H. Berlin, Springer-Verlag, 1991c, pp 110–126

Kestenberg JS: The diversity of child survivors of the Holocaust, in Children: War and Persecution. Proceedings of Congress Hamburg, September 26–29, 1993. Edited by Stiftung für Kinder. Osnabrück, Germany, Secolo Verlag, 1995

212 The Last Witness: The Child Survivor of the Holocaust

Kestenberg JS: Kinder unter dem Joch des Nationalsozialismus (Children under the Nazi yoke). Jahrbuch der Psychoanalyse 28:179–209, 1992
Kestenberg JS: Spätfolgen bei verfolgten Kindern (Late sequelae of persecuted children). Psyche 8:730–742, 1993b
Kestenberg JS: What a psychoanalyst learned from the Holocaust and genocide. Int J Psychoanal 74:1117–1129, 1993c
Kestenberg JS: The diary from the ghetto in Krakow. Echoes of the Holocaust (Bulletin of the Jerusalem Center for Research Into the Late Effects of the Holocaust, Talbieh Mental Health Center) 3:21–39, 1994a
Kestenberg JS: Overview of the effect of psychological research interviews on child survivors, in Children During the Nazi Reign: Psychological Perspectives on the Interview Process. Edited by Kestenberg JS, Fogelman E. Westport, CT, Greenwood, 1994b
Kestenberg JS: Prägenitale Grundlagen des moralischen und des korrupten Uber-Ich sowie Vermutungen über das Wesen des nationalsozialistischen Uber-Ich (Pregenital bases of the moral and corrupt superego and some considerations on the nature of the National Socialist superego), in Ererbte Traumata. Edited by von Louis MT and Wiesse J. Göttingen, Germany, Vandenhoeck & Ruprecht
Kestenberg JS, Borowitz E: On narcissism and masochism in the fetus and the neonate. Pre-Peri-Natal Psychology 5:87–94, 1990
Kestenberg JS, Brenner I: Children who survived the Holocaust: the role of rule and routines in the development of the superego. Int J Psychoanal 67:309–316, 1986
Kestenberg, JS & Brenner I: Le narcissisme au service de la survie. Revue Française de Psychoanalyse 6:1393–1408, 1988
Kestenberg JS, Brenner I: The mutual influences of psychoanalysis and related research. Paper presented at the winter meeting of the American Psychoanalytic Association, New York, December 1989

Kestenberg JS, Fogelman E (eds): Children During the Nazi Reign: Psychological Perspectives on the Interview Process. Westport, CT, Greenwood, 1994

Kestenberg JS, Gampel Y: Growing up in the Holocaust culture. Isr J Psychiatry Relat Sci 29:129–146, 1983

Kestenberg JS, Kestenberg M: The background of the study, in Generations of the Holocaust. Edited by Bergmann MS, Jucovy ME. New York, Basic Books, 1982, pp 33–45

Kestenberg JS, Kestenberg M: Child killing and child rescuing, in Origins of Human Aggression. Edited by Neumann GG. New York, Human Sciences Press, 1987, pp 139–154

Kestenberg JS, Kestenberg M: Die Verfolgung von Kindern durch die Nazis (Persecution of children by Nazis), in Spuren der Verfolgung (Traces of Persecution). Edited by Hardtmann G. Gerlingen, Germany, Bleicher Verlag, 1992, pp 80–92

Kestenberg JS, Kestenberg M, Hogman F, et al: Jewish-Christian relationships as seen through the eyes of children before, during and after the Holocaust, in Remembering for the Future: Jews and Christians During and After the Holocaust. Oxford, UK, Pergamon, 1988a, pp 622–636

Kestenberg JS, Kestenberg M, Amighi J: The Nazis' quest for death and the Jewish quest for life, in The Psychological Perspectives of the Holocaust and Its Aftermath. Edited by Braham RL. New York, Social Science Monographs, 1988b, pp 13–44

Kestenberg JS, Koorland V: Als eure Grosseltern jung waren (When Your Grandparents Were Young). Hamburg, Verlag Dr. R. Kramer, 1993

Kestenberg JS, Sossin KM: The Role of Movement Patterns in Development, Vol 2. New York, Dance Notation Bureau, 1979

Kestenberg M: Discriminatory practices in the German restitution program. Victimology 5:421–427, 1980

Kestenberg M: Discriminatory aspects of the German indemnification policy: a continuation of persecution, in Generations of the Holocaust. Edited by Bergmann MS, Jucovy ME. New York, Basic Books, 1982, pp 62–79

Kestenberg M: Legal aspects of child persecution during the Holocaust. J Am Acad Child Psychiatry 24:381–384, 1985a

Kestenberg M: Poland Without Jews. Newsletter of the Jerome Riker International Study of Organized Persecution of Children 1:1–2, 1985b

Kestenberg M: The healing power of creativity. Echoes of the Holocaust 1:51–59, 1992

Kestenberg M: The effect of interviews on child survivors; child survivors revisited, in Children During the Nazi Reign. Edited by Kestenberg JS, Fogelman E. Westport, CT, Greenwood, 1994, pp 57–71

Kestenberg M, Kestenberg JS: The sense of belonging and altruism in children who survived the Holocaust. Psychoanal Rev 75:533–560, 1988

Kichler L: One Hundred Children. New York, Doubleday, 1961

Kichler L: Hiding in a bunker, passing as an Aryan: Manya's unforgettable story, in The Lost Generation: Children in the Holocaust. Edited by Eisenberg A. New York, Pilgrim Press, 1982, pp 118–123

Kinsler F: A Survey of Dutch Child Survivors in Los Angeles. Paper presented at the meeting of the International Society for Traumatic Stress Studies, Amsterdam, June 23, 1992

Kisker KP: Die psychiatrische Begutachtung der Opfer nazionalsozialistischer Verfolgung, in Psychiatria et Neurologia. Edited by Koyr D. Dresden, Germany, Geselloch, 1961

Klein C: Poems of the Holocaust. Jerusalem, Gefen, 1985

Klein O: Young people in Terezin, in Terezin. Prague, The Council of Jewish Communities in the Czech Lands, 1965, pp 74–85

Klimkowa-Deutschowa E: Neurologische und psychische Fogezustande des Krieges und der Verfolgung bei Kindern und Jugendlichen, in Spätschaden nach Extrembelastungen (Late Damages After Extreme Burdens). Edited by Herberg HJ. Herford, Germany, Nicolaische Verlagsbuchhandlung, 1971, pp 252–262

Kos-Robes M: Children in need, I: children in camp Theresienstadt. Zeitschrift für Psychiatrie 2:232–239, 1964

Kosinski J: A Painted Bird. New York, Bantam Books, 1978

Krall H: Sublokatorka. Pismo II 5:61–77, 1983

Krall H: Sublokatorka. Paris, Librairie Libella SARL, 1985

Kraus OB: A Diary. Unpublished manuscript, March 1990

Krell R: Therapeutic value of documenting child survivors. J Am Acad Child Psychiatry 24:397–400, 1985

Kris E: The recovery of childhood memories in psychoanalysis, in Selected Papers of Ernst Kris. New Haven, CT, Yale University Press, 1975, pp 301–340

Krystal H: The genetic development of affects and affect regression. Annual of Psychoanalysis 2:98–126, 1974

Krystal H: Integration and Self-Healing: Affect, Trauma, Alexithymia. New York, The Analytic Press, 1988

Kubica H: Dzieci w Oswiecimie (Children in Auschwitz). Unpublished manuscript, May 1991

Kurek-Lesik E: Wojenne nawrocenia zydow i rola matki boskiej Czestochowskiej. IV Sesja Jasnogorska 12:137–141, 1985

Kurek-Lesik E: Udzial zenskich zgromadzen zakonnych w akc ji ratowania dzieci zydowskich w Polsce w latach 1939–1945 (The role of convents in saving Jewish children in Poland in the years 1939–1945. Newsletter of the International Study of Organized Persecution of Children 8:11–13, 1991 (published by Child Development Research)

Kurek-Lesik E: Gdy Klasztor Znaczyl Zycie (When the Convent Meant Life). Cracow, Wydawnictwo, 1992

Lauscherova I: The children of Terezin, in Terezin. Prague, The Council of Jewish Communities in the Czech Lands 1965, pp 88–101

Lazar A: The babies who wouldn't cry, in The Lost Generation: Children in the Holocaust. Edited by Eisenberg A. New York, Pilgrim Press, 1982, pp 274–277

Lempp R: Die Bedeutung organischer und psychischer Insulte in Krieg und Verfolgung wahrend der Kindheit und Jugend, in Spätschaden nach Extrembelastungen. Edited by Herberg HJ. Herford, Germany, Nicolaische Verlagsbuchhandlung, 1971, pp 245–251

Lempp R: Extrembelastung im im Kindes- und Jugendalter. Bern, Verlag Hans Huber, 1979

Lempp R: Die Langzeitwirkung psychischer Traumen im Kindes- und Jugendalter, in Schicksale der Verfolgten (Fates of the Persecuted). Edited by Stoffels H. Berlin, Springer-Verlag, 1991, pp 89–97

Lempp R: Seelische Verfolgungsschaden bei Kindern in der ersten und zweiten Generation, in Spuren der Verfolgung. Edited by Hardtmann G. Gerlingen, Germany, Bleicher Verlag, 1992

Levi JS: The combined effect of interviews and group participation by the interviewer, in Children During the Nazi Reign: Psychological Perspectives on the Interview Process. Edited by Kestenberg JS, Fogelman E. Westport, CT, Greenwood, 1994

Levinson BM: The pet and the child's bereavement. Mental Hygiene 51:197–200, 1967

Levy C, Tillard P: Betrayal at the Vel d'Hiv. New York, Hill & Wang, 1976

Lichtenberg EF: On being interviewed about the Holocaust, in Children During the Nazi Reign: Psychological Perspectives on the Interview Process. Edited by Kestenberg JS, Fogelman E. Westport, CT, Greenwood, 1994

Ludowyk-Gyomroi E: The analysis of a young concentration camp victim. Psychoanaly Study Child 18:484–510, 1963

Mazor A, Gampel Y, Enright RD, et al: Survivors: coping with post-traumatic memories in childhood and 40 years later. Journal of Traumatic Stress 3:1–14, 1990

Mazurczyk J, Zawanowska K: Cziecinstwo i Wojna (Childhood and War). Warsaw, Czytelnik, 1983

McDougall J: Theaters of the Mind. New York, WW Norton, 1985

Meloch K: Cezarego Gawrysia Turkowice Smierc i ocalenie (The death and the saving of Cezary Gawrys in Turkowice). Wiez 33:14–53, 1987

Meloch K: Wszystko co Turkowickie (Everything that is from Turkowice). Wiez 33:164–167, 1990

Meloch K: Spuscizna (Heritage). Wiez 32:96–100, 1989

Meyers O: The return of the secret Jews, in Remembering for the Future: Jews and Christians During and After the Holocaust. Oxford, UK, Pergamon, 1988, pp 1123–1132

Moskovitz S: Child survivors as parents. Paper presented at the 10th annual International Congress of the International Association for Child and Adolescent Psychiatry and Allied Professions, Dublin, July 1982

Moskovitz S: Love Despite Hate. New York, Schocken Books, 1983

Moskovitz S: Longitudinal follow up of child survivors of the Holocaust. J Am Acad Child Psychiatry 24:401–407, 1985

Moskovitz S: Barriers to gratitude, in Remembering for the Future: Jews and Christians During and After the Holocaust. Oxford, UK, Pergamon, 1988, pp 494–505

Moskovitz S: Wrestling with the ogres: When the past invades the present. Paper presented at the annual meeting of the ISTSS, Amsterdam, June 1992

Moskovitz S, Krell R: Child survivors of the Holocaust: psychological adaptations to survival. Isr J Psychiatry Relat Sci 27:81–92, 1984

Mrkalj M: Sjenicak: Kronika Kordunaskog Sela (Sjenicak: A Chronicle of a Village in Kordun). Karlavac, Yugoslavia, Historijski Arhiv u Karloveu, 1980. Excerpts translated by Damir Mirkovic and published in The Newsletter of the Jerome Riker International Study of Organized Persecution of Children 7:3–5, 1990 (published by Child Development Research)

Niederland WG: The problem of the survivor. Journal of the Hillside Hospital 10:233–247, 1961

Niederland WG: Clinical observations on the "survivor syndrome": symposium on psychic traumatization through social catastrophe. Int J Psychoanal 49:313–315, 1968

Niederland WG: Folgen der Verfolgung: Das Uberlebenden-Syndrom (The Consequences of Persecution: The Survivor Syndrome). Frankfurt am Main, Edition Suhrkamp, 1980

Nir Y: The Lost Childhood. New York, Harcourt Brace Jovanovich, 1989

Offer D: Adolescent development: A normative perspective, in The Course of Life, Vol. 4: Adolescence. Edited by Greenspan DI, Pollock GH. Adelphi, MD, National Institute of Mental Health, 1991, pp 181–199

Oliner S: Restless Memories: Recollections of Holocaust Years. Berkeley CA, Judah I. Magnes Memorial Museum, 1979

Oliwa F: Dom ocalonych dzieci w Otwocku (1945–49) (The home of the saved children in Otwock). Biuletyn Zydowskiego Instytutu Historycznego 3:89–105, 1986

Orbach E: Kinder, die nicht leben wollen (Children Who Don't Want to Live). Göttingen, Germany, 1990

Papanek E, Linn E: Out of the Fire. New York, William Morrow, 1975

Pearlstein C: Unpublished poems, 1942

Pisar S: Of Blood and Hope. Boston, Little, Brown, 1979

Podrizki R: A first interview with a child survivor of the Holocaust, in Children During the Nazi Reign: Psychological Perspectives on the Interview Process. Edited by Kestenberg JS, Fogelman E. Westport, CT, Greenwood, 1994

Pollock GH: The mourning process and creative organization change. Am J Psychiatry 25:3–34, 1977

Pollock GH: On siblings, childhood sibling loss, and creativity. Annual of Psychoanalysis 6:443–448, 1978

Pollock GH: The mourning-liberation process and creativity: the case of Käthe Kollwitz. Annual of Psychoanalysis 10:333–353, 1982

Poltawska W: And I Am Afraid of My Dreams. New York, Hippocrene Books, 1989

Poltawska W, Jakubik A, Sarneck J, et al: Wyniki badan psychiatrycznch osob urodzonych w dziecinswie w hitlerowskieh obozach koncentracyjnych (Results of psychiatric examinations of persons born or incarcerated in their childhood in Hitler's concentration camps). Przeglad Lekarski 22:1–49, 1966

Quindeau I: Narration as a construction of identity, in Children During the Nazi Reign: Psychological Perspectives on the Interview Process. Edited by Kestenberg JS, Fogelman E. Westport, CT, Greenwood, 1994

Quindeau I: Trauma und Geschichte. Kassel, Gesamthochschule Kassel-Universität, 1995

Risen SE: The psychoanalytic treatment of an adolescent with anorexia nervosa. Psychoanal Study Child 37:433–459, 1982

Robinson S: Late effects of persecution in persons who as children or young adolescents survived Nazi occupation in Europe. Israel Annals of Psychiatry and Related Disciplines 17:209–214, 1979

Robinson S, Rapaport J, Durst R, et al: The late effects of Nazi persecution among elderly Holocaust survivors. Acta Psychiatr Scand 82:311–315, 1990

Robinson S, Rapaport-Bar Sever M, Rapaport J: The present state of people who survived the Holocaust as children. Acta Psychiatr Scand 89:242–245, 1994

Rosen D: The Forest My Friend. New York, Bergen-Belsen Memorial Press, 1971

Rosenthal G: Narrated life stories of Holocaust survivors in Israel, in Jewish Identity. Edited by Kashti I. Tel Aviv, 1990

Rosenthal PA, Rosenthal L: Holocaust effect in the third generation: Child of another time. Am J Psychother 34:572–580, 1980

Rosh L, Jäckel E: Der Tod ist ein Meister aus Deutschland (Death Is a Master From Germany). Hamburg, Hoffmann und Campe Verlag, 1990

Rossberg A: Das Trauma der Kinder mit einem judischen Elternteil in Deutschland vor 1945 und danach (The trauma of children with one Jewish parent in Germany 1945 and later), in Children: War and Persecution. Proceedings of Congress Hamburg, September 26–29, 1993. Edited by Stiftung für Kinder. Osnabrück, Germany, Secolo Verlag, 1995

Rowe JW: The clinical impact of physiologic changes with aging, in Geriatric Psychiatry. Edited by Busse EW, Blazer DG. Washington, DC, American Psychiatric Press, 1989, pp 35–64

Schur J: Comments on the metapsychology of somatization. Psychoanal Study Child 10:119–164, 1955

Sender RM: The Cage. New York, Macmillan, 1986

Shappell N: Rescuing children from the ghetto in soup pots, in The Lost Generation: Children in the Holocaust. Edited by Eisenberg A. New York, Pilgrim Press, 1982, pp 244–246

Shtrigler M: Nerot Meukolim (Burnt-Out Lights). Jerusalem, Am Oved, 1946, pp 103–110 (Also in English, in The Lost Generation: Children in the Holocaust. Edited by Eisenberg A. New York, Pilgrim Press, 1982)

Siegler IC, Poon LW: The psychology of aging, in Geriatric Psychiatry. Edited by Busse EW, Blazer DG. Washington, DC, American Psychiatric Press, 1989, pp 163–201

Sloan J (ed): Notes From the Warsaw Ghetto: The Journal of Emmanual Ringelblum. New York, Schocken Books, 1974

Spitz R: The First Year of Life: The Psychoanalytic Study of Normal and Deviant Development of Object Relations. New York, International Universities Press, 1965

Spitz RA, Wolf KM: Anaclitic depression: an inquiry into the genesis of psychiatric conditions in early childhood, II. Psychoanal Study Child 2:313–342, 1946

Stoffels H: Schicksale der Verfolgten (Fates of the Persecuted). Berlin, Springer-Verlag, 1991

Strzelecki A: Wyzwolenie Oswiecimia in Zeszyty Oswiecimskie, Vol 3. Oswiecim (Auschwitz), Poland, Wydawnictwo panstwowego Muzeum w Oswiecimiu, 1974

Szwajger AB: I Remember Nothing More: The Warsaw Childrens Hospital and the Jewish Resistance. New York, Pantheon Books, 1990

Terr L: Remembered images and trauma. Psychoanal Study Child 40:493–533, 1985

Treplin V: A fortuituous meeting: an interviewee becomes an interviewer, in Children During the Nazi Reign: Psychological Perspectives on the Interview Process. Edited by Kestenberg JS, Fogelman E. Westport, CT, Greenwood, 1994, pp 137–154

Tyndel M: Beitrag zur Kasuistik und Psychopathologie der wahrend der nationalsozialistischen Verfolgung geborenen Kinder, in Spätschaden nach Extrembelastungen. Edited by Herberg HJ. Herford, Germany, Nicolaische Verlagsbuchhandlung, 1971, pp 266–269

Valent P: Child Survivors: Adults Living with Childhood Trauma. Melbourne, William Heinemann Australia, 1994a

Valent P: A child survivor's appraisal of his own interview, in Children During the Nazi Reign: Psychological Perspectives on the Interview Process. Edited by Kestenberg JS, Fogelman E. Westport, CT, Greenwood, 1994b

van Dam H: Female sexual development at puberty: the Anne Frank diaries reexamined. Paper presented at the annual meeting of the American Psychoanalytic Association, New York, December 1992

van Dam H: The Jewish identity of Anne Frank. Paper presented at the Freud Lectures, New York, February 1993

van der Kolk B: The trauma spectrum: the interaction of biological and social events in the genesis of the trauma response. Journal of Traumatic Stress 1:273–290, 1988

Vegh C: Je ne lui ai pas dit au revoir (I did not have a chance to say good-bye). Paris, Gallimard, 1979

Virag T: Children of the Holocaust—and their children's children: working through parent trauma in the psychotherapeutic process. Dynamic Psychotherapy 2:47–60, 1984

Volkan V: Linking Objects and Linking Phenomena. New York, International Universities Press, 1981

Volkan V: The Need to Have Enemies and Allies: From Clinical Practice to International Relationships. Northvale, NJ, Jason Aronson, 1988

Wangh M: National Socialism and the genocide of the Jews. Int J Psychoanal 45:386, 1964

Wangh M: Die Beurteilung von Wiedergutmachungsanspruchen der als Kleinkinder Verfolgten, in Spätschaden nach Extrembelastungen. Edited by Herberg HJ. Herford, Germany, Nicolaische Verlagsbuchhandlung, 1971

Wiesel E: Night. New York, Avon Books, 1969

Wiesel E: A Jew Today. New York, Vintage Books, 1979

Wiesse J, Olbrich E (eds): Ein Ast bei Nacht kein Ast. Göttingen, Germany, Vandenhoeck & Ruprecht, 1994

Winick M: Hunger Disease. New York, Wiley, 1979

Winnicott DW: Transitional objects and transitional phenomena. Int J Psychoanal 34:89–97, 1953

Winnik HZ: Traumatization through social catastrophe. Int J Psychoanal 49:298–301, 1968

Witkowski J: Hitlerowski Oboz Koncentracyjny dla Maloletnich w Lodzi (Hitler's Concentration Camp for Minors in Lodz). Wroclaw (Breslau), Poland, Ossolineum, 1975

Wolfenstein M: How is mourning possible? Psychoanal Study Child 21:93–123, 1966

Wolfheim N: Pychoanalyse und Kindergarten. Basel, Ernst Reinhardt Verlag, 1966

Ziemian J: Vazatorii de Tigari din Piata Celor Tre Cruci (The Cigarette Sellers of 3 Cross Square). Jerusalem, Yad Vashem, 1963

Zweig J: Mein Vater, was machst Du hier . . . ? (My Father, What Do You Do Here?). Frankfurt am Main, Dipa Verlag & Druck Gmbh, 1987

Index